The Rise of the Midwestern Meat Packing Industry

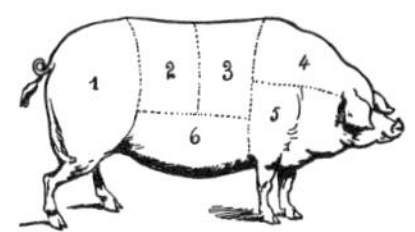

MARGARET WALSH

The Rise of the Midwestern Meat Packing Industry

THE UNIVERSITY PRESS OF KENTUCKY

Scholarly publisher for the Commonwealth
serving Berea College, Centre College of Kentucky,
Eastern Kentucky University, The Filson Club,
Georgetown College, Kentucky Historical Society,
Kentucky State University, Morehead State University,
Murray State University, Northern Kentucky University,
Transylvania University, University of Kentucky,
University of Louisville, and Western Kentucky University

Editorial and Sales Offices: Lexington, Kentucky 40506-0024

Library of Congress Cataloging in Publication Data

Walsh, Margaret.
The rise of the Midwestern meat packing industry.

Bibliography: p.
Includes index.
1. Pork industry and trade–Middle West–History.
2. Meat industry and trade–Middle West–History.
3. Packing-houses–Middle West–History. I. Title.
HD9435.U53A14 1982 338.4'76649092'0977 82-40184
ISBN 0-8131-1473-X

Contents

List of Tables *vi*

List of Maps *viii*

Preface *ix*

1 The Significance of the Midwestern Meat Packing Industry in the Mid-Nineteenth Century *1*

2 Supply, Process, Markets: The Dominance of Seasonal Elements in the Pioneer Years *15*

3 Railroads and the Challenge to River Dominance in the Antebellum Years *39*

4 Changing Patterns of Urban Concentration in the Civil War Period *55*

5 The Emergence of a Permanent Industry *71*

6 The Dimensions of Midwestern Pork Packing *89*

Appendix. The Sample of Midwestern Pork Packers Used for Biographical Illustrations *93*

Notes *107*

Selected Bibliography *149*

Index *175*

Tables

1 Manufacturing in the United States by Region, 1850-1870 *2*

2 Measures of Manufacturing in the United States by Region, 1850-1870 *3*

3 Growth of Manufacturing in the United States by Region, 1850-1870 *4*

4 Manufacturing Profile of the West, 1850-1870, for Selected Industries *5*

5 Leading Industries in the United States, 1850-1870 *6*

6 Pork Packing in the Midwest, 1847-1877 *8*

7 Population Growth in the Midwest, 1840-1870 *10*

8 Hogs Raised in the Midwest, 1840-1880 *11*

9 Pork Packing in Major Midwestern Cities, 1847-1877 *20*

10 Pork Packing in Secondary Midwestern Points, 1847-1866 *22*

11 Exports of Pork and Bacon from Cincinnati, 1847-1873 *34*

12 Westward Movement of Pork Packing, 1847-1877 *40*

13 Concentration of Pork Packing in the Leading Midwestern Cities *58*

14 Changing Distribution of Hog Packing in Principal Midwestern Cities during the Civil War *59*

15 Pork Packing in Secondary Midwestern Points, 1858-1877 *68*

A1 Principal Packing Points in the Midwest, Mid-1840s *94*

A2 Principal Packing Points in the Midwest, Late 1850s *94*

A3 Principal Packing Points in the Midwest, Mid-1860s *96*

A4 Principal Packing Points in the Midwest, Mid-1870s *97*

A5 Number of Packing Establishments in the Midwest, Mid-1840s *98*

A6 Number of Packing Establishments in the Midwest, Late 1850s *99*

A7 Number of Packing Establishments in the Midwest, Mid-1860s *100*

A8 Number of Packing Establishments in the Midwest, Mid-1870s *101*

A9 Components of the Collective Biography *102*

Maps

1 Pork Packing Points in the Midwest in the Mid-1840s *16*

2 Pork Packing Points in the Midwest in the Late 1850s *42*

3 Pork Packing Points in the Midwest in the Mid-1860s *56*

4 Pork Packing Points in the Midwest in the Mid-1870s *76*

Preface

This study examines the process of industrial growth and change in a developing region. The original impetus developed from an earlier book, *The Manufacturing Frontier: Pioneer Industry in Antebellum Wisconsin, 1830–1860,* which suggested that further useful information on the Midwestern economy in the mid-nineteenth century would be forthcoming from an in-depth treatment of one particular branch of manufacturing. Pork packing is a good tool of analysis because agricultural processing early disseminated an industrial experience to newly settled farming country.

The search for materials for this study has been long and widespread and I could not have completed this work without the generous help of numerous librarians. I am most grateful to the staff of the following Libraries: in England, the University of Birmingham; in Illinois, the Newberry Library, the University of Illinois at Chicago-Circle, the University of Chicago, Northwestern University, the University of Illinois at Champaign-Urbana, and the Illinois State Historical Society; in Indiana, the Indiana State Library, the Indiana Historical Society, and Indiana University at Bloomington; in Iowa, the State Historical Society of Iowa, the University of Iowa at Iowa City, and Iowa State Historical Department; in Kansas, the Kansas State Historical Society and the University of Kansas at Lawrence; in Kentucky, the Filson Club, the Louisville Free Public Library, the University of Louisville, the University of Kentucky, and the Kentucky Historical Society; in Massachusetts, the Harvard Business School; in Michigan, the Michigan Historical Collections at the University of Michigan at Ann Arbor; in Minnesota, the Minnesota Historical Society; in Missouri, the Missouri Historical Society, Washington University, the St. Louis Mercantile Library Association, the State Historical Society of Missouri, and the University of Missouri at Columbia; in Nebraska, the State Historical Society of Nebraska and the University of Nebraska at Lincoln; in New York, the Albert R. Mann Library, Cornell University; in Ohio, the Ohio Historical Society, Ohio State University at Columbus, the State Library of Ohio, the Cincinnati Historical Society, the Public Library of Cincinnati, the University of Cincinnati, and the Western Reserve Historical Society; in Washington, D.C., the National Archives and the Library of Congress; and in Wisconsin, the State Historical Society of Wisconsin, the University of Wisconsin at Madison, the Milwaukee Public Library, and the Milwaukee Historical Society.

I could not have carried out the extensive traveling and undertaken the additional expenses without substantial financial assistance. I express my deep appreciation to the American Council of Learned Societies, the Social Science Research Council, and the University of Birmingham.

What appears here is the result of the rewriting of various drafts. I owe a large debt of gratitude to several of my colleagues who read parts or all of one version: Peter J. Cain, Charlotte J. Erickson, Linda J. Jones. Irene D. Neu, and Mary A. Yeager. I also wish to thank Susan Kennedy and Shirley Swann, who typed and retyped the manuscript.

Finally I wish to express my gratitude to the editors of *Agricultural History* and the *Journal of Historical Geography* for permission to use portions of articles which have appeared in their journals.

1

The Significance of the Midwestern Meat Packing Industry in the Mid-Nineteenth Century

Historians have traditionally discussed the economic development of the Middle West in the mid-nineteenth century in an agrarian context.[1] Though the Jeffersonian image has been updated and qualified by studies of the rapid growth of commercial farming, of the national importance of forest and mineral resources, and of the rise of cities, little systematic research has been conducted on the development of a manufacturing sector. Presumably western industrial enterprises were either missing or trivial.[2] Any understanding of the rise of industrial America should properly be directed toward New England and the Middle Atlantic states.[3]

Certainly these two regions formed the nation's main manufacturing belt. They were responsible for over two-thirds of the country's value added, employment, and capital (Table 1). They also led, by a large extent, in size of establishments and output per capita (Table 2). But other parts of the United States cannot be ignored in any aggregate analysis. The absolute and relative contributions of the West grew impressively between 1850 and 1870 with marked increases in the 1860s (Tables 1 and 2). By most measures this region expanded at the fastest rate (Table 3), suggesting that the West was already laying the foundations of the Great Lakes' manufacturing complex which would

Table 1. Manufacturing in the United States by Region, 1850–1870

Region[1]	No. of Estab-lishments	% of U.S.	Capital Invested ($1,000)	% of U.S.	No. of Hands Employed	% of U.S.	Value Added[2] by Manufac-ture ($1,000)	% of U.S.
1850								
New England	22,487	18.1	165,695	31.1	312,719	32.7	130,249	28.1
Middle Atlantic	54,024	43.9	235,586	44.2	420,615	44.0	207,042	44.6
West	28,530	23.2	74,707	14.0	132,049	13.8	75,156	16.2
South	16,896	13.7	55,294	10.4	88,390	9.2	38,308	8.3
United States[3]	123,025	100.0	533,245	100.0	957,059	100.0	463,983	100.0
1860								
New England	20,671	14.7	257,478	25.5	391,836	29.9	223,076	26.1
Middle Atlantic	53,287	37.9	435,062	43.1	546,243	41.7	358,211	41.9
West	36,785	26.2	194,213	19.2	209,909	16.0	158,988	18.6
South	20,631	14.7	95,975	9.5	110,721	8.4	68,988	8.1
United States[3]	140,433	100.0	1,009,856	100.0	1,311,246	100.0	854,257	100.0
1870								
New England	32,352	12.8	489,656	23.1	526,969	25.7	404,164	23.2
Middle Atlantic	83,606	33.2	905.773	42.8	806,094	39.3	730,467	41.9
West	91,929	36.5	552,477	26.1	528,458	25.7	470,128	27.1
South	33,369	13.2	109,883	5.2	155,834	7.6	92,327	5.3
United States[3]	252,148	100.0	2,118,209	100.0	2,053,996	100.0	1,743,898	100.0

Sources: U.S., Congress, Senate, Document 39, *Senate Executive Documents,* 35 Cong., 2 sess. (1858/59); *U.S. Census,* 1860, vol. 3, *Manufactures*; 1870, vol. 2, *Wealth and Industry.*

[1] Regions as defined in the 1860 Census: *New England:* Maine, New Hampshire, Vermont, Massachusetts, Rhode Island, Connecticut; *Middle Atlantic:* New York, New Jersey, Pennsylvania, Delaware, Maryland, District of Columbia; *West:* Ohio, Indiana, Michigan, Illinois, Wisconsin, Iowa, Minnesota, Nebraska, Missouri, Kansas, Kentucky; *South:* Virginia, North Carolina, South Carolina, Georgia, Florida, Alabama, Mississippi, Louisiana, Texas, Arkansas, Tennessee, and West Virginia (for 1870).

[2] Obtained by subtracting the cost of the materials from the value of the product.

[3] Manufacturing in the Far West is not shown but is included in the U.S. total.

Table 2. Measures of Manufacturing in the United States by Region, 1850–1870

Region	Capital per Establish-ment ($)	No. of Hands per Establishment	Value Added per Establish-ment ($)	Value Added per Capita ($)
1850				
New England	7,368	13.9	5,792	47.7
Middle Atlantic	4,361	7.8	3,832	31.3
West	2,619	5.2	2,634	11.8
South	3,273	5.2	2,267	5.4
United States	4,334	7.8	3,771	20.1
1860				
New England	12,456	19.0	10,792	71.2
Middle Atlantic	8,165	10.3	6,722	43.0
West	5,280	5.7	4,322	15.5
South	4,652	5.4	3,344	7.6
United States	7,191	9.3	6,083	27.4
1870				
New England	15,135	16.3	12,493	115.9
Middle Atlantic	10,833	9.6	8,737	94.2
West	6,010	5.7	5,114	32.9
South	3,293	4.7	2,767	9.3
United States	8,401	8.1	6,916	45.8

Sources: U.S., Congress, Senate, Document 39, *Senate Executive Documents,* 35 Cong., 2 sess. (1858/59); *U.S. Census,* 1860, vol. 3, *Manufactures;* 1870, vol. 2, *Wealth and Industry.*

reach maturity at the end of the century. Indeed, by 1870 the West was responsible for 27 percent of the nation's value added.[4]

The region made the most progress toward industrialization in mid-century in the processing branches–lumber planing and sawing, flour and grist milling, brewing, distilling, leather tanning and currying and meat packing (Table 4). These activities have, for the most part, been ignored or dismissed as being merely pre-industrial even though they were of major importance (Table 5). The contributions of lumber processing, which ranked first in 1850 and second in both 1860 and 1870, or that of flour milling, which ranked fourth in both 1850 and 1860 and fifth in 1870, have generally been neglected. These and other agricultural processing industries were much more important to

Table 3. Growth of Manufacturing in the United States by Region, 1850–1870 (Percentage Changes)

Region	No. of Establish-ments	Capital Invested ($1,000)	No. of Hands Employed	Value Added ($1,000)	Capital per Establish-ment ($)	No. of Hands per Establishment	Value Added per Establish-ment ($)	Value Added per Capita ($)
1850–1860								
New England	-8.08	55.39	25.30	71.27	69.06	36.69	86.33	49.27
Middle Atlantic	-1.37	84.67	29.87	73.01	87.23	32.05	75.42	37.38
West	28.93	159.96	58.96	115.44	101.60	9.62	64.09	31.36
South	22.11	73.57	25.26	80.09	42.18	3.85	47.51	40.74
United States	14.15	89.40	37.01	84.11	65.92	19.23	61.31	36.32
1860–1870								
New England	56.51	90.17	34.49	81.18	21.51	-14.21	15.76	62.78
Middle Atlantic	56.90	108.18	47.57	103.92	32.68	-6.80	29.98	72.56
West	149.91	184.47	151.76	195.70	13.94	0.00	18.32	112.26
South	61.74	14.49	41.29	38.83	-29.21	-12.96	-17.25	22.37
United States	79.55	109.75	56.64	104.14	16.83	-12.90	13.69	67.15

Sources: U.S., Congress, Senate, Document 39, *Senate Executive Documents,* 35 Cong., 2 sess. (1858/59); *U.S. Census,* 1860, vol. 3, *Manufactures;* 1870, vol. 2, *Wealth and Industry.*

Table 4. Manufacturing Profile of the West, 1850–1870, for Selected Industries (Value Added in $1,000)

	1850			1860			1870		
Industry	Value Added ($1,000)	West as % of U.S.	Industry as % of West	Value Added ($1,000)	West as % of U.S.	Industry as % of West	Value Added ($1,000)	West as % of U.S.	Industry as % of West
Processing branches									
Cooperage	1,886	42.08	2.51	3,017	41.68	1.90	6,949	49.52	1.48
Flour milling	9,153	39.76	12.18	18,019	44.95	11.33	39,614	51.05	8.42
Leather	2,554	17.22	3.40	3,142	46.34	1.98	5,788	16.78	1.23
Liquors	3,397	43.00	4.52	10,504	13.79	6.61	23,035	51.18	4.90
Lumber	8,313	26.88	11.06	19,957	37.25	12.55	56,408	46.93	12.00
Meat packing	1,946	76.88	2.59	3,802	53.61	2.39	8,753	61.85	1.86
Heavy industries									
Agricultural implements	1,393	31.68	1.85	6,280	52.50	3.95	17,639	57.66	3.75
Iron & iron goods	4,875	18.94	6.49	9,102	19.55	5.73	34,189	25.33	7.27
Machinery	2,104	12.65	2.80	7,323	22.49	4.61	18,485	23.75	3.93
Household consumer branches									
Blacksmiths	2,549	23.31	3.39	2,052	29.95	1.29	11,117	38.83	2.36
Boots and shoes	3,311	10.99	4.41	5,747	11.69	3.61	14,551	16.52	3.10
Clothing	2,924	12.95	3.89	6,878	16.55	4.33	17,162	22.31	3.65
Furniture	2,872	24.81	3.82	5,360	30.71	3.37	15,619	36.12	3.32
Tinware	1,930	19.86	2.57	2,626	29.11	1.65	7,568	35.09	1.61
Total Manufacturing of West	75,156	16.20	. . .	158,988	18.61	. . .	470,128	26.96	. . .

Sources: U.S., Congress, Senate, Document 39, *Senate Executive Documents*, 35 Cong., 2 sess. (1858/59); *U.S. Census*, 1860, vol. 3, *Manufactures;* 1870, vol. 2, *Wealth and Industry*.

Table 5. Leading Industries in the United States, 1850–1870

Industry	1850 Value Added ($1,000)	1850 % of U.S.	1860 Value Added ($1,000)	1860 % of U.S.	1870 Value Added ($1,000)	1870 % of U.S.
1. Lumber, planed and sawed	30,927	6.7	53,570 (2)[1]	6.3	120,267 (2)	6.9
2. Boots and shoes	30,119	6.5	49,161 (3)	5.8	88,062 (3)	5.1
3. Cottons	27,724	6.0	54,671 (1)	6.4	65,927 (7)	3.8
4. Flour and grist mills	23,020	5.0	40,083 (4)	4.7	77,593 (5)	4.5
5. Men's clothing	22,581	4.9	36,680 (5)	4.3	61,533 (8)	3.5
6. Iron manufactures	22,004	4.7	35,689 (6)	4.2	134,952 (1)	7.7
7. Machinery	16,631	3.6	32,566 (7)	3.8	78,096 (4)	4.5
8. Woolens	14,936	3.2	25,032 (9)	2.9	57,891 (9)	3.3
9. Leather	14,837	3.2	22,786 (11)	2.6	33,727 (14)	1.9
10. Furniture	11,574	2.5	13,451 (15)	1.6	43,236 (11)	2.5
United States Totals	463,982		854,257		1,743,898	

Sources: U.S., Congress, Senate, Document 39, *Senate Executive Documents,* 35 Cong., 2 sess. (1858/59); *U.S. Census,* 1860, vol. 3, *Manufactures;* 1870, vol. 2, *Wealth and Industry.*

1. Rank shown in parentheses for 1860 and 1870.

American development than has been assumed, for they directly disseminated an industrial experience and a modern technology to newly settled parts of the country and indirectly stimulated high levels of construction and city growth.[5]

Within the Middle West, processors, using the rich lumber and mineral resources of the Great Lakes area and the increasing farm outputs of the prairies, initially catered to neighborhood markets in their small mills and shops. These entrepreneurs gradually built up their capital and sales expertise and shipped increasing outputs by water or by rail outside the region to national and even international markets. Older manufacturing centers in the Northeast did not pose a strong competitive threat because the cost of freighting low-value bulky commodities over long distances made western processing more profitable, particularly at transshipment points. Even when interregional rail links eased and speeded the flow of raw materials from west to east, improved handling facilities, economies of scale, and business reorganization assured the western manufacturers of their importance both to regional development and to national outputs.[6]

Meat packing was a prominent branch among these midwestern processing industries.[7] Though its output was not as valuable as that of other agricultural-based activities like flour milling or liquors, its contribution must not be underrated. The census coverage of this industry is defective. Difficulties of distinguishing between manufacturing and commerce and the seasonal nature of packing were responsible for the omission of many establishments from the tabulations. Value-added figures would better reflect the extent of the industry if they were raised by at least 25 percent.[8] A more reliable quantitative description is available, however, in the annual statistics generated by local commercial bodies. While these lack a comparative framework they do indicate not only an upward but a fluctuating growth in pork packing in the Middle West throughout the nineteenth century (Table 6).[9]

This growth is significant for any understanding of midwestern or even national economic history because the details of its dimensions, shape, and style provide information on the process of change in a developing region and in an industry which has been essentially regarded as pre-modern. Analysis of the market conditions of supply and demand, of the steady improvements in transportation, and of the critical role of small merchant capitalists demonstrates the main features of the evolving industry. Progress might be gradual and piecemeal rather than swift and dramatic, but in the space of a generation, between the early 1840s and the mid-1870s, meat packing was transformed from its pioneer commercial status to the threshold of a genuine manufacturing activity.

The simple mercantile orientation of meat packing in the late colonial and early national eras was transferred across the Appalachians in the wake of the expanding westward frontier. In the opening decades of the 1800s innumerable farmer-packers either killed animals and cured meat for their own use during the winter months or took their surpluses in the form of "dead" meat or livestock to local market towns on the Ohio-Mississippi River system. Here merchants would assemble cargoes of meat for dispatch downriver as part of their all-purpose trading. Their functions were seldom clearly defined because the meat business was both seasonal and erratic. Depending on such imponderables as the weather, the size of the hog crop, the supply of salt, the

Table 6. Pork Packing in the Midwest, 1847–1877 (No. of Hogs)

Season	Winter Months	Annual Percentage Change	3-Year Moving Average (Winter)
1847/48	1,710,000	. . .	. . .
1848/49	1,560,000	-8.77	. . .
1849/50	1,652,220	+5.91	1,640,740
1850/51	1,457,396	-11.79	1,446,539
1851/52	1,562,580	+7.22	1,556,539
1852/53	2,044,005	+30.81	1,687,994
1853/54	2,473,807	+21.03	2,026,797
1854/55	2,124,404	-14.12	2,214,072
1855/56	2,489,502	+17.19	2,362,571
1856/57	1,818,468	-26.96	2,144,125
1857/58	2,210,778	+21.57	2,172,916
1858/59	2,465,552	+11.52	2,164,933
1859/60	2,350,822	-4.65	2,342,384
1860/61	2,155,702	-8.30	2,324,025
1861/62	2,893,666	+34.23	2,466,730
1862/63	4,069,520	+40.64	3,039,629
1863/64	3,261,105	-19.87	3,408,097
1864/65	2,422,779	-25.71	3,251,135
1865/66	1,785,955	-26.29	2,489,946
1866/67	2,490,791	+39.47	2,233,175
1867/68	2,781,084	+11.66	2,352,610
1868/69	2,499,173	-10.14	2,590,349
1869/70	2,595,243	+3.84	2,625,167
1870/71	3,717,084	+43.23	2,937,167
1871/72	4,875,560	+31.17	3,729,296
1872/73	5,451,254	+11.81	4,681,299
1873/74	5,462,700	+0.21	5,263,171
1874/75	5,561,226	+1.80	5,491,927
1875/76	4,887,999	-12.11	5,303,975
1876/77	5,068,992	+3.70	5,192,172
1877/78	6,502,446	+28.28	5,486,479

Sources: *Cincinnati Prices Current,* 1845–1877; Cincinnati Chamber of Commerce, *Annual Reports,* 1847–1878.

Table 6 (continued)

Season	Full Year	Annual Percentage Change	3-Year Moving Average (Full Year)
1847/48	...	...	...
1848/49	...	...	...
1849/50	...	...	...
1850/51	...	...	...
1851/52	...	...	...
1852/53	...	...	...
1853/54	...	...	...
1854/55	...	...	...
1855/56	...	...	...
1856/57	...	...	...
1857/58	...	...	...
1858/59	...	...	...
1859/60	...	...	...
1860/61	...	...	...
1861/62	...	...	...
1862/63	...	...	...
1863/64	...	...	...
1864/65	...	...	...
1865/66	...	...	...
1866/67	...	...	...
1867/68	...	...	...
1868/69	...	...	...
1869/70	...	...	...
1870/71	3,784,507	...	...
1871/72	4,921,637	+30.05	...
1872/73	5,946,968	+20.83	4,884,371
1873/74	6,500,806	+9.31	5,789,804
1874/75	6,728,885	+3.51	6,392,220
1875/76	6,116,405	-9.10	6,448,699
1876/77	7,376,858	+20.61	6,740,716
1877/78	9,045,566	+22.62	7,512,943

Table 7. Population Growth in the Midwest, 1840–1870

State	1840		1850		1860		1870	
	Population (1,000)	State as % of Midwest Total	Population (1,000)	State as % of Midwest Total	Population (1,000)	State as % of Midwest Total	Population (1,000)	State as % of Midwest Total
Ohio Valley States								
Ohio	1,519	36.78	1,980	31.01	2,340	22.83	2,665	18.65
Indiana	686	16.60	989	15.48	1,350	13.18	1,681	11.76
Kentucky	780	18.88	982	15.38	1,155	11.28	1,321	9.25
Total	2,985	72.26	3,951	61.87	4,845	47.29	5,667	39.66
Mississippi Valley States								
Illinois	476	11.53	852	13.33	1,712	16.71	2,540	17.78
Missouri	384	9.29	682	10.68	1,182	11.53	1,721	12.05
Iowa	43	1.04	192	3.01	675	6.59	1,194	8.35
Wisconsin	31	0.75	305	4.79	776	7.57	1,055	7.38
Total	934	22.61	2,031	31.81	4,345	42.40	6,510	45.56
Other West								
Michigan	212	5.13	398	6.23	749	7.30	1,184	8.29
Minnesota			6	0.09	172	1.68	440	3.08
Kansas					107	1.05	364	2.55
Nebraska					29	0.28	123	0.86
Total	212	5.13	404	6.32	1,057	10.31	2,111	14.78
Total Midwest	4,131	100.00	6,386	100.00	10,247	100.00	14,288	100.00

Source: *Ninth Census, 1870, A Compendium* (Washington, D.C., 1872), 8–9.

anticipated demand, and the availability of finance, packers might buy livestock directly from the farmer or the drover, might purchase meat from the farmer, might slaughter, pack, and cure, or only undertake the two latter tasks, and then might sell the meat on their own account or on commission. The limited qualitative and quantitative evidence available suggests an active and growing interest in packing in the 1820s and 1830s which was focused on Cincinnati but spread out along navigable water routes as far as western Illinois.[10]

As population continued to move west in the mid-nineteenth century the close but uncertain relationship of packing with the atomistic rural agrarian economy becomes easier to define. Family-sized food-producing farm units underpinned the structure of the Middle West. The rapid expansion of population and farms brought a growth in the numbers of livestock and also improvements in their quality (Tables 7 and 8).[11] There was thus an increasing supply of animals for processing. But farmers were sufficiently profit-oriented to react to market forces, here in the shape of two- to three-year fluctuations in the corn-hog cycle. They would cut hog production when corn was in short supply and commanded a high price, and would increase hog production when corn was plentiful and cheap. Numerous individual assessments of how to measure the vagaries of the market in fact meant that the hog crop oscillated throughout the period. Packers

Table 8. Hogs Raised in the Midwest, 1840–1880 (1,000s)

State	1840	1850	1860	1870	1880
Ohio	2,100	1,965	2,252	1,729	3,141
Indiana	1,624	2,264	3,099	1,872	3,186
Kentucky	2,311	2,891	2,331	1,838	2,225
Illinois	1,495	1,916	2,502	2,703	5,170
Iowa	105	323	935	1,354	6,034
Missouri	1,271	1,703	2,354	2,306	4,553
Wisconsin	51	159	334	513	1,129
Kansas	–	–	138	207	1,788
Midwest Total	8,957	11,221	13,945	12,522	27,226
United States Total	26,301	30,354	33,513	25,135	47,682

Sources: *U.S. Census,* 1840, 1850, 1860, 1870, 1880.

could never be certain about the size and quality of raw materials, let alone their price.[12]

The expanding but diffuse urban demand for meat products, both at home and abroad, presented different organizational problems and created more uncertainty for packers throughout the period. While in 1830 more than 90 percent of the country's population lived in rural areas of fewer than 2,500, by 1870 this proportion had dropped to less than 75 percent.[13] The growth of cities, particularly in the Northeast but also in the Midwest and to a lesser extent in the South, created a concentrated demand for food supplies, which western processors were ready to fill. Unfortunately this demand varied between and within cities and regions, and packers had to make estimates. They had to anticipate not only the purchasing power of consumers and the amounts to be sold but also the cut, quality, and cure of the product and the competition of rival packers. Growing markets for western meat in Europe, and especially in Britain, further complicated assessments, for not only was the distance involved in shipping a semi-perishable commodity greater and the information flow less reliable, but consumers preferred to buy different cures and cuts of meat. Packers faced constant difficulties in forecasting sales with accuracy.[14]

If the market conditions of supply and demand remained tenuous elements within the meat-packing industry, improvements in the transportation network offered better opportunities for gaining more effective control and making more progress toward modernization. But this progress was neither smooth nor uninterrupted. While the early movement of livestock was restricted to droving and the early shipment of meat products was confined to waterways, processing took place in entrepôts scattered along the length of the Ohio-Mississippi River network and some of the Great Lakes. The weather could then have a major impact in altering the flow and speed of commodity movements on natural waterways.[15]

The advent of railroads in the 1840s and early 1850s initially widened the agricultural hinterland of the river ports by acting as feeder lines. But soon the advantages of rails in terms of speed of movement, seasonal reliability, and flexibility of route enabled new packing points to emerge as well as old centers to flourish. By the early 1860s the primacy of rail transport was clearly established in the form of increasing centralization of packing plants at main termini. This concentration, however, did not take place without an interregional as well as an intraregional struggle, for eastern city packers, now also able to ship western livestock relatively quickly and smoothly, had better access to urban markets. Western packers were forced to improve railroad handling facilities and internal business organization to survive this competition. The changing transportation network was very important in shaping the way in which meat packing contributed to western development.[16]

The role of the entrepreneur in making piecemeal but cumulatively effective changes is also critical in understanding industrial growth in a rural-agrarian economy. In the early period of western settlement unspecialized and ubiquitous storekeepers handled pork packing and shipments as part of their general trade. Indeed, they were the only men who could command the working capital and experience needed to carry on the business. These all-purpose merchants gradually found that they had to specialize more if they were to stay in operation. They increased their meat trade, but because of the seasonal factors it remained comparatively small-scale and part-time.[17]

Merchants continued to be active during and after the Civil War period, at which point they were joined by newcomers who saw packing as a profitable enterprise in which to invest. There was no clear-cut division between the two styles of capitalists, for the industry was still seasonal and subject to fluctuations. Both slowly made improvements to plants and increased product flow until the technological breakthrough of ice packing encouraged the newer arrivals to forge ahead of the traditional merchants. The latter did not disappear: they remained active but on a secondary level. This slow transition from merchant to manufacturer was part of the process by which industrial experience and modern business operations were disseminated to developing regions.[18]

A variety of externalities—economic and institutional crises, the circulation of information, the role of urbanization and of seasonality—helped to shape the emergent meat-packing industry and to determine its role in the economy of the Middle West. Regional and national instability resulting from general panics and depressions such as those of 1857 and 1873, or the incidence of specific phenomena, most noticeably the Civil War, compounded the short-term fluctuations arising out of the corn-hog cycle. The meat industry was thus plagued with more instability than its counterparts in agricultural processing, let alone in other branches of manufacturing. The improvements in newspaper and telegraphic information flow on the market prices of animals and meat products within and beyond the Middle West helped packers predict business conditions more accurately. Though they were never able to match the demand with their supplies, they gained greater knowledge about and control over opportunities. The growth of packing in cities, the concentration of the industry in large cities, and their ensuing rivalry not only illustrate the significance of access to transportation facilities but throw light on the evolving urban network both within the Middle West and in the United States. Finally, the impact of the weather, primarily in the length of the packing season but also during the antebellum years in the frequency and duration of snow, frosts, and rain, was influential in determining whether pork merchants survived and flourished.

In the mid-nineteenth century the meat packing industry rose to prominence as a leading branch of American manufacturing. Like many other branches, its rapid growth reflected abundant supplies and expanding markets, particularly urban markets for consumer perishables. But the growth was peculiar for its oscillations, which stemmed not only from general economic and institutional crises but also from the agrarian supply base. Moves toward concentration and centralization were evident in the displacement of merchants by manufacturers and in the development of the regional economy, but even with more sophisticated technology and information flow, the erratic course of development would remain. The industry matured but it still remained on the threshold of modernization.

2

Supply, Process, Markets: The Dominance of Seasonal Elements in the Pioneer Years

In the fall of 1846 two merchants, Charles B. Coons and Jno. P. Dobyns, undertook to engage in packing pork in Maysville, Kentucky, a small town on the Ohio River some sixty miles above Cincinnati.

> The undersigned owners of the large Pork Establishment known as the "Lower Pork House" situated half a mile below the city on the Germantown Turnpike and near the bank of the River where there is a first rate landing at all times for boats and a good paved road leading to the premises, inform the public that they will be prepared to slaughter and pack any number of hogs the approaching season. . . . Salt, Barrels and Kegs furnished at lowest rates. . . . The business will be under the control and supervision of a Packer who has had long experience in Cincinnati and for the last two years has been engaged in the business at this place. . . . Charges will be as low as it can be done in Cincinnati and warranted to be done as well. . . . Good pens for keeping Hogs will be in readiness and corn furnished at the lowest rates, to feed when necessary. We ask a call of those having Hogs to slaughter and are now prepared to contract for the slaughtering of any number.[1]

1. Pork Packing Points in the Midwest in the Mid-1840s

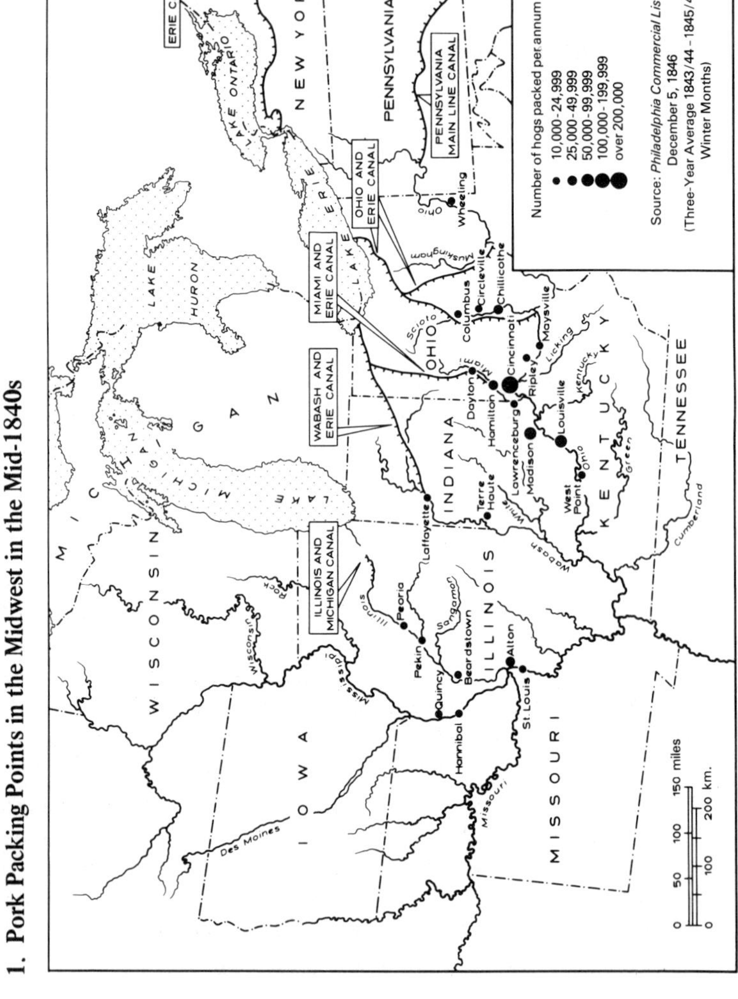

For them, processing was an organized business in which they slaughtered animals and put up meat either on their own account or for farmers to whom they had offered credit facilities. They then stored the meat products while the river was closed to trade and forwarded them in the spring either to Cincinnati or to some more distant large city.

But meat packing was neither their only nor their most important function. The partners more properly considered themselves to be wholesale grocers and western produce and commission merchants. They carried a varied stock of manufactured goods and groceries like cotton yarns, Madeira, Windsor glass, white lead, sugar, coffee, tea, salt, and pepper, which they sold to local residents and farmers or bartered in exchange for such produce as pork, bacon, whiskey, hemp, and tobacco. They were in fact intermediaries for receiving, selling, processing, and shipping all kinds of products imported into and exported from the northeastern section of Kentucky. They engaged in packing a few thousand hogs in the winter months primarily as a means of increasing sales to western farmers and as a means of paying for goods bought in the East. They then liked to be called pork merchants.[2]

Coons and Dobyns were not atypical. Other entrepreneurs in towns and cities located on the banks of the Ohio River and its tributaries differed only in the variety of services they offered to their pioneer communities. Most men who packed pork in Chillicothe, Hamilton, Circleville, Ripley, Maysville, Terre Haute, and Lafayette were merchants conducting a dry goods, wholesale grocery, general forwarding, or commission trade, and they had had some previous experience of handling small consignments of meat among their western produce (Map 1). When hog raising improved and increased in the Miami, Scioto, and Wabash River valleys they seized the opportunity to advertise their willingness to slaughter hogs and put up pork for those farmers who wanted to trade locally rather than in some distant but central market. They had the capital and could command the credit needed to engage in this seasonal and fluctuating activity, but they usually refrained from specialization because they considered that the pork trade was highly speculative.[3]

Farther west in the more recently settled parts of Illinois and Missouri, similar patterns of mercantile activity held true. General storekeepers familiar with the river trade of both the flatboat and the steamboat variety first consolidated small cargoes of local produce and then started processing. Their capacity to trade as pork men in the Upper Mississippi Valley depended on their commercial reputation, their skills in assessing seasonal factors, and their ability to capture trade from local competitors. Business rivalry was more noticeable here than in Ohio and Kentucky because the absence of a central packing point on the Mississippi River meant that most drovers and farmers sold their animals and wagon pork to a nearby merchant in a river town. Choice of both the port and the dealer fluctuated with the prices and the services offered in any given year. Rural merchants had to be flexible.[4]

Many of their urban counterparts in the larger packing centers like Madison, Indiana, Louisville, or even in "Hogopolis" itself, Cincinnati, operated under not dissimilar constraints (Tables 9 and 10). They too ran a general store throughout the year and put up a few thousand hogs in the winter as part of their trade. They may have gained some locational advantages from having better access to financial and information services and through proximity to by-products plants, but they also suffered greater competition for livestock in the central markets where larger capitalists worked.[5] But even this small group of leaders was more noticeable for its conformity to rather than its deviation from the general pattern of a part-time and temporary commitment to meat packing. Certainly these entrepreneurs packed 10,000 to 15,000 hogs, or two to three times the number put up by the average rural businessman. They also assembled cargoes of upriver produce along with their own goods for forwarding to eastern wholesale houses, and they occasionally became involved in manufacturing by-products, but they still retained their foothold in a general western trade and relied upon their long-distance commercial links for access to cash and credit.[6] In the 1840s there were few specialist pork merchants, let alone manufacturers. The midwestern meat industry was in the hands of all-purpose traders who annually adapted to the conditions peculiar to their locality.

The temporary and fluctuating character of early meat processing in the 1840s stemmed primarily from the seasonality of business operations and transport facilities. This seasonality started with decisions made by thousands of individual pioneers when the weather turned cold and animals needed winter feed. Most farmers in the Middle West kept hogs because they were cheap to raise, easy to produce, looked after themselves, and provided the household with meat for most of the year. Their first hogs were frequently those "razorbacks" which met with such derision from foreign and eastern visitors alike, not only on account of their shape and appearance but because they provided such low quality meat.

> [They] . . . have long-peaked snouts, coarse heads, thin chests, narrow shoulders, sharp heads, slab sides, meagre diminutive hams, big legs, clumped feet, the hide of a rhinocerous, the hair and bristles of a porcupine, and as thick and shaggy as a bears; they have no capacity for digesting and concocting their food in the stomach for nourishment; there is nothing but offal, bones, rind, bristles and hair, with a narrow streak of gristle underneath, and a still narrower line of lean, as tough and rank as white leather.[7]

Their edibility, or lack of it, resulted from foraging in the woods for a diet of nuts, acorns, and apples, commonly known as "mast." Even though they were often fattened for several weeks at the start of winter, usually on corn but occasionally on barley meal or distillery slop, the end result was poor quality—soft, oily, and hard to preserve—and not suited to long distance trade.[8]

Farmers soon learned that they could command more sales and better prices for their hogs, either as livestock or as wagon pork, if they bred and fed these animals. Following the lead of their counterparts east of the Appalachians, they introduced a variety of foreign pigs, such as the Suffolk, Berkshire, Yorkshire, Irish Grazier, Poland, Essex, Chinese, and Chester Whites, in the 1840s. They debated the merits of the different breeds of pure blood, noting, for example, that the Berkshire was a good breeder and could stand neglect and hard usage, that the Suffolk was an excellent feeder, fattened quickly and easily, dressed out a high quality carcass, and was easy to manage, while the Chinese, whether black or white, also fattened rapidly and gained great weight in proportion to its bone and offal; unfortunately it was small-boned and not symmetrical—fattening too much on the belly and not enough on the back. The defects of particular strains could be countered by crossbreeding, a practice that most farmers quickly advocated. Even in the 1840s "lard" hogs, which fattened quickly and easily, became numerous in midwestern livestock markets.[9]

Table 9. Pork Packing in Major Midwestern Cities, 1847-1877 (No. of Hogs)

Year (beginning Oct.)	Cincinnati	Louisville	St. Louis
1847/48	498,160	97,200	65,924
1848/49	410,000	179,000	89,400
1849/50	401,755	184,000	124,000
1850/51	334,529	196,414	85,000
1851/52	362,048	193,000	47,000
1852/53	361,000	301,000	60,000
1853/54	431,188	407,033	90,000
1854/55	357,286	283,788	89,830
1855/56	405,396	332,733	93,700
1856/57	344,512	245,830	71,531
1857/58	446,677	253,803	98,000
1858/59	382,826	288,590	57,500
1859/60	434,499	251,870	70,326
1860/61	433,799	198,751	79,800
1861/62	474,467	91,335	84,093
1862/63	608,457	116,000	175,000
1863/64	370,623	103,267	240,099
1864/65	350,600	92,409	185,894
1865/66	354,079	90,519	116,760
1866/67	462,610	157,071	176,800
1867/68	366,831	140,980	237,323
1868/69	356,555	167,209	224,341
1869/70	337,330	182,000	241,316
1870/71	500,066	242,135	305,600
1871/72	656,841	309,512	419,032
1872/73[1]	720,565	310,746	637,063
1873/74[1]	669,648	226,947	595,948
1874/75[1]	696,317	273,118	613,208
1875/76[1]	682,142	223,147	432,319
1876/77[1]	644,789	214,862	545,905
1877/78[1]	766,718	299,214	657,817

Sources: *Cincinnati Prices Current,* 1845-1877; Cincinnati Chamber of Commerce, *Annual Reports,* 1847-1878.

1. Totals include summer packing.

Table 9 (continued)

Chicago	Indianapolis	Milwaukee	Kansas City
26,682	1,500	...	...
...	12,000	...	...
11,500	14,000	...	...
20,000	18,400	...	...
22,036	29,000	...	...
50,000	27,000	30,000	...
60,000	44,900	43,000	...
73,684	34,476	34,000	...
70,000	65,030	37,500	...
89,050	27,160	15,000	...
96,252	40,480	16,000	...
172,000	33,217	32,000	...
166,000	32,276	52,000	...
231,335	58,781	51,000	...
514,118	42,100	94,761	...
970,264	77,000	182,465	...
904,659	66,400	141,091	...
750,147	55,888	107,130	...
501,462	36,000	87,853	...
635,732	53,739	133,370	...
796,225	52,645	159,463	2,500
567,954	56,466	129,094	16,000
685,959	55,474	172,626	25,500
919,197	105,000	240,344	36,200
1,212,276	170,824	313,118	83,000
1,425,079	291,317	303,500	203,750
1,826,560	555,634	594,000	150,348
2,136,716	482,765	248,197	78,500
2,320,846	412,346	184,604	74,500
2,933,486	577,819	286,425	132,792
4,009,311	474,414	426,767	266,165

Table 10. Pork Packing in Secondary Midwestern Points, 1847–1866 (No. of Hogs)

Season (beginning Oct.)	Madison	Chillicothe	Terre Haute	Peoria	Quincy	Keokuk
1847/48	98,000	55,000	47,500	26,000	21,650	10,500
1848/49	95,500	64,756	47,000	19,500	18,400	18,000
1849/50	87,709	32,785	59,544	21,000	29,000	19,000
1850/51	96,349	21,000	65,548	30,000	20,000	22,000
1851/52	97,202	42,000	62,651	17,000	17,500	10,000
1852/53	137,000	53,294	108,884	38,000	15,000	14,000
1853/54	122,450	54,496	78,169	19,812	20,500	9,000
1854/55	94,000	28,000	69,976	30,000	32,443	20,000
1855/56	77,465	23,964	48,562	55,000	43,600	31,000
1856/57	50,706	14,152	49,150	24,200	38,806	27,000
1857/58	58,000	14,250	49,131	30,790	39,640	25,500
1858/59	54,918	16,665	44,297	52,000	59,800	53,600
1859/60	59,889	13,199	41,755	29,548	58,583	49,600
1860/61	58,410	23,678	41,138	20,150	49,800	48,500
1861/62	59,000	19,262	60,268	35,325	53,500	40,000
1862/63	32,775	22,705	80,593	80,000	100,000	113,479
1863/64	10,500	14,010	49,674	42,700	72,130	95,100
1864/65	3,000	10,600	29,007	31,527	50,000	54,000
1865/66	310	5,500	14,408	19,527	26,162	31,000
1866/67	24,121	7,500	31,532	34,600	38,438	34,100

Sources: *Cincinnati Prices Current*, 1845–1867; Cincinnati Chamber of Commerce, *Annual Reports*, 1847–1867.

Farmers aimed to sell their hogs aged between sixteen and twenty months, and weighing upwards of 200 pounds, which was the standard set for "heavier" animals and higher prices. But their ability to reach these targets varied annually, for the degree of fattening undertaken depended on the size and price of the corn crop. From their reading of farm journals and local newspapers and from their own practical experience, farmers knew how much weight gain might be expected from feeding one bushel of corn to hogs, and they had on hand a table of pork and corn equivalents which approximated the value of corn when sold in the form of pork. They had to decide in the autumn which was the more profitable way in which to market their crops–in the kernel or on the hoof. If the price of corn was high, then they sold the grain, used hogs on the farm, and refrained from bringing many to market. If the price of corn was low, they fed the grain to the animals and sold as many hogs as they could fatten to either a reasonable or a heavy weight. The supply of well-fed "lard" hogs was potentially large, but its availability was at least partially dependent on midwestern farmers' perceptions of relative prices.[10]

The oscillations of pork-packing operations, both from season to season and within specific seasons, were connected to still more farmers' decisions. Having fattened their animals for periods ranging from three weeks to three months in the fall and winter, they next had to choose whether to sell them gross or net, or as live animals or "dead" meat. Farmers might carry out their own slaughtering on the farm and sell the packer dressed pork or they might also cure meat and sell "country bacon" if they were dissatisfied with the market price for livestock and could afford the labor. The price differentials between gross and net pork varied, but generally net realized between $0.75 and $1.00 more per 100 pounds. Premiums of between $0.25 and $0.60 offered by slaughterers might offset some of the higher price, but generally wagon pork was easier to transport and lost no weight en route. Packers might prefer not to take farmers' pork because of the variation in cuts and cures and the problems of frozen carcasses and "soft meat," but while the industry was still in its infancy they did not refuse to handle dressed pork.[11]

Alternatively, if farmers sold hogs live, their transportation to market, either by the farmer himself or by a drover who collected several lots into one herd, presented more uncertainty for the packer.

In the first place, the vagaries of the weather frequently interfered with a smooth and steady flow. Rain and mild weather following snow were highly inconvenient because they reduced the roads or tracks to a sea of mud through which it was virtually impossible to move. Heavy snow falls presented problems in acquiring enough feed to prevent weight loss and also were likely to obstruct travel. A sharp frost might harden the road surface and accelerate movement, but it also froze the rivers sufficiently to allow passage to other markets, thus stimulating competition between packers and between cities. The weather afforded no assurance of regular supplies on foot.[12]

In the second place, the distance of the journey to market was an unknown variable. Unlike cattle, hogs were difficult to control en masse when being driven. Although tales of stitching hogs' eyelids or roping their hind legs to dampen their roaming spirit may well be apocryphal, midwestern farmers and drovers favored short distances, whether for the razorback which traveled reasonably well or for the carefully bred hog whose progress was likely to be more sluggish. There was no fixed definition of a short distance. Some drovers would travel two or three hundred miles to reach the central packing point of Cincinnati: others preferred forty or fifty miles or less to the local and dispersed "porkopoli" of the central Ohio Valley and the Upper Mississippi Valley. Some recorded journeys of fifteen to twenty days at a daily rate of five to ten miles; others were more optimistic. All would get their hogs to market, but there was no guarantee when or where.[13]

While the broadly seasonal character of agrarian life in a developing region subjected the packing industry to certain restraints of supply, business operations were entirely circumscribed by cold weather. The commercial killing of animals and the cutting and preserving of meat for future use was a winter activity in which low temperatures were essential.[14] Some pork merchants started limited work in late October or early November to send "early" cargoes of new season's meat downriver before ice prevented navigation. Others might begin packing in early November if there was a cold snap. But the pork packing season proper rarely opened before mid-November and even then it was subject to interruptions as the typical newspaper comment below suggests:

> Early in the week the weather turned cool and there have since been one or two days when it was cool enough to pack Pork, but it was not at any time favorable and there has of course been but little done. Hogs have commenced coming in and the arrivals so far embrace about 3500 to 4000 head, of which probably 1500 have been slaughtered and all but one small lot packed on drovers' accounts. . . . We hear of several lots being on the way and in the course of the ensuing week there will be a good many droves in the vicinity, where they will chiefly remain until the weather is such as to admit of packing.[15]

The season continued from two to four months at the outside with a concentration of activity between late November and early January.[16]

Conditions varied geographically as well as between years. The packing season was likely to be shorter in more southerly points like Louisville or Cincinnati than in either the Illinois River towns of Peoria or Beardstown or the Mississippi River towns of Keokuk and Quincy, whose packing might last well into February.[17] But local variations in weather were always likely to prevent a steady, let alone continuous, process. A mild spell was the most frequent hazard, lasting anywhere from two days to two weeks. Then hogs accumulated at the pens with delay and loss to the owner, or carcasses were spoiled. Rains and floods were another seasonal hazard; occasionally the rivers would rise high enough to flood the pork houses otherwise conveniently located on the bank. A bitterly cold spell or snowstorms could also retard slaughtering by making working conditions impossible. The sequence of weather interruptions was neither regular nor predictable, but it was inconvenient and contributed to the fluctuating and temporary character of early meat processing.[18]

While the seasonality of the pork trade might deter some would-be western capitalists from participating in an uncertain business, it fitted in well with the ventures of both western merchants and nonlocal meat entrepreneurs looking for new sources of supply. Meat processing and wholesaling was an attractive and potentially profitable operation for these groups because it could be undertaken with a small investment of fixed capital and an extension of existing commercial arrangements for obtaining extra working capital as credit flows. Some businessmen who were well aware of the idiosyncracies of dealing in western produce with its irregular and individualistic sources of supply, or of specializing in provisions for a growing urban or foreign market, were eager to risk the seasonal vagaries in return for high profits.[19]

Little finance was needed to build an early meat-processing plant. As rivers were closed to navigation during the winter months, merchants had spare capacity in their warehouses, so they hastily and temporarily fitted them up with the simple tools of the trade, such as cutting instruments, tables, pickling vats, and lard kettles or tanks. If they had insufficient space to improvize hog pens and slaughter yards, or if nuisance ordinances prevented their presence within the city boundaries, packers could rent some land nearby and transport carcasses to their converted warehouses or they could hire the services of the local butcher either for the benefit of retaining the offal or on commission.[20]

When the initial commitment to the pork trade proved profitable, merchants might construct new pork houses with some of the profits from the previous year's crop, but these buildings were rarely elaborate structures and contained little sophisticated equipment. They were usually erected in stone or brick rather than the cheaper but combustible wood so as to minimize the hazards of fires, and they were generally located on riverbanks to avoid drayage costs. Most houses consisted of two stories: the lower floor, often leading directly to the river, was used for storing bulk pork and barrels; the upper floor contained the cutting tables and the pickling vats, and occasionally the lard kettles or tanks, though these might be housed in a separate building. As more money was plowed back into the premises, adjoining slaughter yards were opened and a smokehouse was built. Such improvements, however, rarely necessitated major expenditures and few rural pork houses were capital intensive.[21]

Some city entrepreneurs, already beginning to call themselves pork packers and curers as well as pork merchants, either by themselves or in partnership with eastern or foreign capitalists, did invest in larger well-designed and fireproof buildings in the late 1840s and early 1850s. In Cincinnati these establishments were of two varieties, those housing the full disassembly line and those specializing in curing green meats. Their size ranged from 150 feet by 50 feet to 360 feet by 160 feet and from three and a half to six stories high, but all were constructed of brick or stone, had fireproof roofs and walls separating the smokehouse and rendering rooms from other floors, and had extensive cellars paved with brick to retain cool temperatures for storing. In the "integrated" house the cutting tables and brine tanks were on the first two levels while the storage area for cooperage, salt, and other articles was above, with the slaughtering and pens on the top floor. The smoke and rendering houses either abutted onto or ran parallel with these units. In the "ham" establishments the curing and drying apartments and smokehouses were more extensive and the top floors were used for canvassing, coloring, and decorating. The pork houses of Louisville mirrored the integrated variety of Cincinnati, while the establishments in Madison and St. Louis were less sophisticated.[22] But whatever their size or range of equipment, the improved pork houses of the late 1840s and early 1850s were not capital intensive when compared to machinery plants or textile factories.[23]

If the fixed costs of pork packing were relatively low, the cash or credit required for working operations was extensive. A country pork merchant in the Middle Ohio Valley in the mid-1840s might need $45,000 to process 6,000 hogs. If he paid $2.50 per 100 pounds for live hogs weighing 200 pounds and some $0.75-$1.00 more per 100 pounds for dressed meat, and if he bought approximately 70 percent of his hogs live, then a Chillicothe packer could pay $35,000 for meat. He also needed some $5,000-$6,000 for other packing materials. If he employed fifteen laborers for ten weeks at a daily rate of $1.00 each, the wage bill would come to $900. Assuming that meat products were shipped by water to New Orleans at $0.80 per barrel, transport and insurance might add another $3,000. Working costs were never constant owing to fluctuations in hog prices, but allowing for some imponderables in calculations, the rural pork man in the older Middle West needed to command $50,000.[24]

Farther west in the Upper Mississippi Valley where packers were not subject to Cincinnati prices, capital investments were not significantly different. A pork merchant in a river town like Quincy required only slightly smaller finances. His hog purchases might cost $0.25 per 100 pounds less, but other materials and labor charges would be similar. Transport expenses by steamer—or even by flatboat—to New Orleans might not involve notably higher sums because St. Louis, like Cincinnati, was a well-established port with frequent services even to the more distant packing points of Beardstown, Pekin, and Peoria. Overall the rural packer of the riverine era of the mid-1840s would require $40,000-$50,000 to pack 6,000 hogs.[25]

The city capitalist in Cincinnati, Louisville, or Madison might process 15,000 hogs. In Cincinnati these hogs, selling for $3.25 net, would place the value of meat inputs at $97,500. Cooperage, salt, curing, and pickling materials would amount to $17,025, while the wages for a work force of twenty men would total between $1,200 and $1,500. In Louisville or Madison, where slaughtering and packing were usually carried out in the same premises, there were probably twice the number of workers, and labor costs rose accordingly. However, since two-thirds of the hogs may have been purchased live, the value of pork materials only amounted to $82,500. Should the city packer convert all his pork into bacon at 70 percent of the weight of the hog, freight costs on 210,000 pounds of meat packed into hogsheads and forwarded in spring would approximate $6,300. If, more likely, he decided to barrel half the pork, transport charges would be marginally lower; if he rendered lard, further freight expenses would be incurred. Allowing small sums for inspection and insurance, a city pork merchant needed between $100,000 and $125,000 to carry out his season's work in the mid-1840s.[26]

Few if any entrepreneurs in the pioneer Midwest had financial reserves of these dimensions. Yet contemporary sources boast of the proliferation of pork packers throughout the region. The apparent anomaly can be explained through the general activities of western merchants, through their ability to command credit both from local financial institutions and from distant wholesalers, and through the injection of capital by eastern or foreign venturers interested in acquiring western meats. Given these resources many persons were willing to engage in a trade which at first sight seemed to consume large sums which they did not possess.

In the early years of the pork business when storekeepers packed only a few hundred animals or forwarded small shipments of pork and bacon, they negotiated their meat purchases in a variety of ways. They bartered farmers' produce for manufactured goods, they offered credit at their store, or they paid in negotiable paper or cash. As all-purpose merchants they stocked basic commodities like coffee, tea, spices, sugar, salt, iron, nails, or glass which they were willing to exchange. They also provided their own notes as security for other items which farmers might want to buy locally. When cash was required by farmers to pay taxes or mortgages, the merchant used approved negotiable paper like county orders and town scrip or state bank notes or even hard specie. This last medium was preferable because of the possibility of heavy discounts on bank notes and commercial paper which originated at a distance and whose reputation was unknown. The general western produce merchant had to have a stock of goods, a sound reputation, and credit facilities before he could make any headway in meat packing.[27]

Those tradesmen who started to specialize in meat packing by building a pork house had to establish standings capable of generating large amounts of capital at short notice in the autumn and winter when contracts were made and hogs were marketed. The profits of last year's pork trade or of a more general and well-run business were insufficient sums with which to start. These had to be augmented by greater use of bank notes and commercial paper. A solid relationship with the local bank, such as Indianapolis pork men had with the branch of the Indiana State Bank in that city, was desirable. At mid-century this bank loaned out some $600,000 to resident packers and eastern operators in the pork business. But more often western packers relied on wholesale merchants in the major East Coast ports or sometimes in the larger regional entrepôts to provide them with short-term loans repayable in the sale of meat products. Long-distance commercial links were essential for access to cash and credit.[28]

The enterprise run by Charles B. Coons and Jno. P. Dobyns—either together, singly, or in partnership with other venturers—illustrates the general pattern of mercantile behavior. Dobyns had been in the grocery, produce forwarding, and commission business in Maysville, Kentucky, since the 1830s. During the 1840s he built up an extensive knowledge of trade in northeastern Kentucky and acquired commercial connections and property in the vicinity. At various times he was associated with Charles Coons, another grocery and provisions merchant with real estate in Maysville. When Dobyns turned his attention to the hemp trade in 1851, Coons joined with other entrepreneurs of sound financial standing and continued to run a profitable pork business alongside his other activities. Here was an establishment that had commercial connections of long standing and had tangible real estate as collateral for short-term cash borrowings.[29]

These Maysville businessmen were not exceptional. Similar examples of men who developed a wide mercantile experience and backed it with property holdings in the vicinity can be found in other would-be porkopoli of the riverine era. Jacob D. Early was but one of several emerging Wabash River pork packers. Having gained considerable experience in the dry goods trade in Flemingsburg, Kentucky, he moved to Terre Haute in 1835, where he took over his brother's business in general trading and pork packing. Together with Joseph Miller he did a thriving commission trade in the late 1830s and early 1840s and soon felt confident enough to build his own pork house. By the mid-1840s he had facilities to pack 10,000 hogs annually and was gaining a reputation as a pork man as well as a general merchant. Well-established mercantile connections with forwarding and commission houses and a solid standing with nearby banks, together with a shrewd eye for the fluctuations of the corn-hog cycle, were the keys to his success in the pioneer days of the meat industry.[30]

More generally entrepreneurs in the leading rural packing points of both the older and newer Midwest exhibited like patterns of behavior. Moses R. Bartlett of Chillicothe, Ohio, Bingham & Wilson of Hamilton, Ohio, John L. Reynolds of Lafayette, Indiana, Samuel Wade of Alton, Illinois, and Gano & Shields of Hannibal, Missouri, were all well-established dealers in their communities and were able to secure a packing activity ranging from a few thousand up to 13,000 by virtue of their general trade and credit extension facilities. They were not fully committed to the pork trade because they thought it was a highly speculative business. Indeed, several of these men faced financial difficulties at different times consequent on the short-term fluctuations of the corn-hog cycle. But in an era when poor transportation restricted the movement of bulky farm produce to short distances they were sufficiently flexible to respond to local agrarian conditions. The rural all-purpose merchants with their commercial credit links were essential to the growth of the pioneer meat industry.[31]

Their counterparts in larger cities were in a more fortunate position for gaining access to funds because the existence of more banks in places like Cincinnati, Louisville, and St. Louis offered additional and alternative arrangements for borrowing funds. Indeed, Cincinnati boosters frequently attributed the Queen City's ascendancy in meat packing to superior financial institutions. Certainly the branch of the

Second Bank of the United States, which reopened in 1825, attempted to cater to the needs of pork men, while the appearance of several new banks in the early 1830s further improved existing arrangements. By the early 1840s some entrepreneurs who were well-established in the trade could state that they were bank directors. Though a packing presence among the executive officers of a bank did not automatically ensure either a direct or a steady line of credit to the majority of the trade, it did mean that many banks were at least responsive to the seasonal and cyclical needs of the growing industry. Just when and how many banks became active in financing packing is difficult to ascertain, and some financial institutions were always reluctant to become involved in what they considered to be a highly speculative business, but given the profits that could be made and the importance of provisions in the economy of the region, most banks were unable to avoid some commitment.[32]

City pork merchants, who needed larger amounts of working capital both for themselves and for extending to upriver traders, also looked to substantial credit flows from direct links to or partnership arrangements with eastern wholesalers and eastern or foreign capitalists. Taking advantage of their location in major western entrepôts they were well placed to negotiate with distant outlets.[33] The Davis Brothers of Cincinnati doubtless maintained the Boston connections which their father had established in the meat trade there before he came west in the mid-1830s. John J. Roe, who entered the provisions trade in St. Louis in the mid-1840s, had previously been engaged for several years as a boat owner and builder on the Ohio-Mississippi River. He soon made partnership arrangements advantageous to his meat trade in New Orleans, New York, and Liverpool, England. Other city traders acted as agents for large forwarding firms and were paid a commission in the form of either a specified fee or a fixed percentage of the profits. While eastern and foreign firms also negotiated working relationships with merchants in smaller interior midwestern towns, they were much more likely to deal with pork men in large cities where the urban infrastructure and circulation of information were more effective.[34]

There were many opportunities for individual advancement in the pioneer meat industry of the Middle West, provided that the would-be pork men had access to large funds primarily for the purchase of hogs but also to pay labor costs and to obtain a pork house. Their substantial seasonal demands could often be accommodated through extensions of mercantile credit or through short-term bank loans. But these were not likely to be forthcoming unless venturers either had built up commercial confidence, had a sound local reputation, had personal assets that could be used as collateral, or came west already well armed with capital and financial references. In other words, most men who entered the pork trade with any prospect of remaining in business had to be either experienced merchants or persons of means or preferably both.

Their ability to become successful entrepreneurs, however, depended not only on commercial background, capital availability, and familiarity with and flexibility in dealing with supplies of livestock, but also on some vision in gauging the demand for western provisions. This demand varied annually in both quantity and quality. Markets, especially those in cities, were expanding at an unknown rate and they could be intermittently curtailed by economic and institutional crises. Consumer tastes for specific cuts and cures of pork differed noticeably with income and between geographic areas. In view of the distance to most markets and the slow flow of information, packers were rarely able to ascertain requirements several weeks or even months in advance. Thus collectively or individually they had little chance of forecasting their sales prospects accurately and they worked on previous years' sales patterns, making adjustments for the fluctuations in the supply of western hogs.

Early each season packers faced the problem of how best to process animals into specific meat products both ahead of and uncertain of consumer demand. When they had slaughtered and cleaned the hogs and had removed their head, feet, and leaf lard, they would cut the carcasses into three main sections—hams, shoulders, and middles or sides. They would first trim the hams and shoulders according to popular demand and the comparative price of lard. When pork was cheap it was profitable to render a higher proportion of the hog down to lard.[35] They would then process bulk meat either by salting or by salting and smoking, and would barrel meat by pickling in a brine solution. Small cargoes of lightly salted "new" or "green" meat were offered for prompt sale if the rivers were navigable in the early winter, but most bulk meat remained in heavy salt in the cellars or cool basements for several weeks or even months, and was sold, often after smoking, as bacon, in hogsheads weighing between 800 and 900 pounds each, or as shoulders in casks or in canvas.[36] Quality hams were more carefully cured and were sold individually.[37] Barreled pork in 200-pound containers consisted of various cuts identifiable by three main inspection categories: clear, mess, and prime.[38] Midwestern packers had several alternative ways of processing their meat.

They also had several outlets to consider because the pork trade was national and international rather than regional. Assuming that most of the domestic demand for commercially processed meat was urban, that the western hog pack comprised 70 percent of the national pack, and that the average American per capita consumption of pork was 122 pounds, then midwestern packers would have a plentiful and expanding market for their products.[39] Add the rising but uncertain foreign trade in pork products, and venturers seemed to be well placed.[40] But they had to disaggregate this overall market position into five distinct parts, the local or western, the southern, the northeastern, the institutional, and the foreign, each of which had differing needs. Furthermore the particular demands of each section were complicated by the distance factor, measured both by transport and by information flow.

Packers paid least attention to local outlets. As livestock was available for most of the year, many regional urban centers contained butchers' stalls supplying adequate amounts of fresh meat. These were supplemented, in season, by direct sales of wagon pork brought in from the farms. Certainly processors sold a small proportion of their output in the vicinity, for during the summer months when butchers only conducted a light business, the former released bulked or barreled meat from their storerooms. In addition there was always some demand for bacon, for particular brands of ham, and for lard. But this trade was rarely large enough to deserve mention in the local press.[41]

There was also a limited and fluctuating demand for salted meat within the expanding region of the Middle West. Some frontier entrepôts which were built in advance of the growth of their agricultural hinterlands depended on commercial links with more mature areas for a large proportion of their provisioning requirements. St. Louis was such a case, for merchants there continued to look to the Ohio Valley for their supplies until 1840, and they themselves did not become involved in cutting and curing until the mid-1840s. At the other end of the developmental spectrum, entrepreneurs who had started packing in

Table 11. Exports of Pork and Bacon from Cincinnati, 1847-1873 (in Pounds[1])

Year (Sept. 1-Aug. 31)	Via Canals and Railways[2]	South by Water
1847/48	3,713,411	60,693,890
1848/49	3,120,855	60,084,696
1849/50	4,253,718	52,177,460
1850/51	3,103,653	46,949,270
1851/52	7,722,290	52,091,795
1852/53	16,000,158	45,730,213
1853/54	20,846,302	30,520,803
1854/55	18,296,681	30,597,358
1855/56	30,470,305	21,046,450
1856/57	36,605,369	20,832,550
1857/58	36,301,109	24,291,150
1858/59	31,941,045	30,056,500
1859/60	38,872,984	38,649,300
1860/61	30,135,498	40,205,831
1861/62	74,149,768	7,263,750
1862/63	100,002,521	10,423,400
1863/64	47,413,245	14,827,675
1864/65	29,070,721	18,642,370
1865/66	28,189,376	34,671,309
1866/67	28,391,427	46,536,230
1867/68	32,369,475	34,592,650
1868/69	37,968,992	32,009,873
1869/70	49,241,486	32,604,050
1870/71	50,136,710	36,907,852
1871/72	79,701,336	33,659,317
1872/73	76,517,888	38,815,170
1873/74	87,799,143	30,863,134

Sources: Cincinnati Chamber of Commerce, *Annual Reports,* 1847-1874.

1. Barrel = 200 lbs.; tierce = 300 lbs.; box = 500 lbs.; hogshead = 850 lbs.

2. Other destinations reported for Cincinnati produce are "Upriver" and "By Flatboat."

the small river towns in the 1830s and 1840s were increasingly unable to withstand the competition of their counterparts in larger cities. Merchants in Columbus and Circleville on the Scioto River, or in Hamilton and Dayton on the Miami River were already importing some meat and lard from Cincinnati in the 1850s. Two further intraregional outlets warranted periodic attention. Lead miners in the Upper Mississippi Valley created an irregular demand for bacon and pickled meat, while canal and railroad construction crews and westward migrants also provided a transient market for various packers in different cities. Yet, as a whole, pioneer pork packers usually sold only a small proportion of their output within the region.[42]

They traded a much larger share of their products southward. Merchants had long sent bulk meats directly to downriver ports for sale to plantations and to New Orleans, where they were either redistributed immediately to urban markets or to plantations upriver and on the coast, or were stored for later use. Hams of both the common and superior quality were also in demand in the southern cities and for the planters' personal consumption, as were small amounts of midwestern lard and lard oil. Indeed, only the high quality barreled "mess" pork did not feature markedly in southern shipments.[43] The South may not have been dependent on midwestern food supplies in the 1840s and early 1850s, but estimates suggest that between one-third and one-fifth of the provisions shipped downriver may have remained in the region.[44]

Part of the remainder was forwarded by coastal steamer to northeastern ports, either directly by eastern operators who had come west or through western agents and their intermediaries in New Orleans. Other midwestern meat was shipped east by lake and canal or by river and canal or later by rail (Table 11). Once in the main markets of New York, Boston, Philadelphia, and Baltimore, this meat was sold for local consumption in the cities themselves, was retailed in adjacent areas, or was exported if the terms of trade were favorable. All types of pork products were sent east. Fancy hams from Cincinnati and Louisville commanded the attention of high-class clientele, while "mess" pork also retailed well. Sales of bacon and lard were more general, and bulk pork suited the incomes of the lower end of the market. Though there is no specific evidence to support the proposition that the urban-industrializing Northeast was the main center of consumption in the 1840s and early 1850s, both descriptive and quantitative sources suggest that expanding food requirements here focused highly in midwestern packers' calculations.[45]

Another smaller but significant domestic outlet for western meat was the navy, army, and merchant marine. The regular demands for both barreled and bulk pork provided an important stimulus to the early growth of western packing. Though some entrepreneurs hesitated to bid for contracts because the government laid down stringent regulations and required guaranteed deliveries, many were anxious to supply ships and forts. The merchant marine featured most noticeably in the shape of the New England fishing fleets, whose taste for high quality "clear" pork and Chicago mess beef warranted special attention. Other oceangoing vessels and steamboats on inland waterways needed more general victualing. The "institutional" demand might at times be erratic, but it warranted notice in any consideration of packers' markets.[46]

Another fluctuating, though larger, market for midwestern meat lay abroad; in the 1830s the United States replaced Ireland as the world's leading source of cheap provisions. The lowering of British tariffs on livestock and food products in the early 1840s stimulated American interest in this trade. Packers quickly learned to process products suited to British consumer tastes. Bacon was singed or dry-salted in boxes, hams were mildly cured and canvassed, mess pork was placed in a special pickle to preserve a better color, middle cuts were dispatched boneless, and beef was put up in eight-pound pieces in tierces. Already in the 1840s bacon and ham exports alone reached 166 million pounds.[47] Of the other foreign markets, the West Indies featured notably for its demands of lard for both cooking and eating but also for smaller imports of bacon and barrels of prime and cargo pork. France similarly warranted attention because of lard imports, but these were packed in cans rather than kegs or packages. While it is impossible to estimate the relative importance of the foreign markets, individual packers were clearly aware of their potential.[48]

The variation in specific markets often threatened the endeavors of individual merchants who engaged in pork-packing ventures. Though previous patterns of meat consumption might offer some guide, seasonal price fluctuations for different cuts and cures were problematic. The market reports for major coastal and interior cities could throw some light on prospects, but until the widespread use of the telegraph, they were frequently a poor guide to accurate forecasting. Even then, packers had to make allowances for the time taken to ship salted meat to distant parts. Sudden rushes or declines in buying or even abundant stocks of old meat at the start of a new season could disrupt well-laid plans for interregional and international trade. All in all it was very difficult to predict the course of meat sales.[49]

In the pioneer era, when the midwestern meat industry was focused on the river ports of the Ohio and Mississippi network, packers were still primarily merchants. In terms of commercial experience and ability to command cash or credit, they were the best placed personnel to undertake potentially lucrative but highly risky ventures. They could engage in seasonal operations because they conducted other western trade which provided some income and a sound reputation and because they had physical facilities in the shape of empty warehouses. Of more importance, they could command the large working capital needed for the purchase of raw materials, either by borrowing from local banks on their own security or from large mercantile operators on a credit basis, or by working on a commission. Furthermore, as merchants they were well aware of the problems of selling a semiperishable commodity in a dispersed market while lacking full information and depending on imperfect transportation networks. Economies of scale resulting from capital investment and centralization of facilities were not yet substantial and though city processors in Cincinnati or Louisville ran larger operations than their rural counterparts in Circleville or Terre Haute, they all shared the problems of working on a seasonal basis in a developing agrarian economy. Midwestern packing was still in the hands of all-purpose traders who were sufficiently flexible to adapt to seasonal variations and to conditions peculiar to their locality.

3

Railroads and the Challenge to River Dominance in the Antebellum Years

In the 1850s seasonal elements continued to shape the behavior of midwestern packers, who remained predominantly merchants. Furthermore, water transport to markets was still the main factor determining the location of these entrepreneurs. But change as well as continuity underwrote the fluctuating growth of the industry. As population moved west so processors followed, extending the geographical base of packing. The increasing supply of animals throughout the region further stimulated the expansion of individual enterprises. Of more lasting significance, however, the advent of the railroad altered the flow of livestock and pork products to new as well as old places and pointed to developments which would change the shape of the industry in future years.

Regional packing outputs rose by 61 percent from 1,457,396 in 1850/51 to 2,350,822 in 1859/60 (Table 6). Of this total, an increasing proportion originated in the Mississippi Valley states (Table 12). Packers in this newer Midwest, like their counterparts in the earlier settled parts of the region, had put up small quantities of pork products in numerous dispersed locations in the 1840s and had exported these by water. In the 1850s they increased their activities relatively quickly so that packing points like Peoria, Quincy, and Beardstown, all in

Table 12. **Westward Movement of Pork Packing, 1847–1877 (By Percentage of Regional Total[1])**

	Ohio Valley States				Mississippi Valley States				
Period	Ohio	Indiana	Kentucky	Total	Illinois	Missouri	Iowa	Wisconsin	Total
1847–1851	35.86	22.90	10.77	69.53	15.08	7.89	3.15	–	26.12
1852–1856	27.32	24.73	18.17	70.22	17.70	6.17	4.34	–	28.21
1857–1861	27.48	17.58	12.53	57.59	23.52	7.16	6.29	1.74	38.71
1862–1866	22.82	10.02	4.88	37.72	36.71	9.60	7.43	4.59	58.33
1867–1871	19.31	11.47	6.99	37.77	33.12	13.76	5.33	6.12	58.33
1871–1876	15.85	11.31	5.20	32.36	35.45	12.93	7.06	5.23	60.67

Souces: *Cincinnati Prices Current,* 1845–1877; Cincinnati Chamber of Commerce, *Annual Reports,* 1847–1878; Chauncey M. Depew, ed., *One Hundred Years of Commerce* (New York, 1895), 2: 384.

1. States reported for the West but not included here are Kansas, Michigan, Minnesota, Nebraska, Tennessee, and West Virginia.

Illinois, and Keokuk and Burlington in Iowa, came to be included among the leading packing centers of the West (Map 2; Table 10). Using the growing hog supplies of Illinois, Missouri, and Iowa, merchants in river towns in the Mississippi Valley flourished (Table 8).

But their pattern and range of operations were remarkably similar to those pioneer merchants active in the 1840s. Indeed, some pork men worked throughout the period and found little reason to change their business conduct. In the early fall they advertised their willingness to put up hogs or dressed pork or to supply packing materials. Once the weather turned cold enough, they started slaughtering and packing and continued to work at high speed for about six weeks. They stored the salted and cured meat ready for shipment downriver in the spring. During the rest of the year they conducted a western produce and dry goods trade.

These country merchants were, however, likely to need large sums of working capital both to purchase increased numbers of hogs and to pay higher prices for these animals. In Peoria live hogs cost $4.00-$4.25 per 100 pounds in the late 1850s, while dressed animals were generally $0.75-$1.00 more. Barrels, salt, sugar, saltpeter, and coal would cost 15 percent of the value of the raw materials, and day laborers worked for about ten weeks at $1.00 daily. Entrepreneurs who packed 8,000 hogs—the average size of a midwestern operation—of which two-thirds were purchased live, and who employed ten to twelve workers, each outlaid $83,000. Assuming that alternative routes to market through Chicago rather than St. Louis did not significantly alter freight costs, then the typical Peoria merchant would require funds amounting to some $90,000.[1]

The experiences of Maxwell & Johnson, the leading packing firm in Alexandria, Missouri, in the late 1850s, confirm the demand for substantial working capital.[2] In the 1857/58 season when they packed 13,369 hogs, they spent $100,401 on the purchase of animals alone. Assuming that these made up 85 percent of the value of the materials, that wages cost $1,000, and that freight charges on pork products added another $6,000, then the Alexandria enterprise required $125,000 during a three- to four-month period from late October to late February. Though the panic of 1857 brought financial stringencies in the Middle West, this year was not exceptional. In the 1855/56 season Maxwell & Johnson paid $110,225 for 11,770 hogs.[3]

2. Pork Packing Points in the Midwest in the Late 1850s

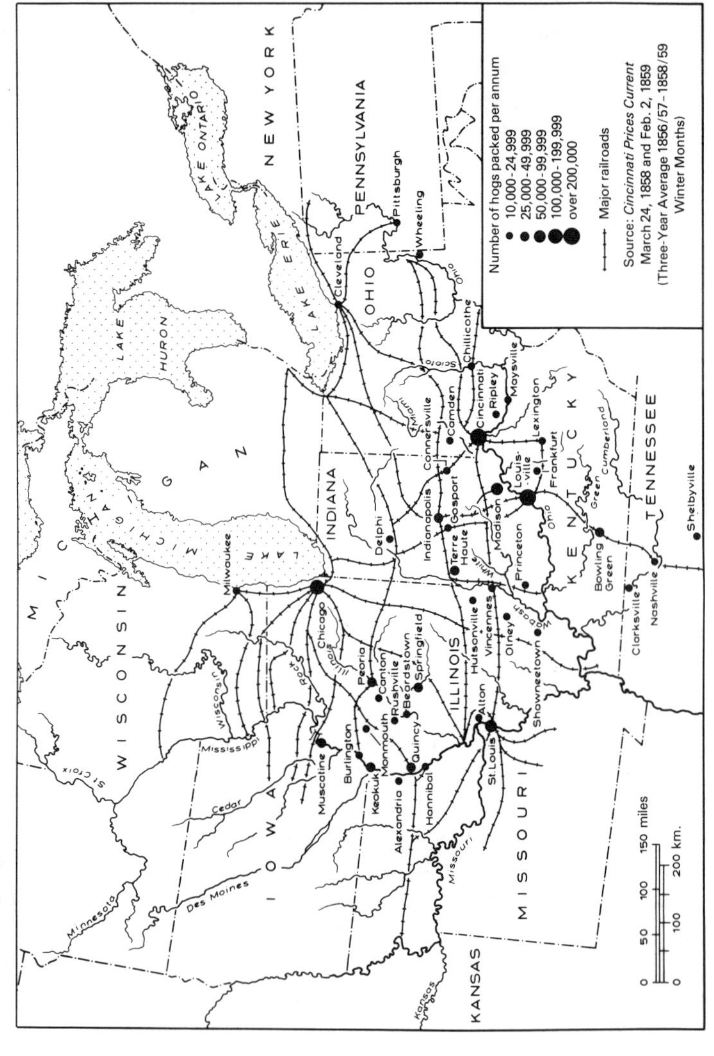

As in earlier years, merchants gained access to financial resources through extending their credit with wholesale firms in large entrepôts, through a sound relationship with nearby banks, or even through acquiring a rich partner. The working arrangements of Maxwell & Johnson provide some detailed insights into mercantile financing. During the 1857/58 season they frequently requested funds from the wealthy commission and wholesale grocer, John J. Roe of St. Louis, who was also engaged in packing pork. Rose had far-flung trade connections in New Orleans, New York, and Liverpool, England, and he frequently lent money on his own account or using eastern funds to country customers. Indeed, he frequently sent large sums upriver to Alexandria, and Maxwell & Johnson rapidly disbursed these to farmers and drovers and in payment of temporary loans. In the following season, when competition from rival packers in nearby Keokuk forced the entrepreneurs to make early contracts with farmers, they started receiving lump sums of $5,000-$10,000 as early as late September. They put up 18,000 hogs in 1858/59 because they were able to command funds whereas packers in interior Iowa towns suffered from a shortage of money.[4]

Not all pork merchants were as fortunate as Maxwell & Johnson, but a considerable number relied on some outside relationship. The Milwaukee butchers Frederick Layton and John Plankington borrowed $3,000 from the bankers Marshall & Ilsley to fund their entrance into the packing trade in 1852. The Peoria merchant Alexander G. Tyng, who processed both lumber and pork in the early 1850s, was not only connected with the wealthy entrepreneur G.W. Higginson of Chicago, but also married into the moneyed Brotherson family. Eventually in 1856 he went into partnership with his father-in-law P.R.K. Brotherson. In nearby Pekin the produce dealer T.N. Gill, already a reputable businessman in the late 1840s, received an injection of confidence and financial support from the backing of C. and G.H. Rupert, since Gideon Rupert, a landowner and banker, was one of the wealthiest men in Tazewell County. Although by 1851 Gill already ran the largest business in Pekin, his reputation grew stronger during the decade due to his affluent associations.[5] Western merchants such as these may have been able to run their pork operations alone in the 1850s, but their progress was considerably aided by their partners' capital.

Other packers in the Upper Mississippi Valley river towns started off their western careers as general merchants and built up the credit capacity needed for meat processing through their position in the community. Edward Wells arrived in Quincy in the mid-1830s and was active first as a cooper and then in the general provisions trade. He took a larger interest in packing around mid-century, but he still retained a healthy involvement in the general economic life of the community. In a similar fashion Horace Billings, who arrived in the Illinois River town of Beardstown in 1842, plunged into several types of trading and into real estate transactions. His commitment to meat packing remained limited partly because of his other interests but also partly because he specialized in curing hams. In Keokuk the merchants Patterson & Timberman started packing in 1848 by working on a commission basis. They built up their pork trade considerably during the next decade, relying on their real-estate holdings as collateral and their reputation as shrewd and careful businessmen.[6] Other than in the size of their operations, these venturers were remarkably similar to their counterparts in the Ohio Valley packing points of the mid-1840s.

Furthermore those packers in the older Midwest who remained in operations throughout the two decades also demonstrated the continuity of mercantile enterprise. In Terre Haute, where the pork trade fluctuated considerably, Jacob D. Early remained active (Tables 10 and A2). But he also reserved his general interest in city ventures, thus weathering the relative decline in packing. Even in "Hogopolis" itself, Cincinnati, where leading entrepreneurs expanded their business despite falling city outputs, higher production rarely meant abandoning old and well-established habits. The Davis Brothers, Evans & Swift, and John Child, now a partner in the firm of J. Rawson & Company, might call themselves pork packers and curers, but they were content to make steady progress by combining their processing with being produce, commission, and forwarding merchants.[7]

Though merchants continued to dominate antebellum pork packing with little change in their behavior other than increasing the size of their operations, the structure of the region's industry was gradually altered by the advent of the railroad. Initially this faster and more reliable form of land transport carried large numbers of hogs from interior places in Ohio and Indiana, which had not previously participated in commercial activity, to rail termini like Cincinnati, Madison, Indiana, and Indianapolis, which were well situated to remain or become packing centers. Indeed, good rail connections became crucial in controlling intraregional traffic in livestock. Soon lines radiated through Illinois, Wisconsin, and eastern parts of Iowa and Missouri, bringing in animals to Chicago, Milwaukee, and St. Louis. Furthermore, even in the 1850s rails forged new and improved links to interregional markets by facilitating the direct shipment of meat products to Atlantic ports, which were absorbing a larger share of western output, both on their own account and for re-export. However, railroads also increased the movement of livestock out of the region to supply either the fresh meat trade or the eastern packing industry. Midwestern entrepreneurs thus found early that rails provided a double-edged impetus to improve their facilities if they wished to remain competitive.[8]

The railroad first made its impact felt in the shipment of hogs to packing points in the Ohio Valley. Before the construction of tracks in Ohio and Indiana, hogs were driven by road to local markets from adjacent hinterlands. In the case of Madison, the city was the nearest outlet for animals raised in central and southern Indiana. All-purpose traders and commission merchants had turned their attention to packing as early as the late 1830s and early 1840s, and they carried out an active, if fluctuating, business. But their prospects were considerably enhanced when the building of the Madison and Indianapolis Railroad in the mid-1840s tied this rich and fertile area more firmly into their catchment zone. By 1845/46 when Madison's pork merchants processed 63,000 hogs—making the city the region's third largest packing point, after Cincinnati and Louisville—75 percent of the animals slaughtered and put up were transported by rail. This proportion increased in the late 1840s, and by 1850/51 entrepreneurs were packing 97,000 hogs, practically all of which were shipped by rail.[9]

But the early benefits of improved access to larger numbers of animals soon disappeared as other lines shipped hogs not only to the larger terminus of Cincinnati but also to Indianapolis. Already by 1852/53 Madison packers were unable to process all the hogs brought into their city. They could not expand facilities fast enough to meet demand, and outputs declined markedly after the bumper season of 1853/54 (Table 10). Entrepreneurs had certainly risen to the new challenge. Messrs. White, Cunningham & Company built up a robust business in the well-equipped Mammoth Cave Pork House early in the decade, and when the plant was taken over by Powell, McEwen & Company in

1856, these wealthy and experienced businessmen ran one of the largest packing enterprises in the West (Table A2). But they were alone. Other pork merchants in Madison put up only a few thousand hogs on a part-time basis. When rail links were opened to Cincinnati, many farmers preferred the better security and commercial services of the central market, while others opted to move their hogs to Indianapolis.[10] Madison packers, either as individuals or collectively, did not fully exploit the opportunities arising from the increased flow of hogs by railroads.

A similar situation held true in Burlington, Iowa, later in the 1850s. Located at a convenient point on the Mississippi River, merchants started processing local hogs and shipping noteworthy quantities of pork downriver in the late 1840s. They built up a fluctuating business in the early 1850s, since Burlington was only one of several competing river ports to which Iowa, Illinois, and Missouri farmers drove their animals. But the impetus to improve facilities and expand operations was provided by an upsurge of railroad building in mid-decade.

In 1855 the completion of the Burlington and Chicago line enlarged the hog supply and provided connections both to a growing midwestern entrepôt and to eastern markets. In 1856 the opening of the Burlington and Quincy road on the east side of the Mississippi and the Burlington and Missouri as far as Mount Pleasant, Iowa, on the west side of the river extended the city's hinterland. Then in 1857 the link between Burlington and Peoria further enhanced business opportunities. Burlington's promoters quickly predicted that the city would become the great porkopolis of the Northwest. Certainly outputs increased dramatically in 1854/55 and again in the following season. Unfortunately, however, local entrepreneurs failed to prevent hogs passing through as well as coming to the would-be packing center. Already by 1856 the number of hogs that were shipped to the bustling central market of Chicago from Iowa and western Illinois equaled the number that were slaughtered and put up in Burlington. And the city's pork packing declined rapidly in 1856/57 and again in 1857/58. Though pork merchants recovered in the last two seasons of the 1850s, they could not guarantee any long-lasting security. The railroads that had initially promised so much to Burlington's packers failed to encourage any large-scale activity.[11]

By the 1850s railroads were both stimulating and checking growth, at least in the smaller riverine entrepôts. They also had a double-edged impact on smaller landlocked cities like Indianapolis. Though located on the White River and in the center of the state, Indianapolis remained a small town until the late 1840s, when the arrival of the railroad marked the start of an era of expansion. Some merchants had already sent early shipments of salted pork downriver in the 1840s, but these were not significant since the White River was not a major water route. The upsurge in city packing followed the opening of the Madison and Indianapolis Railroad in 1847 (Table 9). Then two mercantile firms, the Mansur family and Benjamin I. Blythe, seized the new opportunities of increased supplies of hogs to build up trade. When Blythe sold out in 1853, the Mansurs dominated production. As respected grocery store and commission merchants of good standing, they quickly capitalized on improved conditions. Indeed, pork packing was becoming a major industry in Indianapolis, reaching an antebellum peak of 65,030 in the 1855/56 season.[12]

Progress did not continue unchecked, however. Indianapolis's packers struggled to maintain their share of the region's outputs in the second half of the 1850s, for other Indiana cities like Terre Haute, Lafayette, and particularly Madison, provided local competition for hogs. Of more importance, as new rail links were opened and improved, Indianapolis pork merchants found that larger numbers of hogs were shipped out of the state, not only directly to northeastern coastal cities but also to Cincinnati. Even though packers agreed to pay Cincinnati prices minus freight charges for hogs, they were unable to increase their business. Rails had brought as much competition as industrial stimulus, if not more.[13]

But what happened to meat packing in those larger midwestern cities where merchants might practice economies of scale and benefit from better commercial services? Did the advent of railroads secure a better supply base, strengthen ties with an enlarged hinterland, accelerate the shipment of pork products to markets, and generally improve business prospects? The examples of Cincinnati and Chicago illustrate two patterns of development—the former obtaining initial benefits but not consolidating gains, the latter growing rapidly and achieving dominance.

Cincinnati packers were already preeminent in the western pork industry before the arrival of the railroad. In the mid-1840s the Queen City's annual output of 230,000 hogs produced 22 percent of the region's total pack.[14] Strategic location astride the main transportation route of the Old Northwest, the Ohio River, early brought an active river-and-frontier trade which provided businessmen with assured markets and superior facilities in credit and banking. Easy access to a productive stock-raising region and good supplies of salt, cooperage, and labor further contributed to Cincinnati's packing ascendancy. The construction of canals in the late 1820s and 1830s merely served to consolidate the city's dominance in the Ohio Valley in both general trading and the meat business.[15]

Cincinnatians welcomed railroads as a source of commercial expansion. The first local road, the Little Miami, was in operation as far north as Springfield, Ohio, in 1847, and in that packing season, when the line was still tributary to Cincinnati and not yet connected to the lake port of Sandusky, there was a sharp increase in pork outputs. Other local lines constructed in southern and central Ohio, northern Kentucky, and southeastern Indiana in the early 1850s produced an intricate network of tracks in an area which already looked to the Queen City. These rails soon provided a faster means of moving hogs to market than did the traditional methods of wagon and toll roads. But despite these improvements in transportation, the pork business did not increase then or even later in the 1850s, when further extensions brought most of Indiana and Illinois within reach of Cincinnati. Direct routes to Lake Michigan and the Mississippi River did not provide that vital stimulus needed to encourage new growth. Indeed, in the 1850s Cincinnati pork houses averaged packs of only 384,000 hogs or 19 percent of the midwestern total. These outputs compared unfavorably with packs of 426,000 hogs achieved in the late 1840s, when the city cornered 26 percent of the regional product[16] (Table 9).

Why did the railroads fail to stimulate Cincinnati's most famous antebellum industry? A combination of factors—stability of hog supplies, rivalry with other packing centers, and inertia consequent on the viability of the river route to markets—provide the answer. Though city promotors claimed that 5,631 miles of track led directly to Cincinnati in the mid-1850s, the more limited mileage tapping the hinterland of the Ohio Valley was the main source of livestock. Here hog raising was on the decline because farmers were able to sell more of their cereals directly as a cash crop rather than marketing them indirectly as animals. Cincinnati packers might, in these circumstances, continue to obtain a steady supply at the expense of their counterparts in smaller cities who did not benefit from economies of scale. They could not, however, hope to increase capacity at the expense of other merchants in nearby large cities like Louisville which also had rail links tapping a similar hinterland.[17]

Furthermore, though Cincinnati prices were the best in the older part of the Midwest, farmers could now bypass regional markets and send their hogs live to East Coast outlets, since the railroads that opened up interior Ohio and Indiana to Cincinnati also linked up with trans-Appalachian routes and Atlantic cities. New York was connected to the Great Lakes in 1851, Philadelphia was joined to the Ohio River in 1852, and Baltimore followed suit in 1853. Indeed, by 1853 many places in the Ohio Valley had northeastern termini, and since the cost of shipping hogs east for sale was competitive with sending them to the Queen City, increasing numbers of animals were shipped out of the region. In 1842 about 100,000 hogs, or 11 percent of the total sold, were driven to Atlantic markets. By mid-century approximately 250,000 or 15 percent of those entering commercial activity were driven or freighted east by rail. In 1860 the number was 640,000 or 22 percent of the western hog crop. Cincinnati venturers, like their Madison, Burlington, and Indianapolis counterparts, were not immune to the threat of interregional competition. In point of fact they could not process all the hogs imported into their city. Small exports of livestock–of some 10,000 hogs per annum in the late 1850s–pointed to the difficulties of adjusting to transport innovations.[18]

Another explanation as to why Cincinnati's entrepreneurs failed to fully exploit the opportunities offered by the railroad lies in the existence of a satisfactory alternative route to market. Packers continued to sell most of the Queen City's hog product either through the southern gateway of New Orleans or the eastern gateway via Pittsburgh and the Pennsylvania Canal (Table 11). Though only a third to a half of the midwestern meat which was exported south stayed there, the downriver route remained important until the Civil War blockade forced a reorientation. Cincinnati pork merchants were reluctant to send pork directly east by rail, suggesting an entrepreneurial quiescence satisfied with tradition and "what worked" rather than seeking innovation and "what might be better." In failing to seize the advantage of using the faster land route to market they were guilty of lapsing into initial inertia.[19]

The experiences of several leading Cincinnati pork men substantiate both their conservatism and their modest growth in a period of regional expansion. Three old and well-established firms, Charles Davis & Company, Evans & Swift, and Joseph Rawson & Company, all packed between 20,000 and 25,000 hogs in the 1850s or about 5 percent of the city's total. They continued to be active in the commission trade and in forwarding provisions, but they also increasingly specialized in curing hams for the upper end of the market.[20] Enjoying the confidence of the community as cautious traders, they were able to weather the fluctuations of the corn-hog cycle without difficulty, but they set limits on their business endeavors. Even the relative newcomer, James Morrison & Company, who established their Cincinnati operations in mid-decade, were infected by prudence and did not push ahead rapidly. They certainly took advantage of their Irish connections to sell pork products in Britain, but this foreign market was of long standing. There was no sense of urgency and bustle among Queen City meat packers.[21] By contrast, firms in Louisville like Atkinson, Thomas & Company and the Hamilton Brothers, who were not only engaged in intraurban competition with others but who were also striving to make Louisville the preeminent packing place of the Ohio Valley, pushed ahead rapidly in the early 1850s. Though outputs declined later in the decade, individual enterprises still remained dynamic and forward looking.[22]

Even more forceful and bustling were entrepreneurs in the Lake Michigan port of Chicago, who quickly exploited the improved commercial conditions brought about by the arrival of the railroads. Indeed this new form of transportation underwrote the economic growth of Chicago as the mercantile and manufacturing center of the Northwest. Reaching out into a widening hinterland, Chicago increased rapidly from a population of 29,963 in 1850 to 109,260 a decade later. In 1851 the city was the greatest primary corn market in the United States. Three years later it was the greatest primary wheat center, and in 1856 it attained supremacy as the foremost American lumber market. Then in 1862, due to the increasing numbers of livestock shipped to Chicago, boosters could loudly proclaim that the city was indeed "Hog Butcher to the World."[23]

Merely a lake port, Chicago did not merit distinction as a pork-packing center. The city was, in the late 1840s, on a par with other Illinois towns like Beardstown, Peoria, and Quincy, which recorded annual outputs ranging between 10,000 and 20,000 hogs (Tables 9 and 10).[24] In 1848 the opening of the Illinois and Michigan Canal increased the shipment of pork to Chicago and destroyed the price advantage which packers in the Illinois River towns were able to offer local farmers, but the new all-water route to the South did not boost Chicago's hog processing. At mid-century the city was still only one among several subregional centers.[25] In the next few years, however, the construction of railroads radiating out of Chicago quickly altered this situation.

The first line in operation was the Galena and Chicago, opened in 1848 and extended to Freeport by 1853. Further south, the Chicago and Rock Island, spreading across Illinois to the Mississippi River, was completed in 1854 and bridged the river two years later. Another westward artery, the Chicago, Burlington and Quincy, joined the burgeoning metropolis to the Mississippi by 1856, while still farther southwest a direct line to Alton was in operation by 1854. By 1859 the railroad had reached west to the Missouri River. To the south the Illinois Central, chartered in 1851, entered Chicago the following year and was connected to Cairo by 1856. To the east the Michigan Central and the Michigan Southern competed for early access to Chicago in 1852 and then for through business by agreements or associations with other companies. A third major line, the Pittsburgh, Fort Wayne and Chicago, formed by a merger with other lines, joined Chicago to Pittsburgh and from there ran by courtesy of the Pennsylvania Central to New York. By 1856 there were over 2,400 miles of track in Illinois, all having Chicago as their ultimate destination. Five years later thirteen important lines, with a combined mileage of 4,500, entered the city. Promotors could, with justification, claim that profuse building had made the city a veritable railroad metropolis.[26]

The impact of this improved transport network on the Chicago meat packing industry was both rapid and marked. Already by the 1852/53 season, packers had more than doubled their outputs, mainly as a result of the animals shipped in from the Rock River Valley and from Iowa by the recently opened Chicago and Galena Railroad. In the next few years other lines tapping the Upper Mississippi Valley and central Illinois–the Chicago, Burlington and Quincy, the Chicago, Alton and St. Louis, and the Illinois Central–transported a growing share of the city's rising intake.[27] By the mid-1850s Chicago put up twice as many hogs as Peoria and was Illinois's principal packing center. In the 1859/60 season Chicago entrepreneurs were responsible for 13 percent of the western pack, giving the city regional status (Table 9).

Chicago had, in point of fact, become the leading pork center of the newer Middle West as a result of direct and reliable links to the flourishing hinterland of the western prairies. As a large entrepôt her commercial and financial services were superior to those that could be developed by smaller cities like Keokuk, Burlington, Peoria, Quincy, and Springfield, Illinois, and these services encouraged the centralization of livestock shipment, handling, and processing. Then Chicago's widespread rail network gave the city's entrepreneurs a competitive edge over rivals in other major cities. The new and growing Lake Michigan port of Milwaukee was located north of the corn-hog belt proper, and the old established entrepôt of St. Louis looked primarily to resources west of the Mississippi River. These cities also gained from more assured supplies of animals and more direct connections to East Coast markets, but not on the same scale as Chicago.[28]

But the railroads that were to make Chicago "Hog Butcher to the World" did not create a modern industry overnight. The shape of Chicago's pork packing enterprises in the 1850s reflected that mercantile base so widespread throughout the region. Provision and commission merchants who had put up meat in the 1840s continued active in the trade. Though they increased outputs and enlarged or rebuilt their pork houses, they practiced few economies of scale. Neither they nor newcomers to Chicago packing made substantial changes in organization in the later 1850s.[29]

The progress of Craigin & Company illustrates the continuing mercantile dominance. George D. Craigin & Company operated a successful provisions enterprise in New York City in the early 1850s when they decided to establish a western branch house to secure better control over supplies of meat. To this end they formed a partnership with John L. Hancock, a beef packer in Westbrook, Maine, who moved to Chicago in the spring of 1854. In his position as manager, Hancock built a substantial packing house with a capacity of 300-400 cattle or 1,000 hogs daily, and within the first year of business, Craigin & Company, Chicago, conducted a large trade. Despite the panic and depression of the late 1850s, outputs continued to grow, reaching 22,055 in the 1859/60 season. Using the sound credit facilities and capital supplied by the New York house, the Chicago plant concentrated on processing meat for retail in the Northeast and in Europe.[30] But any impetus to internal organization was dormant or underdeveloped because Craigin & Company and other Chicago packers still retained their broad commercial interests in western produce rather than specializing in manufacturing pork.

Two facets of this wider commitment can be illustrated from the meat trade itself. In the first place, many packers retained their interest in beef packing. Such a development might seem to be a logical step on the path to modernization. Both beef and pork packing could be combined under one roof, particularly since cattle processing started in October and was finished by December, while hog processing often did not begin until late November. But the marketing side of the business was different and in the 1850s when increased supplies of animals gave Chicagoans the opportunity to surge ahead, mixed enterprises weakened rather than strengthened any moves toward structural organization.[31] In the second place, livestock trading also expanded sharply. Receipts of swine increased more than tenfold between 1852 and 1861, reaching a total of 675,902 in the latter year. Receipts of cattle also rose markedly, heading up to 204,259 in 1861. Chicago thereby became the largest and most important western livestock market, attracting provision dealers as well as packers. Indeed, 40-45 percent of the hogs and 40 percent of the cattle received in Chicago in the late 1850s were shipped out, primarily by rail, to East Coast cities. The unprecedented scale of this trade created its own infrastructure of financial and handling services, and some Chicago merchants became involved in shipping as well as slaughtering and packing animals.[32] These opportunities, plus more occasions to participate in the grain and lumber trades as well as in Chicago real estate transactions, meant that many entrepreneurs retained their mercantile base rather than concentrating on pork processing.

The railroads affected the midwestern meat industry in three ways.

First, they replaced droving as a faster and more reliable method of moving hogs to pork-packing points. Though packers often continued to ship pork products by water, they were increasingly dependent on rails for hog supplies, and only those river ports which had good rail connections flourished. But railroads also enabled some towns that were not located on the Ohio-Mississippi River system to reach markets. Thus the stranglehold of river dominance was broken and even lake ports emerged among the leading packing points. Second, rails also encouraged concentration in larger termini. Once animals were loaded on trains, farmers often preferred selling at a central rather than a local market on the assumption that prices were more favorable and that payment would be faster. The city packer might not practice any economies of scale in comparison to the country packer, but the opportunities provided by the urban infrastructure encouraged more and larger-scale operators to congregate in major railroad entrepôts. Third, rails facilitated interregional shipment of hogs. A higher proportion of midwestern animals entering commerce were taken to the Northeast for slaughter either by butchers for immediate city use or by packers to be processed. No matter in which midwestern packing point an entrepreneur worked, he always lost a proportion of his potential supply either to larger midwestern or to northeastern cities. Railroads were sponsoring a modified pattern of spatial diffusion and structural concentration.

Yet despite these changes the character of the industry remained remarkably like that of the earlier decade. Merchants continued to be the dominant entrepreneurs. In the smaller cities and towns these men might still be all-purpose traders who ran a dry goods store as well as dealt in western provisions. In the larger cities they were more likely to be western produce merchants, some of whom specialized in packing and curing pork. But while seasonal elements continued to shape the behavior of midwestern packers, these men were still mainly interested in the distribution of goods rather than their manufacture. Indeed, processing was only part of the wider commercial web through which salted meat reached the final consumer. Merchants remained in the ascendancy in the antebellum pork packing industry in the Middle West.

4

Changing Patterns of Urban Concentration in the Civil War Period

In the Civil War period, 1860-1867, midwestern pork packers consolidated the superiority of railroad termini as packing points, confirmed the growth of the Upper Mississippi Valley region as the center of activity, and accelerated the ascendancy of larger cities in general and of Chicago in particular (Map 3). Though traditional patterns of seasonal and mercantile activity continued to shape the character of the hog industry, structural reorganization was much more pronounced and pointed the way toward future developments. The war itself, by disrupting transport flows and by stimulating altered market arrangements and some artificial demands, served as an agent to accelerate trends that were already in motion. By the mid-1860s the meat industry was on the threshold of internal organization.

The advantages of the railroad as a means of shipping livestock and pork products were already well established when the conditions of trade were upset by the outbreak of war in 1861. This occurrence strengthened the hold of the railroad entrepôts as packing points by channeling traffic from the Mississippi River network to alternative land and water routes. Lake-port rail termini like Chicago and Milwaukee flourished under the impact of increased livestock flows, while major river ports like Cincinnati and St. Louis had to strengthen their rail

3. Pork Packing Points in the Midwest in the Mid-1860s

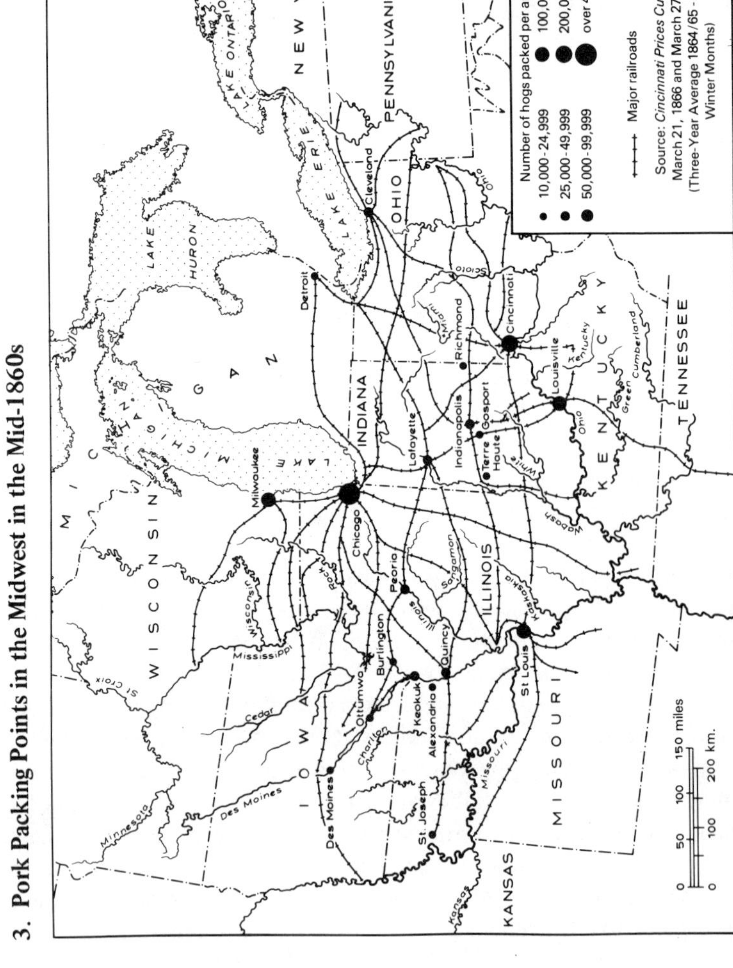

shipments of meat for sale in coastal cities and for re-export abroad. Some of the traditional downriver traffic whose final destination was eastern or foreign markets, was never again dispatched by New Orleans. Other new commerce originating in the Upper Mississippi Valley, which witnessed an upsurge in hog production in the early 1860s, turned to rail shipments straightway. Hog packing was increasingly tied to railroads as the main source of freight movements within the Midwest.

The institutional impact of the Civil War also had a notable, if imprecise, effect on the region's meat industry. A total of 1,556,687 men enlisted in the army at some time during the course of the war, and meat was an essential item in their ration.[1] The commissaries of subsistence bought an estimated 668,398,199 pounds of bacon, salt pork, and salt beef, and 161,290,500 pounds of fresh beef.[2] A considerable proportion of this total originated in the Midwest, since four of the major depots–Cincinnati, Louisville, St. Louis, and Chicago–were located in the region, while the five East Coast depots–Boston, New York, Philadelphia, Baltimore, and Washington–were partly provisioned from the western packing industry. Midwestern packers in major cities who secured army contracts received handsome payments which they reinvested in the business.[3]

These railroad and marketing developments during the Civil War hastened the concentration of packing in a few regional centers which enjoyed good commercial infrastructures. Concentration was not a new development in the 1860s, for two decades earlier nearly half of the midwestern outputs originated in four main centers (Table 13). But the spread of the industry westward in the 1850s had favored a broader dispersion of processing among smaller points. Increasingly, however, these places failed to register among the leading packing points because the threshold of success was relatively higher. Large rail termini were now able to command greater flows of livestock because they provided better handling facilities and financial services both for reshipment to the East and for processing locally. Moreover the system of contracting for army supplies further favored packers in bigger cities. By the mid-1860s the five leading packing points, with a joint production of 63 percent of the regional total, were all metropolitan areas, and this configuration would continue (Table A-3). Small entrepôts could survive in both the older and the newer Midwest, but their trade would have little impact on the future shape of the industry.

Table 13. Concentration of Pork Packing in the Leading Midwestern Cities (Hogs Packed: Percentages of Regional Total)

Season (beginning Oct.)	Four Cities	Six Cities	Season (beginning Nov.)	Four Cities	Six Cities
1843/44	33.34	40.00	1865/66	59.52	66.46
1844/45	41.90	47.31	1866/67	57.50	65.01
1845/46	52.39	58.82	1867/68	56.07	63.58
1846/47	47.09	53.00	1868/69	53.87	61.29
1847/48	44.40	50.40	1869/70	55.74	64.75
1848/49	49.60	56.76	1870/71	51.10	60.38
1849/50	58.94	66.35	1871/72	52.59	62.26
1850/51	48.69	56.52	1872/73	53.08	62.22
1851/52	43.75	49.46	1873/74	52.37	61.90
1852/53	44.42	49.97	1874/75	53.78	63.15
1853/54	42.47	48.06	1875/76	57.46	63.75
1854/55	38.83	45.59	1876/77	56.23	64.72
1855/56	36.52	41.94	1877/78	61.23	69.68
1856/57	41.30	46.79			
1857/58	40.46	45.30	Full-Year Packing		
1858/59	36.54	40.94			
1859/60	39.24	44.28	1872	52.02	62.02
1860/61	43.78	49.26	1873	56.12	64.13
1861/62	40.59	45.92	1874	58.38	66.13
1862/63	47.57	53.21	1875	62.90	69.57
1863/64	50.79	56.88	1876	63.74	71.80
1864/65	57.52	63.64	1877	65.31	73.34

Sources: *Cincinnati Prices Current,* 1845–1877; Cincinnati Chamber of Commerce, *Annual Reports,* 1847–1878; *Philadelphia Commercial List,* Dec. 1846.

1. Estimates only; comprehensive figures for packing points were not reported.

Of the leading midwestern packing centers, Chicago and Louisville experienced the most dramatic change (Table 14). Chicago moved rapidly ahead to produce 17.8 percent of the region's total in 1861/62 and to earn the title "Hog Butcher to the World." During the war years this share increased to 24.8 percent, a proportion that Chicago easily retained for the remainder of the mid-century. By contrast, Louisville, whose location entailed divided loyalties and disruptions both to hog supplies and to meat outlets, faded rapidly. Throughout the war the city was but a shadow of its former self, producing only 3.2 percent of the regional total. Though recovering some momentum at the end of hostilities, Kentucky's leading city would never again reach her antebellum position in the meat trade. Milwaukee and Cincinnati also encountered varying fortunes during the war, but their more moderate shifts reflected the new balance between the Ohio and Mississippi River valleys as major packing areas. St. Louis, despite being a river port in a slave state, was able to overcome these disadvantages by drawing on the increasing supply base of the area west of the Mississippi River. Though the Civil War brought some artificial restraints to both freight movements and market outlets, the patterns that were established during these years were to remain in force when the packing industry experienced integration in the late 1860s and the 1870s.

The Civil War accelerated the superiority of Chicago as a meatpacking center by increasing the rail shipment of livestock to and through the city. As farmers in the Upper Mississippi Valley responded to improved prices for agricultural produce, the Chicago market was inundated with animals. Receipts of hogs rose from 498,029 in the 1860/61 season to 1,410,320 four years later, and while 45 percent of the total remained in Chicago at the earlier time, 62 percent remained in 1864/65. Receipts of cattle rose from 148,300 to 343,726 in the same period, though higher proportions were exported–62 and 76 percent respectively–to supply the butchering trade elsewhere. How much of the threefold increase in meat packing in Chicago resulted from the artifical redirection of trade rather than the natural advantages inherent in being a highly effective rail depot may never be known. Certainly Windy City packers were pushing ahead in the late 1850s and they did

Table 14. Changing Distribution of Hog Packing in Principal Midwestern Cities during the Civil War

City	Average No. Packed, 1857–1860	% of Regional Pack	Average No. Packed, 1861–1864	% of Regional Pack
Cincinnati	424,450	18.49	451,037	14.27
Louisville	248,254	10.81	100,753	3.19
Chicago	166,397	7.25	784,797	24.82
St. Louis	76,407	3.33	171,272	5.42
Indianapolis	41,189	1.79	60,347	1.91
Milwaukee	37,750	1.64	131,362	4.15

Sources: *Cincinnati Prices Current,* 1858–1865; Cincinnati Chamber of Commerce, *Annual Reports,* 1858–1865.

not loosen their grip on the region's industry in the late 1860s. What may be said with confidence is that during the war period, they firmly established Chicago's position as the nation's new packing capital.[4]

How did they achieve this dominance? The number of pork and beef packers increased from twenty-one in the 1859/60 season to fifty-four five years later. But of more significance than the increase in the tally of merchants in the trade was the size of the top firms, which, under wartime conditions, frequently packed over 30,000 hogs each season as well as several thousand cattle. Though their individual contributions rarely exceeded 3 percent of the region's total, these establishments, now companies rather than proprietors or partners, grew increasingly more aggressive as they seized leadership.[5] A few examples of their business operations illustrate the nature of their activity.

Craigin & Company still retained a prominent position among Chicago packers. Though their beef packing declined from 17,359 cattle in the immediate prewar years to 9,270 in the mid-1860s, reflecting the general drop in city activity, their pork outputs more than doubled, from 27,828 to 62,702 hogs, in the same period. Under the dynamic leadership of John L. Hancock, who took a central role in Chicago's commercial life, serving as president of the Board of Trade in 1863 and 1864, helping to institute the new stockyards in 1865, and being a prominent member of the Packer's Association, the company flourished during the war years. Drawing on an ample working capital of \$500,000-\$750,000, sound business arrangements with the parent company in New York, and the increased supply of animals to Chicago, the firm both expanded sales in the northeastern markets and conducted a large trade with the government commissariats at New York and Chicago. Indeed, Craigin & Company gained such a strong footing during the war years that they earned a national reputation—producing 2.2 percent of the packing of the West—or an output greater than that of the city of Indianapolis (Tables A 3 and A 9). Despite some speculative losses in the later 1860s, the firm was never seriously threatened. Their business reputation, always judged to be sound, had improved in the buoyant war years.[6]

The Chicago establishments of Culbertson, Blair & Company and A.E. Kent & Company were even more outstanding than Craigin & Company (Table A 9). The former company was a relative newcomer to the Windy City, but its members had long experience in the pork trade.

Daniel A. Jones and Charles M. Culbertson had run a successful general store and packing operation in Newport, Indiana, in the 1840s and early 1850s. Then, seeking better opportunities in the newer West, they moved first to Muscatine, Iowa, in 1856 and then, within a year, to Chicago. Here, using their abundant capital and business skills, they straightway became leading packers. By the early 1860s they were annually putting up 19,250 hogs, and, under the stimulus of wartime contracts, outputs rapidly increased. Indeed, in the 1864/65 season when the firm reorganized as Culbertson, Blair and Company to admit the experienced merchant and banker Lyman Blair, packing amounted to 56,473 hogs and 10,033 cattle. Progress continued such that by the late 1860s the firm processed 88,039 hogs annually, or 3.4 percent of the western total, thereby outstripping the combined products of smaller places such as Terre Haute and Peoria. These businessmen had combined the opportunities of increased livestock traffic with their sound commercial standing to engage in a lucrative trade during a boom period.[7]

A.E. Kent & Company were also relative newcomers to the Chicago meat industry who rapidly rose to prominence in the early 1860s. The members, however, had different backgrounds and experience from those of Culbertson & Blair, thus suggesting the permutations of ingredients underlying success. Albert and Sydney Kent were young Connecticut men who came west to seek their fortunes. Sydney taught school in Kane County, Illinois, and then in 1854 became a clerk in the Chicago wholesale dry goods house of Savage, Case & Company. Two years later he started to work by himself as a broker and shipper of grain. His brother Albert, who had trained for the law, had meanwhile joined a commission house dealing in furs. Then in 1860 they decided to join forces and start packing meat. Using the finance accumulated in their early ventures, they conducted a large business and reaped substantial profits in their first year. Expanding meat sales to both the Union army and northeastern cities, they boldly opened a commission house in New York in 1862. By the last wartime season of 1864/65, business reached a total of 62,135 hogs and 14,394 cattle. Though trade fluctuated in the second half of the 1860s, A.E. Kent & Company still ran one of the largest operations in the country. Entrepreneurial initiative and experience, a buoyant wartime market, and investment in modern plant facilities accounted for the rapid success of the enterprise. The brothers used their financial and mercantile assets well in a speculative industry. In this they demonstrated the positive results of risk-taking in the Middle West.[8]

Not all Chicago packers were so successful. Some, like Reid & Sherwin, ran into difficulties; others, like Gurdon Hubbard and the Houghs, preferred to remain general merchants rather than specialist meat packers. John Reid and his brother-in-law Joseph Sherwin had started packing with a small capital in the 1861/62 season. Taking advantage of the expanding market, they made some quick profits which they reinvested in enlarging their operations and in fitting out a slaughterhouse. They seemed set to take a leading position, since by the 1866/67 season they were putting up 60,393 hogs, or 9.5 percent of Chicago's pork products. But their success was short-lived because they operated heavily on margins. When pressed to make payments, the firm was severely embarrassed, and they were forced to retrench. Success in pork packing could be rapid, but failure would soon follow in the fluctuating conditions of operation if the enterprise was not placed on a sound footing.[9]

Some older established Chicago merchants like G.S. Hubbard and R.M. & O.S. Hough also expanded their business, but they remained committed to the traditional mercantile style of business rather than concentrating on meat processing. Gurdon S. Hubbard was one of Chicago's oldest residents and pioneer meat packers. In the 1820s and 1830s he had been an Indian trader and had supplied the Fort Dearborn garrison with cattle and hogs. In the 1840s and early 1850s he was active as a commission merchant and an insurance agent, and he also slaughtered and packed both hogs and cattle. Indeed his career was typical of the broad commercial approach adopted by pioneer entrepreneurs, and he clearly preferred to maintain widespread interests. He continued to pack in the 1860s, and, combining with the prominent Keokuk firm, Patterson & Timberman, they regularly put up over 16,000 hogs and 2,000-3,000 cattle, or between 2 and 3 percent of the Chicago total. But this output was of small moment, considering the opportunities that were available in the expansive years of the early 1860s.[10]

Roselle and Oramel Hough fared slightly better than Gurdon Hubbard, though they too were constrained by old ways. The brothers had come to frontier Chicago in the late 1830s and had worked with

Sylvester Marsh, a prominent packer. In the 1840s Roselle ran a butcher's store while Oramel was superintendent at the packing house of Wadsworth, Dyer & Company. By using their joint experience of the western meat trade and the capital provided by a wealthy Massachusetts operator, the Houghs started up in business in 1850. Taking advantage of British army demands during the Crimean War, they soon built up a sound reputation, which they maintained throughout the decade. Reorganization in 1862, to include John Worster and Cyrus Dupee of Boston, helped strengthen finances and sales outlets in both Boston and New York. But already newcomers were surpassing the Houghs, who experienced relative decline during the war years. Then in the late 1860s, when outputs fluctuated around the 30,000 mark, the Houghs and more new partners were involved in the lumber trade, railroads, and the running of the Union Stockyards. Such diversified interests diluted the attention given to packing. The company still consisted of creditable businessmen, but their contribution to pork packing faded as leadership was seized by men with a deeper commitment to the meat industry.[11]

In Chicago forward-looking entrepreneurs were emerging to take the lead in midwestern meat packing. Stimulated by increased flows of livestock in the late 1850s and early 1860s and then by army contracts during the Civil War, a small group of men concentrated on processing meat and paid close attention to increasing and improving their facilities. Many were relative newcomers to the city and were not constrained by the traditional exercise of widespread mercantile commitments. Despite the continuing business fluctuations and uncertain conditions of operation, they planned to move ahead and gain economic status through specializing on a large scale.

Their momentum and that of Chicago packers generally stands in contrast to the relative quiescence of their Cincinnati counterparts. To be sure, the locational problems facing entrepreneurs in Cincinnati during the war period demanded different solutions, but these men seemed content to consolidate their past achievements rather than forging ahead to new horizons. Cincinnati packers maintained their outputs but failed to make any marked progress.

Already in the late 1850s, under the threat of direct rail shipments of hogs to northeastern outlets and the emergence of rival packing centers in the newer Midwest, Queen City men were struggling to maintain their dominant position in the region's industry. Then the outbreak of war disrupted the traditional river route to markets and forced both temporary and longer-term adjustments. Location farther up the Ohio River than Louisville might result in less local sympathy for the Confederate cause, a less visible military presence, and less interference with the supply of animals, but uncertainty and doubt were still more prominent features of entrepreneurial decisions than in peacetime. When businessmen emerged from the initial disruptions of military engagements and financial stringencies, they packed an increased output in 1861/62 and a bumper crop in the following year. They found alternative outlets to the truncated markets of New Orleans and the downriver ports both abroad and in the Union Army, and they now shipped all meat products to Atlantic ports by rail. Railroads initially carried more than double and then triple their former tonnage in the first two years of the war (Table 11).

Subsequent declining outputs during the later war years reflected partly the cyclical fluctuations in the industry and partly the difficulty of obtaining hog supplies from Kentucky. Cincinnati packers certainly looked out for business opportunities in 1863/64 and 1864/65, but they failed to increase their share of the regional market. Only after the war, when the southern demand was large, did Cincinnati men push forward. But even this surge was temporary and packers seemed content to settle at a lower threshold—at some 13 to 14 percent of midwestern output. There were no new initiatives to stimulate growth. Merchants were satisfied to tread well-worn paths.[12]

Charles Davis & Company continued to rank among the leading Cincinnati pork packers in the 1860s. Though the outbreak of war disrupted traditional southern sales, the firm shortly adjusted to new trading relations and was even able to improve its standing. The company's ample financial backing and solid reputation provided the means to transact a heavy business in the Northeast and abroad and also to negotiate contracts with the United States commissariats. Indeed, even in the poor packing season of 1863/64, the enterprise was estimated to be worth between $200,000 and $300,000. When the war ended, Charles Davis & Company quickly reestablished southern outlets, but they also continued to trade directly by rail to Atlantic Coast cities. There were no difficulties in surviving the fluctuating conditions of the 1860s, but neither were there any significant innovations. The firm rarely packed and cured more than 20,000 hogs annually—outputs that matched the figures of a decade earlier. Thus when the Davis Company's progress is measured against some of its Chicago counterparts, its contribution to the western pork industry fades. Paying more attention to curing hams, Davis remained content to opt for the quality rather than the quantity market.[13]

Evans & Swift, another well-known Cincinnati company, continued to remain active during the turmoil of the early war years. Though the redirection of pork sales entailed some temporary problems, they were easily able to withstand the stress on account of their banking connections. In 1863 the entrepreneurs dissolved their partnership, but neither man left the meat trade. Briggs Swift first joined forces with his brother Abraham and then two years later carried on in the commission trade in meat by himself. Jason Evans first associated with his son Benjamin, W.J. Lippincott, and S.C. Newton in carrying on a large business, and he then continued in operation as Evans & Newton. Despite these firms' reorganizations in a difficult period, they both flourished, but there were no changes of direction or new initiatives.[14] Though marketing arrangements altered by necessity, Cincinnati men retained the same style and similar thresholds of operation.

A third large Cincinnati concern, Joseph Rawson, also experienced internal reorganization when John Child retired in 1861. The capacity of the new enterprise was not affected, however, for Rawson made profits from his substantial operations during the war years. As a careful and prudent businessman, he had sought new outlets through provisioning the Union Army and through trading extensively in barreled and cured meats in the Northeast and in neighboring states. At the end of the war he reestablished his southern connections. Despite losing some money in 1866 he was always a first-class business entrepreneur. But he offered no initiatives likely to lead to increased long-term business. Rawson followed the pattern typical of leading Cincinnati firms, namely, of searching out quality rather than quantity markets.[15] This continuing emphasis on high-class products, particularly cured meat, combined with necessary adjustments in trading during and after the Civil War, impeded any dynamic changes in production. Cincinnati merchants, unlike their Chicago contemporaries, did not seize the opportunities for rapid expansion in the 1860s.

But Cincinnati merchants usually maintained their outputs; their

Louisville counterparts, in contrast, suffered serious reversals. For much of the war Kentucky and Louisville were regarded as being more Confederate than Union in sentiment, and trade here was frequently influenced by war destruction and by regulations imposed by the locally quartered Federal army. Crippled by divided loyalties, cut off from southern markets, and plagued by interference with supplies of hogs, Louisville packers undertook much less business and proceeded cautiously. Production, which was already declining in the late 1850s, dropped to a nadir of 91,335 hogs in 1861/62—a figure that had been surpassed fourteen years earlier. Throughout the war, packers averaged 100,753 hogs annually, or 36.6 percent of the mean achieved in the previous decade. Loyal men, like Hamilton & Brothers, sold much of their output to the Union troops and the army hospitals and had little incentive to look elsewhere. The army presence prevented both the smooth flow of hogs into Louisville and the dispatch of pork products to interregional markets. At the end of the war those entrepreneurs, like Hamilton & Brothers, who were still active, turned back to traditional southern outlets, but though their production increased, outputs in the second half of the 1860s only averaged 147,556 per annum, or 53.6 percent of that of the prewar decade (Table 9). Louisville men were slow to develop strong rail links to both old and new markets and were ill prepared to withstand competition from St. Louis and Kansas City merchants, who were now shipping their products south by rail.[16] Henceforth meat packing would contribute only a small share to the commercial life of Louisville.

In St. Louis, the other major packing center located in a slave state, entrepreneurs fared much better than their Louisville counterparts. Though the commercial difficulties of living in Missouri and having major waterway connections with the South impeded much of the city's normal operations, packers pressed forward not only in the bumper season of 1862/63 but throughout the war (Table 9). Having proved their loyalty early in the war by supplying troops without payment, prominent firms like Henry Ames & Company successfully contracted for army supplies not only in St. Louis but also in Louisville. But government markets alone were insufficient to explain the rapid growth of meat packing, which was about the only St. Louis industry that did not suffer from wartime dislocation. Forced to abandon some of their general western trade and to specialize in processing meat, leading merchants followed the example of Chicago venturers. They turned to forging better direct rail links to northeastern cities for consumption there and for re-export. Taking advantage of the growing supply of hogs in Missouri and southern Illinois, packers were able to look to long-term as well as short-term gains. By the end of the war St. Louis entrepreneurs were responsible for 7.7 percent of the hog packing of the Middle West, a proportion they comfortably retained in the next decade.[17]

In Milwaukee, another city in the Upper Mississippi Valley catchment area, packers also made marked headway during the war years and continued to progress thereafter. In the late 1850s growth in the meat industry had been small because much of the farm produce of the new Middle West, which was carried by railroad, headed to Chicago rather than Milwaukee. But the rapid increase in livestock availability in the early years of the war brought new traffic to Milwaukee, and packers like John Plankington rapidly expanded their facilities. As experienced lake-port entrepreneurs they were able to capitalize on western rail links like the Milwaukee and Prairie du Chien and the Milwaukee and St. Paul to bring hogs to market, and they could rely on good routes like the Detroit and Milwaukee line or the lake to ship meat products to Atlantic Coast cities. The subsequent decline and fluctuations in outputs in the 1860s were typical of the cyclical pattern within the region and did not portend a long-term drop in output (Table 9). Led by ambitious and well-financed firms like Plankington & Armour, Milwaukee emerged as one of the West's porkopoli in the later 1860s. Unlike one of its would-be rivals, Keokuk, which also experienced a flurry of activity in the seasons 1861/62 and 1862/63, Milwaukee had a strong enough commercial and financial infrastructure to transform temporary gains into regular business and to become a major midwestern packing center.[18]

Not only did the Civil War years mark a turning point in the differential growth of the principal packing points, but they also witnessed a decline in the total number of packing places and in the contribution of the smaller centers (Tables 13 and A-7). Pork merchants who operated in long-established points like Keokuk, Quincy, Peoria, and Terre Haute could no longer compete effectively against packers who worked in large entrepôts, while those in newer centers like St. Joseph benefited primarily from location near growing sources of supply

Table 15. Pork Packing in Secondary Midwestern Points, 1858–1877 (No. of Hogs)

Season (beginning Oct.)	Keokuk	Peoria	Terre Haute	Cleveland	St. Joseph	Des Moines	Cedar Rapids
1858/59	53,600	52,000	44,297	40,350	11,000	. . .	. . .
1859/60	49,600	29,548	41,755	17,208	15,982	1,800	. . .
1860/61	48,500	20,150	41,138	9,926	7,000	2,500	. . .
1861/62	40,000	35,325	60,268	61,972	4,000	8,800	. . .
1862/63	113,479	80,000	80,593	90,202	8,000	23,500	. . .
1863/64	95,100	42,700	49,674	36,941	28,500	16,500	. . .
1864/65	54,000	31,527	29,007	24,584	22,900	17,000	. . .
1865/66	31,000	19,527	14,408	19,870	24,800	4,017	. . .
1866/67	34,100	34,600	31,532	35,074	20,150	11,141	. . .
1867/68	68,000	46,315	26,345	30,158	30,010	15,016	. . .
1868/69	42,500	32,587	30,737	18,503	29,800	17,000	. . .
1869/70	47,400	15,155	17,309	31,224	61,300	14,500	. . .
1870/71	47,400	48,000	33,280	36,415	74,360	11,809	300
1871/72	57,500	94,664	25,117	35,010	118,155	45,555	15,089
1872/73	71,156	102,500	36,920	60,195	90,744	53,507	36,204
1873/74	62,286	68,150	40,000	86,922	81,642	43,570	72,810
1874/75	72,000	112,750	32,000	80,266	117,050	74,017	54,620
1875/76	29,750	87,991	13,200	88,077	84,390	40,068	75,968
1876/77	57,100	46,500	4,125	121,202	60,974	61,780	76,945
1877/78	50,409	41,500	14,337	107,762	67,320	80,165	125,360

Sources: *Cincinnati Prices Current*, 1857–1877; Cincinnati Chamber of Commerce, *Annual Reports*, 1857–1878.

(Table 15). Those men in the very small packing places like Dayton, Ohio, Logansport, Indiana, and Decatur, Illinois, struggled to survive. Patterns of activity changed throughout the western pork industry in the early and mid-1860s.[19]

Rural packers, who had been the backbone of the pork trade in the antebellum years, continued to operate in both large towns and small cities in the Midwest, but their position was undermined by rivals in major regional entrepôts. The rapid spread of the railroad in the 1850s gradually destroyed the locational strength of local packing ports by freighting hogs to major transshipment points and by providing an alternative means of shipping processed meat to markets. In the river ports of the Upper Mississippi Valley, entrepreneurs, though stimulated to greater activity by rising prices, never counteracted the pulling power of Chicago and St. Louis firms. In Quincy, Adams, Sawyer & Company remained general merchants who preferred to moderate the risks of a speculative business by working on a commission basis. In Peoria, Tyng & Brotherson continued as commission merchants, grain dealers, and pork packers, while in Keokuk, Patterson & Timberman generally worked for larger firms in Chicago and St. Louis. It was becoming increasingly difficult to thrive as an independent small-scale pork merchant in an industry that was becoming more systematically organized.[20]

Pork merchants in the older Midwest were in no better position in the 1860s. Two Wabash River merchants, Jacob D. Early in Terre Haute and Henry T. Sample in Lafayette, are representative. Both were long-time residents and traders who conducted pork operations when prospects looked good. Their calculations were not always correct, but they had sufficient diverse commercial and financial interests that they did not depend on packing for their livelihood. This partial and intermittent commitment, like commission work, may have been the way forward in the pioneer years of the meat industry, but in the 1860s both practices were indicative of the decline of rural participation in agricultural processing.[21]

Builders of the future western meat industry usually resided in larger centers unless they were part of the frontier movement. In St. Joseph the orientation still belonged to the pioneer West. Merchants who lived in this Missouri River departure point for overland emigrants had been in the provisions business for many years. Initially they imported their meat from older parts of the region, but as farmers settled in western Missouri, they paid more attention to packing and curing pork themselves. Their early ventures were small-scale and part-time, but later in the 1860s, when railroads started to widen market horizons, capitalists invested in larger plants. David Pinger & Company was one such example. Pinger had been a western produce trader since the 1850s. Then in 1865 he associated with three other merchants and bankers to form a stronger company ready to expand. Soon they were putting up between 10,000 and 15,000 hogs annually. Their growth, however, was more reminiscent of the extensive variety which was tied to local supplies and a viable route to market than the intensive variety which followed from centralization and improved transportation.[22]

Pork packers in the Civil War period were more likely to thrive in cities with good rail links both to farm supplies and to interregional markets. But some midwestern transshipment points made greater headway as packing centers than others. Location in the catchment area of the Upper Mississippi Valley usually brought an increased flow of hogs in the early 1860s, while the closure of the traditional river route to and through the South favored more northerly cities. Furthermore, those large regional centers which offered better commercial and financial infrastructures were proving to be more attractive to leading venturers, who frequently found themselves well placed to secure army contracts. Of these cities Chicago was clearly the most important, while Cincinnati maintained a prominent position. St. Louis emerged as a noteworthy contributor, as did Milwaukee, but Louisville faded rapidly. Small, and often river, towns still participated in regional trade, but their outputs tended to be limited. The technology of improved transportation, the benefits derived from urban services, and the impact of the Civil War together favored reorganization and centralization in an industry that had previously responded to its local agricultural base. Westward expansion of farming merely strengthened the development of cities in the newer Midwest.

5

The Emergence of a Permanent Industry

The recently created Pork Packers' Association began its annual report of the "Packing of the West" for 1875-1876 with this statement:

> The business of Pork Packing is a large and growing one . . . now involving an outlay of immense capital. . . . For the item of Hogs alone, not less than $95,000,000 were paid by the packers . . . during the Winter season of 1875-6. To this heavy expenditure may be added the cost of cooperage, wages, salt and necessary running expenses. Not less than five hundred cities and towns in the West are directly interested in the prosperity of this branch of industry and as fully as many more cities and towns in the Eastern portion of our country and Europe are dependent to a certain extent on its production. Years ago the business was conducted without regard to system. . . . With the increased business at the larger packing centers, the . . . business has been enlarged to one of our heaviest interests, and is now conducted upon systematic principles in keeping with the enlightenment of the present age and progress of our country.[1]

In the statistical and descriptive information that followed, the association supported the proposition that the meat industry was reaching maturity. Already by the mid-1860s manufacturers were emerging from the welter of pork merchants, and their growing importance was confirmed in the early 1870s. In response first to improvements in railroad transportation and then to advances in business administration and technology in the shape of centralized stockyards, by-products processing, professional associations, improved communications, and ice packing, many entrepreneurs increased their control over factors of production. Indeed, these men changed the shape and character of the industry not only through the sophistication of their packing plants and the growing size of their enterprises but also through their ability to capture a larger share of the national and international market. Though the firms who controlled more than 1 or 2 percent of the Midwest's outputs were few in number, they were increasingly setting the standard for other venturers to follow. Meat packers were adopting more modern forms of organization.

This process, however, was not complete. Connections with the traditional and more widespread pattern of mercantile operations were not yet severed. Contemporary newspapers, journals, and city directories might well boast about large plants served directly by railroads and capable of packing and curing a thousand or more hogs daily, but they could not conceal the fact that many suppliers processed less than a thousand hogs in the course of the season. Certainly these individuals who packed in neighborhood places could be excluded from commercial consideration, since they sold their products mainly to local customers. But other entrepreneurs who put up a few thousand hogs in rudimentary plants which lacked capital investment continued to pack on a seasonal basis primarily for an intraregional market. Their ability to stay in business alongside or behind the leading manufacturers reflected the remnants of a broad participation in agricultural processing, albeit one that would not last much longer as the industry moved toward big business.

The advent of the railroad had instigated the first widespread changes in the structure of the midwestern meat industry in the 1850s and early 1860s. But by the end of the Civil War it was becoming obvious that good rail connections alone were inadequate to create a modern industry. An expanding supply of hogs brought into regional centers might lead to enlarged business operations, but productivity gains stemmed either from better organization or from technological advances. Accordingly packers started to pay greater attention to centralizing shipment and marketing facilities through stockyards. They would thus not only improve flows of livestock and pork products but also relocate their packing plants more effectively.

Chicago clearly pointed the way in 1865 with the opening of the Union Stock Yards. Increased receipts of livestock in the early 1860s had put a strain on the six separate stockyards then in existence in the Windy City.[2] Drovers, commision merchants, packers, butchers, and railroad investors all wanted better handling and transit facilities in order to avoid injury to stock, delay in receiving shipments, and expense in switching cars from one yard to another. When, in June 1864, the city's Pork Packers' Association resolved that operations should be consolidated, they received a positive response, especially from the railroads who subscribed 92.5 percent of the capital stock of the proposed Union Stock Yards and Transit Company. Following incorporation, in February 1865, the new company bought a 345-acre tract in south Chicago. By the grand opening day of Christmas 1865, they had drained the land and built 500 pens, five large water tanks, feeding facilities, and fifteen miles of track connecting the yard with all railroads. A hotel, exchange, and bank were also nearing completion, and cottages for the employees were planned.[3] In the words of a contemporary, the Great Union Stock Yards were "a monument of Western traffic never before equaled and never to be excelled."[4]

Though boosterist in tone, the words were well founded, for the Yards confirmed Chicago's position as the most accessible livestock market and meat-packing center not only in the Middle West but also in the United States. Straightway there were facilities for unloading, accommodating, watering, and feeding 118,200 head of stock. And in 1866, the first full year of operation, the Yards received a total of 1,286,326 hogs and 384,251 cattle, of which 44.8 and 69.9 percent respectively were shipped out. Though these figures do not differ noticeably from those recorded during the war, in the following year hog receipts increased dramatically by 54.5 percent, to 1,987,120, and they continued on an upward spiral during the next decade. Indeed, ten years after the opening of the Yards they had increased to 4,338,628, of which only 27.9 percent were forwarded to other points. Cattle receipts also grew during the same period, and in 1876, 1,096,745 were shipped into Chicago, of which 72.7 percent were redirected elsewhere for the butchering trade. To accommodate this influx, the facilities at the Stock Yards were enlarged and improved. Total animal capacity rose to 147,500 head; yards and pens occupied another forty-nine acres; ten more miles of railroad track, one mile of streets and alleys, and half a mile of water troughs were further added, while a canal providing direct and easy water communication with Lake Michigan was completed in 1872. By 1876 the cost of constructing the huge yards had risen to upward of $3 million, but the expense was worthwhile, for the volume of livestock at the Union Stock Yards was never equaled elsewhere.[5]

An increased and regular flow of animals was not the only benefit which the presence of the Union Stock Yards bestowed on the thriving Chicago packing industry in the postwar decade. The other advantage lay in the new industrial location adjoining the yards. This move not only overcame the problem of the intraurban transfer of stock and meat products, but it also provided a site unhindered by city nuisance ordinances and well served with piped water. Less apparent, the Yards' complex provided a full range of commercial and financial services. The Exchange Building housed offices for company officials and for numerous commission firms. Telegraph facilities were available for rapid communications, while the Post Office furnished a slower means of information flow. The *Daily Drovers' Journal* reported the activity of the Chicago and other livestock markets. The Union Stock Yards National Bank offered widespread services for the transmission of funds and for essential short-term loans. Then, if required, the Transit House or hotel offered high-class accommodation to those in the trade. Chicago packers gained noticeably in a variety of ancillary ways from being first in the field to help promote a centralized livestock market.[6]

It was not long before other midwestern businessmen followed the example set by Chicago entrepreneurs. In 1871 outside capitalists, primarily eastern railroad men, combined to invest $1 million in building the St. Louis National Stock Yards on the east side of the Mississippi River. Having bought a 400-acre site served by the major railroads, they first provided adequate sewage and water supplies and then built pens and sheds to accommodate 35,000 cattle and 20,000 hogs. Commercial offices equipped with telegraph communications were located in the two-story Exchange Building, while the Allerton House offered the comforts of a first-class hotel. A smaller company, with a capital of $325,000, soon built the St. Louis Union Stockyards on the west side of the river in order to tap the southern and southwestern regions. While both yards were designed to improve livestock, especially cattle, flows eastward, they also stimulated the city's packing industry by providing smoother hog supplies and better access to more specialized commercial services.[7]

In 1871 Cincinnati investors organized the Union Railroad Stock Yard Company with a capital of $1,250,000. They first acquired fifty acres of land, which were then graded and supplied with sewers and piped water. Covered pens and sheds had a capacity of 75,000 head of stock, and railroad sidings surrounded by shipping pens ran through a central thoroughfare. Indeed, Cincinnati venturers claimed to have facilities for unloading, holding, feeding, watering, and reloading stock which surpassed the renowned Chicago yards. Human welfare also received attention. The hotel—"Avenue House"—offered handy accommodation for businessmen and housed offices for brokers on the ground floor. Furthermore, the telegraph provided rapid communication with other parts of the country. Not surprisingly, two years after opening, four of the city's largest packing companies built new plants adjoining the stockyards. Though Cincinnati pork packers could not rival the outputs of their Chicago counterparts, they were still well aware of the advantages of more modern methods of handling livestock.[8]

St. Louis and Cincinnati were not the only midwestern cities to build new stockyards.[9] Milwaukee began construction of spacious premises in the Menomonee Valley as early as 1869. The great Bourbon Yards at Louisville were founded in 1875, and the Indianapolis Belt Railroad and Stock Yard Company, organized in 1877, commenced active operations in 1878. Even smaller packing points followed suit in an attempt to retain their share of the region's business. Burlington, Iowa, which claimed to have extensive yards as early as 1867, made additions and improvements in 1876, while the Peoria Union Stock Yards were opened in 1877. By the mid-1870s the systematic management of animal supplies was essential if the packing industry was to survive, let alone thrive. Centralized livestock yards might well bring the transit of animals through a given point, but they were the only efficient method of guaranteeing large supplies of hogs.[10]

The older packing points were not alone in seeking to improve the handling of livestock. They were joined, or in some cases, were antici-

4. Pork Packing Points in the Midwest in the Mid-1870s

Number of hogs packed per annum

- 10,000-24,999
- 25,000-49,999
- 50,000-99,999
- 100,000-199,999
- 200,000-399,999
- 400,000-799,999
- 800,000-1,599,999
- over 1,600,000

Major railroads

Source: Cincinnati Chamber of Commerce, *Annual Report* 1874, 1875, and 1876 (Three-Year Average 1873/74-1875/76 All Year)

pated by newer centers lying west of the Mississippi River. If railroads furnished adequate links to both raw materials and distant markets, and if sufficient investment capital was forthcoming, newer western places like Kansas City (Missouri and Kansas), St. Joseph, Missouri, Des Moines, Iowa, Cedar Rapids, Iowa, Ottumwa, Iowa, and Omaha, Nebraska, could compress the evolutionary stages of packing and directly enter the modern industry (Map 4). Indeed, at some points large integrated packing plants quickly created their own infrastructure and rapidly built centralized livestock facilities. A reversal of the traditional pattern of business organization took place.

In the late 1850s and early 1860s Kansas City was primarily a frontier community where merchants put up salted and barreled pork both for local consumption and for use on the overland trail. They also shipped some cattle eastward by rail. When, in the late 1860s, numerous Texas steers were driven up the long trails, entrepreneurs saw the need to create a livestock market which could handle this trade. Furthermore, they realized that the area tributary to the Missouri River was a potentially rich corn-growing and animal-feeding belt which would generate an active meat business. Hence in 1871 outside capitalists organized the Kansas Stockyards Company to erect and operate a complete feed and transfer yard. At first this small venture with its twenty-six acres, pens, chutes, and shedlike "Exchange Building" was reminiscent of the railroad yards of the older middle West of a decade earlier. Certainly the receipts of hogs and cattle in the first three years of operation, before the Panic of 1873 disrupted trade, were similar to those of Chicago in the late 1850s.[11]

This situation was short-lived. Signs of centralization were already visible in the extensions of and improvements to pens, barns, and offices in the 1870s. Then in 1876 the reorganized Kansas City Stock Yards Company made advances which echoed those of Chicago after the Civil War. They acquired an extra forty-two acres of land, built new covered floors and pens, finished loading docks for all railroads, and started a large exchange building that contained offices, a bank, a restaurant, billiard hall, barber's shop, and bathroom. Two years later they further expanded their facilities. Yet on occasions the yards were still not adequate, and more improvements were made in the 1880s.[12]

Such progress could not have been made had there not been both outside money and an active packing interest. The involvement of eastern railroad financiers in the new Kansas City Stock Yards Company in 1875 was merely the second upsurge of interest and capital. In the early 1870s experienced commission merchants from Chicago migrated to Kansas City to develop the livestock trade. They were joined by a smaller number of meat packers who saw a future "porkopolis" in the Missouri Valley. Plankington & Armour, one of the nation's largest companies, opened a large modern branch plant in Kansas City in 1871. In their first year of operation, 1871/72, they packed 14,000 cattle and 30,000 hogs. By 1875 their product had risen to 21,500 cattle and over 80,000 hogs. Good transportation facilities were essential to the conduct of such a large operation and the firm was active in promoting better stockyards and good ancillary services. Indeed, Plankington & Armour's success was so marked that they attracted the attention of other national packers to Kansas City. In 1880 the Fowler Brothers of Chicago and Jacob Dold & Sons of Buffalo also established branch plants in Kansas City. Swift & Company of Chicago and Kingan & Company of Indianapolis and Belfast followed later in the decade. Kansas City stockyards benefited both directly and indirectly from being a latecomer to the midwestern packing industry.[13]

Kansas City was not alone in rapidly developing centralized stockyards because the livestock trade and the packing industry were already modernized elsewhere. What had been a precondition for turning mercantile operations into manufacturing plants in older parts of the Midwest had, by the 1870s, become an essential adjunct to the profitable running of capital-intensive establishments in the newer Midwest. Though it is difficult to distinguish between the mercantile and manufacturing phases in cities like St. Joseph, which had a packing activity prior to the Civil War, three other places, two in interior Iowa and one in eastern Nebraska, illustrate the compression of the traditional stages of growth. At all of these points one modern packing plant dominated output and effectively created a livestock market through its operations.

In Cedar Rapids, Iowa, in 1870, there was no packing industry to warrant notice. Yet by 1878 the city boasted of being the nation's eighth largest packing center and of having the fourth largest packing house in the world. These claims were based on the operation of one firm—Thomas Sinclair & Company—which came to Cedar Rapids in 1871. Along with their extensive plant, capable of slaughtering 2,500 hogs daily in the winter and 1,200 in the summer, came auxiliary services, one of which was marshaling yards served by two railroads. Ottumwa, Iowa, presented a similar example of the simultaneous development of centralized shipping and packing facilities. Only in 1877, when John Morrell & Company moved their extensive operations from Chicago to Ottumwa, was a stockyard deemed necessary. The building of an integrated plant in 1878 demanded the smooth flow of livestock and meat products. Again in the 1870s, the operation of a large-scale packing enterprise, this time in Omaha, Nebraska, was the instigating force in developing subsidiary functions. James E. Boyd had begun slaughtering on a small scale in 1872, but five years later he had a capital investment of $200,000 and a packing capacity of 50,000 hogs. By this time he was promoting the construction of extensive stockyards commensurate with the growing importance of the trade. When meat packers moved to new locations in the 1870s, they often brought a fully integrated service modeled on operations which had already been modernized in older parts of the Midwest.[14]

Why did many business operations mature into packing plants in the 1870s? Clearly the widespread use of railroads and the subsequent organization of centralized stockyards gave much impetus through providing better access to livestock and faster dispatch of meat products. The changed transportation flows and market arrangements made during the Civil War also favored the growth of large-scale ventures. But other stimuli were required. Those external to the packing industry included the expansion of urban markets and improved personal communications and information flow. Those internal to the industry were better business organization, the use of the new technology of ice packing during the summer months, and the development of professional organizations. Not all midwestern packers adopted these improvements, but among those who did were the leading firms who came to control a large share of the regional product.

The growth of American cities, particularly those in the Northeast and the Midwest, continued to create a concentrated demand for food products which western processors were ready to fill. By 1870, 40.3 percent of the population of the Northeast and 20.8 percent of the population of the Midwest were urbanized. Assuming that all of the 8.1 million city residents in these two regions ate 122 pounds of pork per year each and that western packers supplied 70 percent of their requirements, then domestic demand far outstripped supply.[15] Furthermore the foreign market was expanding, and by 1870, 11.5 percent of western-produced bacon, ham, and barreled pork was exported.[16] Most assuredly packers could sell their increasing meat outputs.

Those among them who had good access to information on particular markets were able to derive the most gain from timely sales. Generally processors in larger cities benefited most from improvements in verbal communications. In the pioneer era of the pork trade, entrepreneurs had found out about hog prices and outputs in other parts of the Midwest and about stocks of provisions in interregional markets through the reprinting of the mercantile sections of different newspapers in the commercial columns of the local press. But this information flow was slow and had a limited impact.[17] The advent of the telegraph accelerated the regular dispatch of commercial news and encouraged the establishment of a more uniform market structure. Appearing with the railroad in the Midwest, the "talking wire" first improved access to data between specific points which were joined together in the first enthusiastic but chaotic burst of building. Then in the middle and late 1850s, and more particularly in the 1860s, more systematic regional and national links were forged. Indeed, when centralized stockyards were built, the telegraph was already an essential service. In the Chicago Union Stock Yards two rooms in the Exchange Building were allotted as telegraph offices. Other cities quickly followed in establishing special commercial telegraph depots because the destruction of the long-standing verbal barriers of time and space was essential in creating greater efficiency in trade in general and in the meat-packing industry in particular.[18]

Another type of general efficiency was generated by the organization of a national association to adopt rules governing meat packers' business conduct. Systematic schemes for regulating the industry were not new. Pork merchants in their capacity as members of local boards of trade and chambers of commerce had, in the late 1850s and 1860s, drawn up guidelines for cutting and packing all varieties of meat. Earlier still, city councils had laid down ordinances which specified both quantity and quality control. But local variations in the guidelines continued to affect standards. In an attempt to improve public relations and to establish their credentials on a nationwide basis, leading businessmen from the major packing centers and from the East Coast provisions markets met in Cincinnati in September 1872 to hold the first convention of the National Pork Packers' Association. Though the representatives of the various cities continued to have differences, the annual meetings of the mid-1870s did succeed in establishing more uniform standards and in promoting a better appreciation of problems within the trade. Meat packers were at last responding to the national market with institutional arrangements.[19]

Of more direct importance to serving the national market efficiently in the postwar decade were improvements in the internal organization of packing plants. Descriptions of enterprises indicated a growing level of sophistication. In 1871 Plankington & Armour's new packing house in Kansas City consisted of "a large rectangular brick [building] of 160 by 170 feet dimensions . . . connected with the Missouri Pacific Railroad by two tracks. . . . The basement is extensive, and is capacious enough for 15,000 barrels, while 6,000 more can be stored. . . . The first floor will be used for . . . rendering lard, tallow, etc., and for the reception of the steam engine, boilers and other machinery. . . . When in full running order, the house will have facilities for the slaughtering and packing of 1,200 hogs or 1,000 cattle, per day, and will have hanging room for 2,000 hogs or 1,600 cattle. . . . The total cost of the erection, not including the railway tracks amounts to about $70,000."[20] While not all modernizing meat packing plants were the same, they often shared common features. Most large enterprises called for the substantial investment of capital in separate buildings which were divided into different departments, often housing the machinery that was becoming an essential part of the manufacturing. These units conducted a full or nearly full "disassembly-line," whereby animals were processed not only for various cuts and cures of meat but also for their by-products, which included lard, oil, soap, candles, sausage casings, glue, brushes, combs, and buttons. The addition of a cooper's shop considerably cut down the costs of packing and, of greater significance, the presence of icehouses extended the packing season from four to ten months.[21] To be sure, only a small number of establishments were modernized in the 1870s, but their contribution to the output of the industry was considerable (Table A 9). The importance of the large integrated firm was already visible.

Division of labor and the manufacture of by-products were not new facets of meat processing in the post-Civil War decade. Indeed, they were a continuation and refinement of activities long in existence, at least on a citywide basis. As early as 1835 observers had commented on the relatively continuous disassembly line of the hog in Cincinnati, and the Queen City was consistently regarded as the best hog market in the antebellum West because packers made productive use of "everything but the squeal." They processed lard, lard oil, soap, candles, glue, bristles, potash, prussian blue, and manure from the residue of animal carcasses.[22] Cincinnati, however, was exceptional. In many packing points, pork houses were frequently warehouses and were not custom-designed for the trade. The by-product business was limited to the rendering of lard. Even in the larger centers like Louisville or Chicago, production facilities were not highly systematized. There was thus room for the adoption and adaptation of economies of scale in the 1860s and 1870s, first in the older establishments in the major packing points, and then in the new plants constructed in the more recently settled Midwest.

Following improvements in the railroad shipment and handling of livestock, packers turned to investing more capital in plant and machinery. Of the fifty-three firms listed in operation in Chicago in the 1864/65 season, eight either had built new houses or had made significant alterations to their existing establishments. Among these firms, two major wartime contractors, Culbertson, Blair & Company and A.E. Kent & Company, substantially improved their interior arrangements. The latter introduced labor-saving circular saws and steam-powered lifting machinery, so that the beef-packing operations matched the efficiency then visible in pork packing. The former reputedly ran one of the nation's largest and most efficient plants. Reid & Sherwin, who owned Chicago's fourth largest enterprise in the 1865/66 season, claimed that their undertaking was so well managed that their labor-force of twenty men easily matched the output of 300 workmen butchering on a well-managed farm. Several other firms made sufficient advances to be able to handle 1,000 hogs or more daily. Then when the packers moved their businesses to the Stockyards complex in the late 1860s and the 1870s, they constructed plants to incorporate all the facilities conducive to steady increases in output. By the 1870/71 season two firms each put up over 100,000 hogs annually, while ten others each packed over 20,000 hogs. The leading firms were taking advantage of streamlined plants to forge ahead in output.[23]

Chicago men were not alone in substituting modern packing plants for warehouselike pork houses. There were other examples of brick or stone buildings divided into separate floors containing the latest fixtures and steam-driven machinery, and adjoined by large warehouses and yards, in all the leading pork packing points. In older centers like Indianapolis or Milwaukee, packers made strenuous efforts to secure internal operating improvements in the 1860s and 1870s. In the former city, modernization dated from 1863, when the Kingan Brothers built their extensive house, which was 185 feet by 115 feet in dimensions and had five stories and a basement. These premises, furnished with up-to-date appliances including a steam-rendering plant, were among the largest and most convenient in the world. When fire destroyed the works in 1865, rebuilding commenced immediately on a three-story building, because the Irish-based company relied on their western branch to furnish meat both for their provisions outlet in New York City and for their European markets. In 1867 Kingan Brothers expanded further by investing in stockyards. Six years later they bought out their local rivals, Messrs. Ferguson & Company, and thereby added another substantial brick building to their property. By the mid-1870s they employed between 300 and 600 operatives in their plant, which was organized so efficiently that Indianapolis was one of the Midwest's leading packing points.[24]

A similar dominance by one integrated plant gave Milwaukee regional stature in the postwar years. Here John Plankington and Philip D. Armour had joined forces in 1864 to conduct extensive operations. Using their long experience in the meat trade and their ample capital, they soon improved and expanded Plankington's Menomonee Valley plant. By 1867 they employed 100 men and had a daily capacity of 1,200 hogs and 400 cattle. But soon even this was insufficient. Plankington & Armour added extensions to the main building in 1870 and 1873. In 1872 they built a new slaughterhouse and in 1873 a new boiler house, as well as a side track to connect to the St. Paul Railroad. Further developments were soon forthcoming in the shape of an icehouse in 1875, a ham house in 1876, a cooperage, a curing house, and two more icehouses in 1877, and then a huge warehouse and a drying room for the conversion of blood and offal into fertilizer in 1878. By this date Plankington & Armour had the capacity for processing 10,000 hogs daily. Though they planned further improvements in the near future, they had already achieved a "full-product disassembly line." Large capital investment in plant and machinery had brought a quadrupling of output since the end of the war. In the 1877/78 season Plankington & Armour packed 255,970 hogs, or 69 percent of Milwaukee's output.[25]

Men of property made similar progress in the construction and operation of packing plants in several cities in the more recently settled parts of the Middle West. Here capital requirements were, if anything, more substantial because latecomers had immediately to adopt all the technological improvements which had gradually been accumulated in older establishments. Capitalists needed to invest $60,000 or more in land, buildings, and machinery if they aimed to sell their meat products in regional and national markets. At first sight this requirement might not seem very demanding, but fixed capital was still only a small proportion of total financial commitments. Any firm contemplating packing 20,000 hogs annually, which was only a medium-sized output scarcely justifying the outlay in fixed investment, would require a regular working capital or credit facilities of at least $200,000.[26] These extensive new businesses meriting laudatory notices in local newspapers were frequently branches of well-established firms or belonged to men who had considerable experience in the trade elsewhere.

Though the individual design varied, most substantial packing plants, whether in Kansas City, Omaha, St. Joseph, Cedar Rapids, or Ottumwa, incorporated common features. A main building of either stone or brick, and at least three stories high, dominated the works, which was usually located at a railroad site large enough to accommodate acres of pens and yards. The slaughtering of animals took place on the upper floor, while the cutting machinery and hanging rooms were on the second floor. Steam engines, boilers, and other machinery used to supply the motive power and to render down lard and tallow were on the ground floor. Every convenience for speeding up work and for economizing on labor was installed, the most notable being a system of wheels and pulleys or semi-tramways for the swift conveyance of carcasses. The basement and warehouses provided ample storage space. Curing houses, icehouses, and a cooperage were, by the mid-1870s, essential features of an integrated plant, and by the end of the decade facilities for converting blood and offal into fertilizer were becoming more common. Large establishments in the newer Midwest could certainly rival those in the older packing centers.[27]

By far the most important innovation in the process of modernizing the meat-packing industry in the postwar decade was the successful introduction and adoption of ice packing and curing. Climatic conditions, which limited operations to the three or four winter months when it was cold enough to put up meat safely, frequently resulted in a part-time business commitment. If packers could extend the season throughout the year, then they might invest more capital in large plants. They might also moderate some of the worst fluctuations in the trade. A few forward-looking venturers had attempted some experiments in cooling packing rooms with natural ice in the 1850s, but these came to nothing. It was not until the early 1870s that summer packing, using natural ice, which had been efficiently cut from local lakes, rivers, ponds, and flooded quarries and which had been stored during the winter months in specially constructed icehouses, was developed as a commercially feasible proposition.[28]

The spread of ice packing was rapid. Midwestern outputs increased fivefold, from 495,714 hogs in 1872 to 2,543,120 hogs in 1877, at which time summer operations contributed 28.1 percent of the annual pack (Table 6). Chicago, Indianapolis, St. Louis, and Cincinnati were the main points of activity, with the former two having a higher proportion of their product in summer packing than the regional average.[29] Within these centers a few large firms dominated because only those companies that conducted business throughout the year were able to take on regional stature. In Chicago several of the leading firms in the mid-1870s were producing substantial amounts of pork from March to September. The top three enterprises—the Chicago Packing & Provision Company, Armour & Company, and Fowler Brothers, who later became the Anglo-American Packing Company—certainly saw the wisdom of ice packing.[30] Elsewhere the presence of one or two full-line establishments indicated the waning importance of seasonal operations. In Indianapolis, Kingan & Company had introduced ice packing as early as 1871 and two years later they were putting up more hogs in the summer than in the winter. In Cedar Rapids, T.M. Sinclair & Company also paid marked attention to ice packing. In 1874, three years after beginning operations, they put up over 70,000 hogs, making them the largest meat firm in Iowa. By 1879 summer packing alone more than doubled that total, placing this newcomer on a par with large-scale packers in major cities.[31]

Smaller and often older firms that continued to pack primarily or only during the winter lagged behind and produced either for a specialized market or only on a local level. In Cincinnati, for example, both Charles Davis & Company and Joseph Rawson & Sons continued to concentrate on curing hams for the quality market. Though the former firm moved to the new Stock Yards complex in 1875, they still continued to place great emphasis on traditional methods and markets. Furthermore, though some Queen City entrepreneurs ventured into ice packing, they seemed to have lost their initiative in the struggle for industrial dominance. Neither Charles Davis & Company nor Joseph Rawson & Sons could hope to rival George W. Higgins & Company of Chicago, let alone the enterprising Chicago Packing & Provision Company (Table A-9).[32] Yet the well-established Cincinnati firms were much better placed in midwestern enterprise than were the pork merchants in smaller river towns like Peoria, Keokuk, and Quincy, who worked within limited horizons. In Peoria, which can be considered the most progressive of the three centers, William Reynolds & Company, a leading firm, only worked during the winter and often on a commission basis.[33]

The meat manufacturers who gradually emerged from the mass of pork merchants in the mid-1860s came to dominate the industry a decade later. In response to increased livestock flows and to improvements in livestock handling at centralized stockyards, entrepreneurs built more sophisticated plants that were capable of processing by-products as well as animals and were capable of operating for ten, if not twelve, months of the year. A handful of large integrated packing houses were in fact responsible for a third of the region's output, and a permanent industry had emerged. But the transition from merchant to manufacturer was not fully completed. Numerous small dispersed and seasonal enterprises still remained in operation. Though their relative contribution to the regional output was falling and would continue to decline, their existence was a reminder of the atomistic nature of early agricultural processing. Many firms still drew on neighboring farm hinterlands and served local markets. By the late 1870s the midwestern meat packing industry had produced a dual economy with giant enterprises at the center, flanked by hundreds of minor establishments on the periphery. Big business would soon take a different form as mechanical refrigeration and the chilled beef trade emerged in the 1880s, but already the shape of modern enterprise was visible.

6

The Dimensions of Midwestern Pork Packing

By the late 1870s a new order was emerging in the midwestern pork packing industry. Not only had outputs increased markedly from 675,000 hogs in 1842 to 9,045,566 in 1877, but the industry's structure and behavior contrasted sharply with the atomistic and unconcentrated direction of energy that prevailed in the riverine period. Pork packing had developed from a general mercantile involvement with western produce to a well-organized industrial operation demanding technological improvements and systematic business organization. Indeed, the progress of this agricultural processing activity reflected the general contours of change in regional manufacturing whereby entrepreneurs, using abundant natural resources and farm outputs and taking advantage of improved transportation and technological innovations, were turning the midwestern prairies into the Great Lakes Manufacturing Belt.

In the antebellum era, when family-sized food-producing farm units underpinned the structure of the regional economy, there was a plentiful supply of animals for processing. There was also an expanding but diffuse urban demand for salted and cured pork in the Northeast, the South, and even abroad. The essential link between this supply and demand was the pioneer merchant who could process animals, finance a long-distance trade, and distribute its products.

Meat packing was necessarily a winter operation in which low temperatures were vital for safe slaughtering and curing, and lack of refrigeration determined that the meat packed was primarily pork, since salted beef met with consumer indifference. Entry into this seasonal activity was easy for merchants because they were involved in other western trade that provided both an income and a business reputation and because they already had physical facilities in the shape of empty warehouses. More importantly, they could command the substantial working capital needed to buy raw materials, either by borrowing from local banks on their own security or, more likely, by extending credit arrangements with eastern or other western mercantile operators. Furthermore, as traders working primarily in the diverse river towns of the region, they were well aware of the problems of selling a semiperishable commodity in a dispersed market while lacking full information and depending on imperfect transportation services. Participation in pork packing in the 1840s and 1850s was geographically widespread and ranged in scale from the rural storekeeper who consolidated farmers' cargoes of wagon pork to the city specialist who operated a virtual disassembly line. The pioneer industry was in the hands of general merchants who were flexible enough to adapt to seasonal variations and to respond to local customs.

These entrepreneurs remained in the ascendancy in the antebellum years, but the advent of the railroad, first in limited areas in the late 1840s and then more widely in the 1850s, paved the way for alterations in the shape and structure of pork packing. In the first place, railroads improved the flow of livestock to packing points. Though merchants still relied mainly on shipping meat products to market by water, they increasingly came to depend on rails for hog supplies, and only those entrepreneurs in river ports which had good rail connections flourished. The stranglehold of river dominance was broken and packers could now flourish in lake ports and interior places. In addition to sponsoring an altered pattern of spatial diffusion, rails also encouraged pork merchants to concentrate in larger termini where they not only had better access to livestock but they benefitted more directly from improved urban services than did their small-town rivals. Furthermore, these city merchants were in a stronger position to compete with eastern packers whose growth was now rendered viable by the interregional rail shipment of hogs. By the onset of the Civil War most midwestern pork packers, even those in the newer points of the Upper

Mississippi Valley, were becoming more dependent on the railroad.

The new departures of the 1850s became established trends in the 1860s: the superiority of railroad termini was consolidated, the growth of the larger cities was accelerated, and the development of the Upper Mississippi Valley as the new center of activity was confirmed. The impact of the war itself hastened the two former tendencies. In the first place, the closure of the Ohio-Mississippi River as a transport network to markets ensured the use of alternative land and water routes, primarily the railroad. Hog packing was increasingly tied to railroads as the main means of freight movement within and from the Midwest. In the second place, the Civil War itself created a notable artificial market, namely, the Union army. Those leading merchants in major midwestern cities who secured army contracts reinforced the move toward urban concentration. Westward expansion of the hog raising belt had begun before the 1860s and continued independent of the war, but the upsurge in activity here in the early 1860s tended to reinforce both the packers' dependency on the railroad and the growing centralization within the industry by channeling trade mainly to Chicago, but also to St. Louis and Milwaukee.

By the mid-1860s manufacturers were emerging from the multitude of pork perchants, and their growing importance was confirmed in the next decade. These leading entrepreneurs, who were often relative newcomers to the Midwest, changed the shape and character of the industry. The increased flow of livestock in the war years encouraged them, in conjunction with commission merchants and railroad operators, to centralize handling and marketing facilities by building new and efficient stockyards and then to develop larger and more integrated packing plants. Looking partly to improved business organization, they systematized production by using a full disassembly line and by paying greater attention to by-products. More importantly, they successfully introduced and adopted ice packing and curing, thereby creating a permanent industry by extending operations from four or five months to ten months or the full year. By the late 1870s a small number of pork manufacturers were starting to dominate regional outputs and were setting new standards of achievement.

In the course of one generation, from the mid-1840s to the late 1870s, pork packing progressed from a general western trade to a specialized manufacturing operation. The industry matured with the region. Small mercantile entrepreneurs initially participated in seasonal processing as part of their all-purpose business, and while their involvement varied annually according to the local supply of hogs and the profitability of previous years' business, it was always a part-time and often a subsidiary endeavor. In the 1850s, when the railroads encouraged larger-scale operations, different types of processors with varying degrees of commitment could still thrive. Even in the mid-1860s Chicago pork men, arguably the most progressive producers, were also frequently livestock commission merchants.

The major technological breakthrough that altered this seasonal involvement was the successful introduction of ice packing during the summer months. In the 1870s those capitalists who had invested in this facility started to move ahead rapidly, leaving the part-time merchant far behind. These merchants still survived, either specializing as curers or serving their local markets, but their share of the expanding national trade was limited. The future belonged to the large-scale entrepreneur who was prepared to devote full attention to packing and who could command the extensive finance needed for investment in plant and working operations.

Some of these emerging big companies moved rapidly ahead and were shortly joined by newcomers in undertaking more technological changes in the late 1870s and 1880s. In pioneering the use of the refrigerated car, they made way for the chilled beef trade. But to sell this new semiperishable commodity they had to overcome the opposition of both established wholesale networks and consumer reluctance by building up their own distribution and marketing organization. Shortly thereafter they developed a full line of products and by-products and gained greater control over supplies. They then rationalized their giant enterprises, creating a centralized, departmentalized administrative structure. By the mid-1890s, with the rapid growth of great vertically integrated establishments, the meat packing industry had become oligopolistic.[1] Big business had truly arrived in the shape of the "Big Five."[2] By now the world of the small pork merchants and their seasonal operations had long disappeared, but their contribution in laying the foundations of the modern industry and in participating in regional economic growth must not be underrated. As agricultural processors, they served long and well in building the bridge to an era dominated by large firms and their corporate descendants.

Appendix. The Sample of Midwestern Pork Packers Used for Biographical Illustrations

Biographical sketches of individual midwestern meat packers are a useful and significant means of illustrating regional developments if they are representative of the whole population. Ideally a random sample of pork merchants would provide the best case studies of entrepreneurial behavior.[1] Unfortunately such a sample is unobtainable because a complete list of operators on an annual or a regular basis is not available.[2] The lack of other quantitative information which can be turned into descriptive variables on known individuals further suggests that systematic biographical analysis is unfeasible.[3] But historical research should not be limited to or by the presence of complete data banks.[4] Attempts must be made to utilize less robust bodies of information by adopting techniques which use the principles of statistics but which draw on extant descriptive material.[5] While the end-results will not obtain the numerical certainty which statistics assert and which statistics as applied to social sciences claim, they can offer sound estimates of past developments.

The most appropriate method of gathering biographical data on midwestern packers is to draw a sample which is stratified both historically and geographically. Because this study spans four decades businessmen illustrating each phase of development—namely, the pioneer

Table A 1. Principal Packing Points in the Midwest, Mid-1840s

Packing Point	No. of Hogs (Average of 3 Seasons, 1843/44–1845/46)	% of Regional Total	No. of Case Studies Chosen
Cincinnati, Oh.	246,827	24.9	5
Louisville, Ky.	67,000	6.8	2
Madison, Ind.	57,667	5.8	1
Chillicothe, Oh.	38,667	3.9	1
Hamilton, Oh.	34,000	3.4	1
Alton, Ill.	25,667	2.6	1
Circleville, Oh.	23,667	2.4	1
Lafayette, Ind.	23,467	2.4	1
Terre Haute, Ind.	22,667	2.3	1
St. Louis, Mo.	19,833	2.0	1
Hannibal, Mo.[1]	17,900	1.8	1
Columbus, Oh.	15,534	1.6	1
Ripley, Oh.	14,519	1.5	1
Pekin, Ill.[2]	13,312	1.3	1
Maysville, Ky.[3]	10,167	1.0	1
Regional Total	991,667		

Source: *Philadelphia Commercial List*, Dec. 5, 1846.

1. Average based on two seasons, 1844/45–1845/46.

2. No descriptive information is available on packers in Lawrenceburg, Ind., with an output of 13,667 hogs (1.4% of regional total). Pekin, Ill., is the next leading packing point.

3. No descriptive information is available for Westport, Ky., with an output of 15,000 hogs, or 1.5 percent of the regional total. Maysville is a substitute packing point south of the Ohio River.

Table A 2. Principal Packing Points in the Midwest, Late 1850s

Packing Point	No. of Hogs (Average of 3 Seasons, 1856/57–1858/59)	% of Regional Pack	No. of Case Studies Chosen
Cincinnati, Oh.	391,338	18.1	4
Louisville, Ky.	262,741	12.1	2
Chicago, Ill.	119,101	5.5	1
St. Louis, Mo.	75,677	3.5	1
Madison, Ind.	54,541	2.5	1
Terre Haute, Ind.	47,526	2.2	1
Quincy, Ill.	42,482	2.0	1
Peoria, Ill.	35,663	1.7	1
Keokuk, Io.	35,367	1.7	1
Indianapolis, Ind.	33,619	1.6	1
Springfield, Ill.	28,787	1.3	1
Muscatine, Io.	28,000	1.3	1
Burlington, Io.	24,300	1.2	1
Beardstown, Ill.	23,810	1.1	1
Cleveland, Oh.	23,486	1.1	1
Milwaukee, Wis.[1]	21,000	1.0	1
Regional Total	2,164,933		

Sources: *Cincinnati Prices Current*, March 24, 1858; Feb. 2, 1859.

1. No descriptive information is available for Bowling Green, Ky., with an output of 27,633 hogs, or 1.3% of the regional total. Milwaukee, Wis., is therefore added to the rank order list of packing points.

years of the late 1830s and the 1840s, when packing was widely dispersed among the river towns; the late 1840s and the 1850s, which witnessed the transportation innovation of the railroad; most of the 1860s, which saw the growing strength of the railroad and experienced the dislocation of the Civil War; and the postwar era, marked by the arrival of new technology and structural reorganization—must appear.[6] A single year or a decade is an unsuitable time-span to use as the basis of these phases given the cyclical nature of the industry. A three-year average of packing seasons interspersed by irregular intervals—namely 1843/44-1845/46, 1856/57-1858/59, 1864/65-1866/67, and 1873/74-1875/76—more accurately reflects the fluctuating character of pork packing.[7]

The geographical distribution of meat packing provides a further necessary stratification of the sampling data. Though no inventory of pork establishments exists, there is an annual record of the packing points of the West from the mid 1840s onward. Entrepreneurs selected from the leading centers listed in rank order promote discussion of a widespread activity—an important criterion when examining an agricultural processing industry in a rapidly expanding area. This selection process also illustrates the gradual concentration and modernization of business in regional cities. There is no perfect correlation between the individuals or firms chosen in the sample and the output of their urban base, but the overall pattern is suggestive of the changing location of the industry (Tables A 1 to A 4).[8]

How many entrepreneurs should be included in the sample? Twenty firms in each period are sufficient to encompass the diversity of packing operations while still being a realistic number to handle in the search for descriptive information.[9] This constant number of businessmen generally denotes a declining percentage of firms at work, but it is possible to estimate this progression. In the mid-1840s twenty firms represent 8.9 percent of the number of establishments, while in the late 1850s they only amount to 5.1 percent of the total. At the end of the Civil War the same number of operations account for 5.9 percent, while eight years later, in the mid 1870s, they have declined to 2.7 percent (Tables A 5-A 8). The small proportion of enterprises suggests that throughout the period, extensive growth and local backward linkages to farming are significant in understanding the dynamics of growth in the meat industry.

Table A 3. Principal Packing Points in the Midwest, Mid-1860s

Packing Point	No. of Hogs (Average of 3 Seasons, 1864/65–1866/67)	% of Regional Pack	No. of Case Studies Chosen
Chicago, Ill.	629,114	28.2	6
Cincinnati, Oh.	389,096	17.4	3
St. Louis, Mo.	159,818	7.2	1
Louisville, Ky.	113,333	5.1	1
Milwaukee, Wis.	109,451	4.9	1
Indianapolis, Ind.	48,542	2.2	1
Keokuk, Io.	39,700	1.8	1
Quincy, Ill.	38,200	1.7	1
Lafayette, Ind.	29,172	1.3	1
Peoria, Ill.	28,551	1.3	1
Cleveland, Oh.	26,509	1.1	1
Terre Haute, Ind.	24,982	1.1	1
St. Joseph, Mo.	22,617	1.0	1
Regional Total	2,233,175		

Sources: *Cincinnati Prices Current,* Mar. 21, 1866; Mar. 27, 1867.

The final choice of particular entrepreneurs depended on data availability. The nature of qualitative historical records indicates that those who were selected were either "middle-level" businessmen who, at a minimum, ran successful operations for several years, or were leading figures who attained local repute.[10] They were never the small-scale entrepreneur whose name might only appear in one or two years and who left no additional evidence. Indeed, they were relatively important in their own communities, and their increasing contributions to the regional hog pack—rising from 20.7 percent in the pioneer years to 32.0 percent by the mid-1870s—suggests that the industry was on the threshold of big business (Table A 9).

This group of meat packers is a flawed and biased sample by statistical standards. It is, however, a "convenience" sample, perfectly acceptable when a more scientific one is impossible. Historically these men represent a broad variety of experience which well illustrates the problems and possibilities of agricultural processing in a developing region.

Table A 4. Principal Packing Points in the Midwest, Mid-1870s

Packing Point	No. of Hogs (Average of 3 Seasons, 1873/74–1875/76)	% of Regional Pack	No. of Hogs (Average of 3 Full Years Mar. 1–Feb. 28)	% of Regional Pack	No. of Case Studies Chosen
Chicago, Ill.	1,600,812	30.2	2,094,707	32.5	6
Cincinnati, Oh.	568,259	10.7	682,702	10.6	2
St. Louis, Mo.	418,645	7.9	547,158	8.5	2
Indianapolis, Ind.	299,096	5.6	483,582	7.5	1
Milwaukee, Wis.	241,389	4.6	242,267	3.8	1
Louisville, Ky.	241,071	4.6	241,071	3.7	1
Kansas City, Mo.	96,116	1.8	101,116	1.6	1
St. Joseph, Mo.	94,361	1.8	94,361	1.5	1
Peoria, Ill.	89,630	1.7	89,630	1.4	1
Cleveland, Oh.	85,088	1.6	187,774	2.9	1
Cedar Rapids, Io.	67,799	1.3	130,186	2.0	1
Keokuk, Io.	54,679	1.0	70,110	1.1	1
Quincy, Ill.	52,552	1.0	54,113	0.8	1
Regional Total	5,303,975		6,448,699		

Sources: Cincinnati Chamber of Commerce, *Annual Reports*, 1874, 1875, 1876.

Table A 5. Number of Packing Establishments in the Midwest, Mid-1840s

	1843/44		1844/45		1845/46	
State	No. of Packing Points	No. of Establishments[1]	No. of Packing Points	No. of Establishments[1]	No. of Packing Points	No. of Establishments[1]
Ohio	47	119	51	104	44	114
Indiana	30	62	29	43	36	59
Illinois	11	28	11	17	10	16
Kentucky	5	18	6	17	6	28
Tennessee	1	3	1	1	7	11
Missouri	1	3	2	7	3	13
Virginia	–	–	1	2	1	3
Iowa	1	1	1	1	1	1
Total	96	234	102	192	108	245

Total number of firms for 1843/44–1845/46 = 224. Sample of twenty firms = 8.9% of total number.

1. Contemporary sources suggest that the average output of a packing plant was 6,000 hogs. Each point listed as having an output under 6,000 hogs was given one establishment. For each point having an output over 6,000, the total was divided by 6,000 to obtain the number of firms; any fraction was recorded as one firm: 6,001 is recorded as two firms.

Table A 6. Number of Packing Establishments in the Midwest, Late 1850s

State	1856/57		1857/58		1858/59	
	No. of Packing Points	No. of Establishments[1]	No. of Packing Points	No. of Establishments[1]	No. of Packing Points	No. of Establishments[1]
Ohio	43	88	49	111	47	110
Indiana	48	68	57	92	58	87
Illinois	41	68	53	87	54	109
Kentucky	14	49	16	56	15	58
Tennessee	4	6	5	7	5	11
Missouri	17	25	21	36	18	30
Iowa	11	22	12	20	14	29
Wisconsin	1	2	1	2	2	5
Total	179	328	214	411	213	439

Total number of firms for 1856/57–1858/59 = 393. Sample of twenty firms = 5.1% of total number.

1. Contemporary sources suggest that the average output of a packing plant was 8,000 hogs. Each point listed as having an output under 8,000 hogs was given one establishment. For each point having an output over 8,000, the total was divided by 8,000 to obtain the number of firms; any fraction was recorded as one firm: 8,001 is recorded as two firms.

Table A 7. Number of Packing Establishments in the Midwest, Mid-1860s

State	1864/65		1865/66		1866/67	
	No. of Packing Points	No. of Establishments[1]	No. of Packing Points	No. of Establishments[1]	No. of Packing Points	No. of Establishments[1]
Ohio	50	90	41	78	54	103
Indiana	46	57	43	53	43	67
Illinois	41	128	36	90	48	113
Kentucky	4	15	2	11	3	18
Missouri	13	35	11	24	15	35
Iowa	14	26	11	18	16	22
Wisconsin	3	13	3	11	2	15
Total	171	364	147	285	181	373

Total number of firms for 1864/65–1866/67 = 341. Sample of twenty firms = 5.9% of total number.

1. Contemporary sources suggest that the average output of a packing plant was 10,000 hogs. Each point listed as having an output under 10,000 hogs was given one establishment. For each point having an output over 10,000, the total was divided by 10,000 to obtain the number of firms; any fraction was recorded as one firm: 10,001 is recorded as two firms.

Table A 8. Number of Packing Establishments in the Midwest, Mid-1870s

State	1873/74		1874/75		1875/76	
	No. of Packing Points	No. of Establishments[1]	No. of Packing Points	No. of Establishments[1]	No. of Packing Points	No. of Establishments[1]
Ohio	82	141	80	114	71	120
Indiana	76	115	66	100	65	105
Illinois	72	210	81	227	76	238
Kentucky	12	30	14	31	13	36
Tennessee	6	7	10	11	8	8
Iowa	35	57	35	51	30	58
Missouri	18	73	21	66	25	75
Wisconsin	22	46	24	43	28	44
Kansas	23	25	20	21	21	22
Michigan	9	12	10	14	12	13
Minnesota	11	12	11	12	11	12
Nebraska	6	7	6	6	5	6
West Virginia	3	3	3	3	3	3
Miscellaneous	2	2	2	2	2	2
Total	377	740	383	701	370	742

Total number of firms for 1873/74–1875/76 = 728. Sample of twenty firms = 2.7% of total number.

1. Contemporary sources suggest that the average output of a packing plant was 12,000 hogs. Each point listed as having an output under 12,000 hogs was given one establishment. For each point having an output over 12,000, the total was divided by 12,000 to obtain the number of firms; any fraction was recorded as one firm: 12,001 is recorded as two firms.

Table A 9. Components of the Collective Biography

Individual or Firm	Packing Point	No. of Hogs Packed	Method of Derivation
1843/44–1845/46			
H. Lewis	Cincinnati	14,810	6% of city total
J.R. Child & Co.	Cincinnati	14,810	6% of city total
Davis & Bro.	Cincinnati	14,810	6% of city total
Evans & Swift	Cincinnati	14,810	6% of city total
J.W. Coleman	Cincinnati	27,070	Contemporary newspapers
A.S. White & Co.	Louisville	10,050	15% of city total
Huffman, Maxcy & Co.	Louisville	10,050	15% of city total
Woodburn & Shrewsbury	Madison	14,417	25% of city total
M.R. Bartlett	Chillicothe	4,500	Various contemporary sources
Bingham & Wilson	Hamilton	13,000	Various contemporary sources
S. Wade & Co.	Alton	10,000	Various contemporary sources
S.H. Ruggles & Co.	Circleville	8,000	Various contemporary sources
J.L. Reynolds	Lafayette	10,000	Various contemporary sources
J.D. Early	Terre Haute	6,347	28% of city total
H. Ames & Co.	St. Louis	1,983	10% of city total
Gano & Shields	Hannibal	8,500	Various contemporary sources
B. Comstock & Co.	Columbus	7,750	Various contemporary sources
E. Collins	Ripley	6,000	Various contemporary sources
T.N. Gill	Pekin	4,500	Various contemporary sources
Coons & Dobyns	Maysville	3,500	Various contemporary sources

These twenty firms packed 204,907 hogs, or 20.7% of the regional total.

Individual or Firm	Packing Point	No. of Hogs Packed	Method of Derivation
1856/57–1858/59			
C. Davis & Co.	Cincinnati	19,567	5% of city total
Evans & Swift	Cincinnati	19,567	5% of city total
J. Rawson & Co.	Cincinnati	19,567	5% of city total
J. Morrison & Co.	Cincinnati	19,567	5% of city total

(continued)

Table A 9 (continued)

Individual or Firm	Packing Point	No. of Hogs Packed	Method of Derivation
1856/57-1858/59 (continued)			
Atkinson, Thomas & Co.	Louisville	32,580	Contemporary newspapers
Hamilton, Ricketts & Co.	Louisville	34,062	Contemporary newspapers
Craigin & Co.	Chicago	25,000	Various contemporary sources
H. Ames & Co.	St. Louis	15,135	20% of city total
Powell, McEwen & Co.	Madison	45,730	Contemporary newspapers
J.D. Early	Terre Haute	16,950	Contemporary newspapers
E. Wells	Quincy	8,496	20% of city total
Tyng & Brotherson	Peoria	8,916	25% of city total
Patterson & Timberman	Keokuk	14,147	40% of city total
Mansur & Ferguson	Indianapolis	15,554	Various contemporary sources
J.L. Lamb	Springfield	18,000	Various contemporary sources
S.O. Butler	Muscatine	10,000	Various contemporary sources
Schenck & Denise	Burlington	11,000	Various contemporary sources
H. Billings	Beardstown	5,953	25% of city total
H.M. Chapin	Cleveland	5,000	Various contemporary sources
Layton & Plankington	Milwaukee	10,500	50% of city total
These twenty firms packed 355,291 hogs, or 16.4% of the regional total.			
1864/65-1866/67			
Culbertson, Blair & Co.	Chicago	67,596	Chicago Board of Trade
A.E. Kent & Co.	Chicago	50,312	Chicago Board of Trade
Craigin & Co.	Chicago	48,936	Chicago Board of Trade
Reid & Sherwin	Chicago	44,329	Chicago Board of Trade
R.M. & O.S. Hough	Chicago	28,237	Chicago Board of Trade
G.S. Hubbard & Co.	Chicago	16,303	Chicago Board of Trade
C. Davis & Co.	Cincinnati	19,455	5% of city total
B. Swift & Co.	Cincinnati	19,455	5% of city total
J. Rawson	Cincinnati	19,455	5% of city total

(continued)

Table A 9 (continued)

Individual or Firm	Packing Point	No. of Hogs Packed	Method of Derivation
1864/65–1866/67 (continued)			
H. Ames & Co.	St. Louis	35,694	St. Louis Merchants' Exchange
Hamilton & Bros.	Louisville	26,067	23% of city total
Plankington, Armour & Co.	Milwaukee	44,913	Milwaukee Chamber of Commerce
Kingan & Co.	Indianapolis	16,181	One-third of city total
Patterson & Timberman	Keokuk	13,233	One-third of city total
Adams, Sawyer & Co.	Quincy	8,566	Contemporary newspapers
H.T. Sample & Co.	Lafayette	9,000	Various contemporary sources
Tyng & Brotherson	Peoria	9,517	One-third of city total
Rose & Prentiss	Cleveland	10,000	Various contemporary sources
J.D. Early	Terre Haute	8,000	Various contemporary sources
D. Pinger & Co.	St. Joseph	8,872	One-third of city total

These twenty firms packed 504,121 hogs, or 22.6% of the regional total.

Individual or Firm	Packing Point	No. of Hogs Packed	Method of Derivation
1873/74–1875/76			
Chicago Packing & Provision Co.	Chicago	389,120	Chicago Board of Trade
Armour & Co.	Chicago	241,844	Chicago Board of Trade
Fowler Bros.	Chicago	162,725	Chicago Board of Trade
H. Botsford & Co.	Chicago	116,693	Chicago Board of Trade
G.W. Higgins & Co.	Chicago	105,869	Chicago Board of Trade
Culbertson, Blair & Co.	Chicago	68,501	Chicago Board of Trade
J. Rawson & Sons	Cincinnati	34,135	5% of city total
C. Davis & Co.	Cincinnati	34,135	5% of city total
F. Whittaker & Sons	St. Louis	60,000	Various contemporary sources
H. Ames & Co.	St. Louis	45,000	Various contemporary sources
Kingan & Co.	Indianapolis	284,000	Various contemporary sources
Plankington & Armour	Milwaukee	137,849	Milwaukee Chamber of Commerce

(continued)

Table A 9 (continued)

Individual or Firm	Packing Point	No. of Hogs Packed	Method of Derivation
1873/74-1875/76 (continued)			
McFerran, Armstrong & Co.	Louisville	48,214	20% of city total
Plankington & Armour	Kansas City	50,000	Various contemporary sources
D. Pinger & Co.	St. Joseph	32,000	Various contemporary sources
Reynolds & Co.	Peoria	43,590	Peoria Board of Trade
Rose & Prentiss	Cleveland	45,000	Various contemporary sources
T.M. Sinclair & Co.	Cedar Rapids	130,186	Various contemporary sources
Patterson & Timberman	Keokuk	23,370	One-third of city total
Adams, Sawyer & Co.	Quincy	7,730	Various contemporary sources

These twenty firms packed 2,060,661 hogs, or 32.0% of the regional total.

Abbreviations

AH	*Agricultural History*
CBT *AR*	Chicago Board of Trade, *Annual Report*
CCC *AR*	Cincinnati Chamber of Commerce, *Annual Report*
CDP *AR*	Chicago Democratic Press, *Annual Review*
CPC	*Cincinnati Prices Current*
HMM	*Hunts' Merchants' Magazine*
IBT *AR*	Indianapolis Board of Trade, *Annual Report*
MBT *AR*	Milwaukee Board of Trade, *Annual Report*
MCC *AR*	Milwaukee Chamber of Commerce, *Annual Report*
PF	*Prairie Farmer*
R.G. Dun & Co.	R.G. Dun and Company Credit Rating Reports Collection
SLCC *AR*	St. Louis Chamber of Commerce, *Annual Report*
SLME *AR*	St. Louis' Merchants' Exchange, *Annual Report*

Notes

Chapter 1

1. The Middle West is here synonymous with the Western Region as defined by the *U.S. Census, 1860.* It consists of Ohio, Indiana, Michigan, Illinois, Wisconsin, Iowa, Minnesota, Nebraska, Missouri, Kansas, and Kentucky. It thus includes all of the current East North Central region, most of the West North Central region, and one state from the South. Middle West (or Midwest) and West are used here interchangeably.

2. Though there is no single volume on the economic history of the Middle West, many monographs and general works have dealt with different parts of the region and its various economic activities during the middle years of the nineteenth century. See, for example, Paul W. Gates, *The Farmer's Age: Agriculture, 1815-1860* (New York, 1951); Clarence H. Danhof, *Change in Agriculture: The Northern United States* (Cambridge, Mass., 1969); Allan G. Bogue, *From Prairie to Corn Belt: Farming on the Illinois and Iowa Prairies in the Nineteenth Century* (Chicago, 1963); John G. Clark, *The Grain Trade in the Old Northwest* (Urbana, 1966); Fred A. Shannon, *The Farmers' Last Frontier: Agriculture, 1860-1897* (New York, 1945); Gilbert C. Fite, *The Farmers' Frontier, 1865-1900* (New York, 1966); George R. Taylor, *The Transportation Revolution, 1815-1860* (New York, 1951); Albert E. Fishlow, *American Railroads and the Transformation of the Antebellum Economy* (Cambridge, Mass., 1966); Harry N. Scheiber, *Ohio Canal Era: A Case Study of Government and the Economy, 1820-1861* (Athens, Ohio, 1969); Robert F. Fries, *Empire in Pine: The Story of Lumbering in Wisconsin, 1830-1890* (Madison, Wis., 1951);

Richard C. Wade, *The Urban Frontier: The Rise of Western Cities, 1790-1830* (Cambridge, Mass., 1959); Carl J. Abbott, "The Divergent Development of Cincinnati, Indianapolis, Chicago and Galena, 1840-1860: Economic Thought and Economic Growth" (Ph.D. diss., Univ. of Chicago, 1971); David Klingaman and Richard Veddar, eds., *Essays in Nineteenth Century Economic History: The Old Northwest* (Athens, Ohio, 1975). Three early monographs provide valuable narrative information on aspects of western manufacturing: Isaac Lippincott, *A History of Manufacturing in the Ohio Valley to the Year 1860* (New York, 1914); Louis C. Hunter, *Studies in the Economic History of the Ohio Valley: Seasonal Aspects of Industry and Commerce before the Age of Big Business* (Northampton, Mass., 1935); Elmer A. Riley, *The Industrial Development of Chicago and Vicinity Prior to 1880* (Chicago, 1911). Three more recent useful studies are Norman L. Crockett, *The Woolen Industry of the Middle West* (Lexington, Ky., 1970); James D. Norris, *Frontier Iron: The Maramec Iron Works, 1826-1876* (Madison, Wis., 1964); and Margaret Walsh, *The Manufacturing Frontier: Pioneer Industry in Antebellum Wisconsin, 1830-1860* (Madison, Wis., 1972). For a broader approach to early western manufacturing see Fred Bateman, James D. Foust, and Thomas J. Weiss, "Large-Scale Manufacturing in the South and West, 1850-1860," *Business History Review* 45 (1971):1-17; and Fred Bateman and Thomas J. Weiss, "Comparative Regional Development in Antebellum Manufacturing," *Journal of Economic History* 35 (1975): 182-208.

3. Most traditional books on American industry focus on the Northeast. See, for example, the classic study by Victor S. Clark, *History of Manufactures in the United States,* 3 vols. (New York, 1929). Since the use of the manuscript censuses of manufacturing became fashionable, general texts have at least acknowledged the existence and contribution of industries in other regions. See, for example, Douglass C. North, *The Economic Growth of the United States, 1790-1860* (Englewood Cliffs, N.J., 1961), 135-55; Harry N. Scheiber, Harold G. Vatter, and Harold U. Faulkner, *American Economic History,* 9th ed. (New York, 1976), 159-66.

4. Recent research has suggested that it may be more appropriate to compare the West with the South rather than with the Northeast, at least for the antebellum years. See Fred Bateman and Thomas Weiss, *A Deplorable Scarcity: The Failure of Industrialization in the Slave Economy* (Chapel Hill, 1981). Problems arise in making such comparisons, partly because Missouri and Kentucky are here regarded as being

in the West rather than in the South and partly because the 1860s saw divergent trends between the South and other sections of the United States.

5. Processing industries are those branches of manufacturing which are basically "first-stage resource users" in the sense that they refine or process a natural resource—agricultural produce, minerals, or lumber—for custom or commercial trade. Some processed goods are consumed in their finished form, for example, flour, beer, or salted meats. Others are fabricated in a "second stage," as, for example, tanned leather is turned into boots and shoes, or lumber sawed and planed is turned into furniture and barrels. The key to processing is first-stage or immediate work done on natural resources. These industries have generally been neglected. See, for example, their brief treatment in Clark, *History of Manufactures.* Albert Fishlow, *American Railroads and the Transformation of the American Economy* (Cambridge, Mass., 1965), 226-28, noted the important role which processing industries played in the transition from a rural agrarian to an industrial economy, but no one has responded to his call for research. Some information can be found in the traditional but dated studies of particular industries, such as Rudolph A. Clemen, *The American Livestock and Meat Industry* (New York, 1923), and Charles B. Kuhlmann, *The Development of the Flour Milling Industry in the United States* (Boston, 1929), but they generally pay scant attention to the mid-nineteenth century. More recent studies dealing with specific industries in the West or specific parts of the West offer more insights. See, for example, Crockett, *Woolen Industry,* or Walsh, *Manufacturing Frontier.*

6. Walsh, *Manufacturing Frontier,* passim; Margaret Walsh, "The Dynamics of Industrial Growth in the Old Northwest, 1830-1870: An Interdisciplinary Approach," in *Business and Economic History: Papers Presented at the Twenty-first Annual Meeting of the Business History Conference,* ed. Paul J. Uselding (Urbana, 1975), 12-29.

7. Meat packing, as reported in the Manuscript Censuses of 1850, 1860, and 1870 encompassed a variety of activities: pork packing and curing, beef packing, sheep packing, slaughtering, butchers, and sausage makers. Pork packing dominated the pre-refrigeration industry because cattle could be transported to market with less weight loss than hogs, and salted beef met with consumer indifference. Butchering was sometimes regarded as a trade and was not reported.

8. The census marshals and their assistants failed to take a full account of meat-packing establishments for two reasons. First, they were instructed to enumerate effective as of June, a time of the year

when meat packers were not working and may have been using their pork houses for other activities. Second, because many packing establishments were run by merchants, these may well have been considered commercial rather than industrial.

There is no consistent pattern of omission or underenumeration in any specific place or in any particular census year. See Manuscript Censuses for Ohio, Indiana, Illinois, Wisconsin, Iowa, Minnesota, Missouri, and Kentucky, 1850 and 1860, Products of Industry, Schedule 5; and ibid., 1870, Products of Industry, Schedule 4. Estimates for inflating the value of meat products to approximate the actual sums can be made using a variety of proxy measurements, but none are really satisfactory.

The least problematic guess ascertains figures for the cost of raw materials by multiplying the relevant annual figures for the "Packing of the West" by an average price for hogs and adds 15 percent for the value of other materials:

Season	No. of Hogs Packed	Average Price of 200-lb. Hog ($)	Cost of Animals ($)	+15% ($)	New Price of Materials ($)
1849/50	1,652,220	5.00	8,261,100	1,239,165	9,500,265
1859/60	2,350,822	10.00	23,508,220	3,526,233	27,034,453
1869/70	2,595,234	20.00	51,904,860	7,785,729	59,690,589

In order to establish the relationship of the value of materials to the value added, it is necessary to examine the printed censuses of manufactures:

Year	Value of Materials ($)	Value of Product ($)	Value Added ($)	Value Added as % of Value of Material
1850	7,334,439	9,279,939	1,945,500	26.53
1860	16,164,343	19,966,346	3,802,003	23.52
1870	47,165,162	55,918,377	8,753,215	18.56

It is then possible to multiply the new price of materials by this relationship to obtain a new value-added figure, which can then be compared to the Census value-added as some measure of underenumeration.

(see table, next page)

The dangers of accepting such notional figures as accurate abound. The main cause for worry is the differing costs of hogs between and within western packing points. The difference of a few cents per 100 pounds

Year	New Price of Materials ($)	Value Added as % of Value of Materials	New Value Added ($)	New Value Added Increase as % of Census Value Added
1850	9,500,265	26.53	2,520,420	29.55
1860	27,034,453	23.52	6,358,503	67.24
1870	59,690,589	18.56	11,078,573	26.57

can be of crucial importance in altering the end-result. These figures also make no allowance for beef backing or butchering. Underenumeration certainly exists, but the degree is a matter of guess work.

9. The *Annual Reports* of the Cincinnati Chamber of Commerce (1847-1880) (hereafter cited as CCC *AR*) and the annual statements of the "Packing of the West," printed in the *Cincinnati Prices Current* (1845-1877) (hereafter cited as *CPC*), provide the most consistent and extensive coverage of western meat packing. Indeed, the annual statements in the *CPC* were used as the basis for drawing up the livestock and provision sections of the CCC *AR* from the mid-1840s until 1871 because William Smith was both editor of the *CPC* and superintendent of the Merchant's Exchange. Only after Smith's death did the two sources diverge. Because CCC *AR* were derived from information supplied by trade associations in major cities and by reliable correspondents elsewhere, they have been used from 1872 forward. Other sources that have been used to check these figures include the Chicago Board of Trade, *Annual Reports* (1858-1878) (hereafter cited as CBT *AR*); the Chicago Democratic Press, *Annual Review* (1852-1860) (hereafter cited as CDP, *AR*); the Milwaukee Chamber of Commerce, *Annual Report* (1858-1880) (hereafter cited as MCC *AR*); the *Annual Reports* of the United States Patent Office for the late 1840s and early 1850s; and those of the U.S. Department of Agriculture (1862-1876).

10. There is no detailed account of the early history of meat packing. For a general summary see Clemen, *American Meat Industry,* 21-46; and Mary A. Yeager, *Competition and Regulation: The Development of Oligopoly in the Meat Packing Industry* (Greenwich, Conn., 1981), 1-25. For more specific information on the industry in the early West, see Thomas S. Berry, *Western Prices before 1861: A Study of the Cincinnati Market* (Cambridge, Mass., 1943), 215-20; Paul C. Henlein, *Cattle Kingdom in the Ohio Valley, 1783-1860* (Lexington, Ky., 1959), passim; and Lippincott, *Manufacturing in the Ohio Valley,* 112-16, 177-82.

11. The nature of midwestern farming is discussed in Gates,

Farmer's Age, passim; Shannon, *Farmers' Last Frontier,* 125-96; Danhof, *Change in Agriculture,* passim; and Bogue, *From Prairie to Cornbelt,* passim. For the growth of the livestock industry see James W. Thompson, *A History of Livestock Raising in the United States, 1607-1860* (Washington, D.C., 1942), 136-37; Charles W. Towne and Edward N. Wentworth, *Pigs from Cave to Cornbelt* (Norman, Okla., 1950), 162-81; James W. Whitaker, *Feedlot Empire: Beef Cattle; Feeding in Illinois and Iowa, 1840-1880* (Ames, Iowa, 1975), 18-34, 55-73. There were more hogs on farms than there were neat (common domestic bovine) cattle. In 1840 there were 3,754,000 cattle in the Midwest; in 1850, 4,850,000; in 1860, 7,448,000; in 1870, 8,105,000. A considerable proportion of these were milch cows and working oxen and were not available for the livestock trade.

12. It is uncertain what percentage of the hog crop was available for commercial slaughter. Crude estimates made by ascertaining the proportion of the number of hogs packed to the number of hogs on farms suggest that only a small percentage entered the hog trade: 14.7 in 1849/50, 16.9 in 1858/60 and 20.7 in 1869/70. Clearly such figures do not take into account the age of the hog at slaughter, hog births in the spring (between the time of slaughter and the June 1 census), cyclical variations, the number of hogs entering the butcher trade, and the number slaughtered for domestic use on farms. For a technical discussion of slaughter ratios see William N. Parker, "Pork Production in the United States, 1840-1910: Estimates and Source Notes" (unpublished paper, 1966). For a theoretical discussion of the corn-hog cycle see Mordecai Ezekiel, "The Cobweb Theorem," *Quarterly Journal of Economics* 52 (1938): 255-80. More practical discussions relating to the Midwest in the nineteenth century can be found in Berry, *Western Prices,* 239-46; and Samuel Benner, *Benner's Prophecies of Future Ups and Downs in Prices* (Cincinnati, 1884), 56-76.

13. E. E. Lampard, "The Evolving System of Cities in the United States: Urbanization and Economic Development," in *Issues in Urban Economics,* ed. Harvey S. Perloff and Lowdon Wingo, Jr. (Baltimore, 1968), 116-25.

14. Margaret Walsh, "Pork Packing as a Leading Edge of Midwestern Industry, 1835-1875," *Agricultural History* 51 (1977):714-17.

15. Margaret Walsh, "The Spatial Evolution of the Mid-western Pork Industry, 1835-75," *Journal of Historical Geography* 4 (1978): 10-12; Hunter, *Studies in Economic History,* 6-32.

16. Walsh, "Spatial Evolution," 1-22.

17. Margaret Walsh, "From Pork Merchant to Meat Packer: The

Midwestern Meat Industry in the Mid-Nineteenth Century," *Agricultural History* 56 (1982): 127–32.

18. Ibid., 132–37.

Chapter 2

1. *Maysville Eagle,* Oct. 29, 1846.

2. Ibid., Nov. 8, 25, 1845; Jan 27, Feb. 28, Nov. 24, Dec. 1, 22, 1846; Feb. 16, Oct. 14, Nov. 11, 1847; Nov. 23, 1850; Jan. 28, 1851; Nov. 6, 11, 1852; R.G. Dun & Co. Collection, Mercantile Credit Rating Reports, Kentucky, 31:13, 31, 247; (hereafter cited as RG Dun & Co.); Lewis Collins, *Collins' Historical Sketches of Kentucky* (Maysville, 1850), 430–33. The most useful general statements about the role of western merchants can be found in Louis E. Atherton, *The Pioneer Merchant in Mid-America* (Columbia, Mo., 1939). Unless otherwise stated, illustrative biographical material describes members of the stratified sample of midwestern pork packers. For details of this sample see Appendix.

3. *Scioto Gazette,* Nov. 24, 1842; Jan. 12, Nov. 9, 1843; *Maysville Eagle,* Jan 6, Oct. 27, Nov. 24, 1846; Mar. 6, 1847; *Terre Haute City Directory* (1864), 21–23; RG Dun & Co., Ohio, 17:159; 19:37; 152: 107; 162:17; ibid., Kentucky, 31:13, 31, 247; ibid., Indiana, 109:23, 80; 119:2; *History of Ross and Highland Counties, Ohio* (Cleveland, 1880), 204; Henry H. Bennet, ed., *The County of Ross* (Madison, Wis., 1902), 148; Stephen D. Cone, *Biographical and Historical Sketches: A Narrative of Hamilton and Its Residents . . .* (Hamilton, Ohio, 1896), 19; *History of Circleville and Pickaway Counties, Ohio* (Cleveland, 1880), 202–3, 247–48; *History of Brown County, Ohio* (Chicago, 1883), 441–42; Blackford Condit, *History of Early Terre Haute* (New York, 1900), 143–48; Charles C. Oakey, *Greater Terre Haute and Vigo County,* 2 vols. (Chicago, 1908) 2:202–3; *Biographical History of Eminent and Self-Made Men of the State of Indiana,* 2 vols. (Cincinnati, 1880), 2:11–12.

4. *Peoria Register,* Dec. 16, 1837; Mar. 10, Aug. 11, Dec. 8, 1838; Mar. 16, Nov. 16, 1839; Dec. 4, 11, 18, 1840; Dec. 3, 1841; Jan. 28, Nov. 25, Dec. 14, 23, 1842; *Peabody's Weekly Markets,* Jan. 23, 1846; *Beardstown Gazette,* Nov. 5, 12, 19, 1847; Oct. 4, 11, Nov. 8, 15, 29, Dec. 20, 1848; *Hannibal Journal,* Nov. 30, Dec. 14, 1848; Jan. 20, 1853. S. August Mitchell, *Illinois in 1837* (Philadelphia, 1837), 115–16; *Peoria City Directory* (1844), 67, 81, 89, 126; *Alton City Directory* (1858), 80, 132; RG Dun & Co., Illinois, 139: 136, 164; ibid., Missouri,

25:256, 257; *History of Peoria County* (Chicago, 1880), 543, 654, 679–80; *Portrait and Biographical Album of Peoria County* (Chicago, 1890), 204–5; Newton Bateman and Paul Selby, eds., *Historical Encyclopaedia of Illinois and History of Cass County,* 2 vols. (Chicago, 1915), 2:680; William H. Perrin, *History of Cass County, Illinois* (Chicago, 1882), 114, 253; Wilbur T. Norton, *Centennial History of Madison County, Illinois* (Chicago, 1912), 1166; *Biographical Encyclopaedia of Illinois* (Philadelphia, 1875), 202; *History of Marion County, Missouri* (St. Louis, 1884), 898–904.

5. *Cincinnati City Directories* (1844), 32–35, 66; (1848), 67–71, 157–58; (1851/52), 303; (1852), 173–74, 175, 294–95; *Cincinnati Business Directories* (1846), 185, 415; (1850), 98–102, 174–75, 177–78; *Louisville City Directories* (1843/44), 72, 96, 103; (1848), 98, 104, 185; Josiah S. Johnston, ed., *Memorial History of Louisville . . .,* 2 vols. (Chicago, 1896), 1:415–16; Henry A. and Kate Ford, *History of Cincinnati, Ohio . . .* (Cleveland, 1881), 328–30.

6. *Cincinnati City Directories* (1844), 32–35, 66; (1848), 68–71, 157–58; (1851/52), 303; (1852), 173–74, 175, 294–95; *Cincinnati Business Directories* (1846), 185, 415; (1850), 98–102, 174–75, 177–78; *Louisville City Directories* (1843/44), 72, 96, 103; (1848), 98, 104, 185; *Madison Weekly Courier,* Nov. 8, 1845; Jan. 31, 1846; *Louisville Courier,* Nov. 20, 1844; Dec. 24, 1846; Nov. 25, 1848; *Peabody's Price Current,* Nov. 2, 1844; May 17, 1845; *Peabody's Weekly Markets,* Feb. 13, 1846; *CPC,* Jan. 1, 1850; Jan. 29, 1851; RG Dun & Co., Ohio, 78:102, 109, 437, 443; ibid., Kentucky, 24:251, 264; ibid., Indiana, 50:36, 39, 393; Manuscript Census, 1850, Products of Industry, Hamilton County, Ohio; ibid., Clark County, Indiana; *City of Cincinnati and Its Resources* (Cincinnati, 1891), 71, 114; M. Joblin & Co., *Cincinnati Past and Present: Its Industrial History . . .* (Cincinnati, 1872), 114–16, 301–3; J.M. Elstner & Co., *Centennial Review of Cincinnati* (Cincinnati, 1888), 116, 149; Charles T. Greve, *Centennial History of Cincinnati and Its Representative Citizens,* 2 vols. (Chicago, 1904), 2:808–9; Johnston, *Memorial History of Louisville,* 1: 415–16.

7. William Youatt, *The Pig* (London, 1847), 37.

8. For a general summary of early hog raising in the West, see Towne and Wentworth, *Pigs from Cave to Cornbelt,* 98–112.

9. Ibid., 162–81; Clemen, *American Livestock,* 47–59; H.D. Emery, "Hogs and Pork Packing in the West," U.S., Congress, House, *Executive Documents* 91, "Agricultural Report," 38 Cong., 1 sess. (1863/64): 198–202; W.F.M. Arny, "Essay on the Best Breeds of Swine," Illinois State Agricultural Society, *Transactions* 1 (1853/54): 554–58. See also

selected issues of *Prairie Farmer,* for example, 1 (1841): 18–19, 27, 31, 45, 50, 63–64, 86 (hereafter cited as *PF*). Considerable information also exists in various state publications; for example, John Ashton, "A History of Hogs and Pork Production in Missouri," Missouri State Board of Agriculture, *Monthly Bulletin* 21 (1923); but it is not given systematically.

10. Farm journals like the *Prairie Farmer,* vols. 1–10 (1840–1850), are full of advice on hog feeding. For tables of corn-hog equivalents see *Hunt's Merchants' Magazine* 35 (1856):376–77 (hereafter cited as *HMM*); *Ohio Valley Farmer* 2 (1857):184; *Madison Courier,* Nov. 10, 1857; *Tazewell Record,* Dec. 3, 1857; and *PF* (1865), 385.

11. Figures for "gross" and "net" pork are quoted irregularly in the local press. See, for example, *Louisville Weekly Courier,* Dec. 5, 1846; *Des Moines Valley Whig,* Jan. 12, 1854; Jan. 11, 1858; *Peoria Transcript,* Feb. 9, 16, 1858; Dec. 8, 1859. In Cincinnati hog prices were usually quoted net and independent slaughterers obtained a premium of $0.25 to $0.60 per hog in the 1850s; *Cincinnati Gazette,* Dec. 15, 1853; *Madison Daily Courier,* Nov. 16, 1858. The percentage of the hog pack which originated as dressed pork is unknown. In Cincinnati, where slaughterers were active, perhaps 10 percent of the city's output originated as dressed pork. In other packing points the proportion of dressed pork put up by packers was probably higher. Figures available for the 1860s show that 21.4 percent of Chicago's hogs were dressed. *Missouri Republican,* Feb. 17, 1843; Feb. 1, 1845; *Liberty Hall,* Feb. 14, 1846; *CPC,* Jan. 9, 1850; CBT *AR* (1860–1870).

12. The commercial columns of local newspapers are the most reliable sources of information on the flow of hogs to market. See, for example, reports for either the 1846/47 season in Hannibal, *Hannibal Gazette,* Nov. 26, Dec. 3, 10, 17, 31, 1846; Jan. 7, 14, 28, Feb. 14, 1847; or the 1852/53 season in Keokuk, *Des Moines Valley Whig,* Nov. 25, Dec. 9, 23, 30, 1852; Jan. 6, 13, 20, 1853.

13. Most information on droving is based on the reminiscences of old-timers who furnished good stories but provided little systematic evidence. Edmond C. Burnett, "Hog Raising and Hog Driving in the Region of the French Broad River," *Agricultural History* 20 (1946): 83–103 (hereafter cited as *AH*); Howard Johnson, ed., *A Home in the Woods: Oliver Johnson's Reminiscences of Early Marion County* (Indianapolis, 1961), 218–22; Gurdon S. Hubbard, *Autobiography* (Chicago, 1911), 178–79; *PF* 9 (1849): 244; Ashton, "Hogs and Pork Production in Missouri," 52–53. Competiton among the river towns for the hog supply of the Upper Mississippi Valley suggested some flexibility in distances of drives; *Peoria Register,* Dec. 4, 11, 1840; *Quincy*

Whig, Nov. 29, 1843; *Des Moines Valley Whig,* Nov. 1, 1858; Alexander Maxwell, "Letterbook, 1857-1859" (Western Historical Collection, Columbia, Mo.), passim.

14. Cold weather was essential for the safe preparation of salted and cured meat. Once killed, the hog had to be hung to remove all traces of body heat. The carcass was then taken to a cool room where it was thoroughly chilled at temperatures of 36°-38°F., preferably for 36-42 hours, before being cut. Estimates of "ideal" temperatures for packing operations varied. If there were hard frosts the frozen meat sections became difficult, if not impossible, to handle, but mild weather could lead to spoilage. The curing process also required storage in cold temperatures, below 40° F., so that the preserving mixtures could penetrate all parts of the meat.

Two contemporary sources offering useful insights are John S. Seaton, "Killing, Curing and Preservation of Meats," in Kentucky State Agricultural Society, *Second Report to the Kentucky Legislature, 1858/59,* 71-78, which discusses meat processing for family rather than commercial use; and John C. Schooley, *A Process of Obtaining a Dry Cold Current of Air from Ice and Its Different Applications* (Cincinnati, 1855) (Cincinnati Public Library, Rare Books Collection), which describes experiments in keeping a curing room cool.

Technical explanations of temperature control in meat processing are more accessible in the descriptions of the more modern packing plants. See, for example, Arthur Cushman, "The Packing Plant and Its Equipment" in American Meat Institute, *The Packing Industry* (Chicago, 1924), 99-130; and "What Changed Meat Packing—Preservation by Cold Enabled a Trade to Become an Industry," in *The Significant Sixty, National Provisioner* 126 (1950):197-222.

15. *Daily Cincinnati Gazette,* Nov. 14, 1850.

16. The best sources for the length of the packing season are the commercial columns of local newspapers. See, for example, *Peoria Register,* Dec. 18, 1840; Dec. 3, 1841; Dec. 9, 1842; *Liberty Hall and Cincinnati Enquirer,* Dec. 8, 15; *Cincinnati Gazette,* Feb. 9, 1843; Nov. 15, 1850; Nov. 22, 1854; *CPC,* Nov. 2, 23, 30, Dec. 28, 1844; Jan. 4, 1845; Nov. 7, 14, 1851; Nov. 5, 1852; Oct. 26, Nov. 2, 1853; *Dayton Transcript,* Nov. 30, 1844; *Louisville Weekly Journal,* Nov. 26, 1845; *Quincy Whig,* Oct. 27, Nov. 3, 1847; Sept. 12, Oct. 31, 1848; Oct. 30, 1849; Oct. 21, Nov. 19, 1851; Oct. 4, 1852; Dec. 12, 1853; *Hamilton Intelligencer,* Oct. 21, 1847; *Wabash Courier,* Dec. 9, 1848; *Des Moines Whig and Register,* Oct. 3, 1850; *Cincinnati Gazette,* Nov. 15, 1850; Nov. 22, 1854; *Daily Louisville Democrat,* Nov. 10, 1853.

17. *Peoria Register,* 1840-1842; *Quincy Whig,* 1840-1856; *CPC,* 1845-1846, 1848-1857; *Louisville Weekly Journal,* 1845; *Louisville Weekly Courier,* 1846-1847, 1848-1849; *Louisville Examiner,* 1847-1848, 1849; *Hannibal Gazette,* 1846-1847; *Hannibal Journal,* 1847-1850; *Des Moines Valley Whig,* 1849-1857; *Louisville Democrat,* 1851-1854.

18. The unpredictability of weather conditions negates any generalizations, but packing was probably halted at least once in the season. See, for example, *Quincy Whig,* 1838-1857; *Scioto Gazette,* 1841-1849; *Wabash Express,* 1842-1860; *Maysville Eagle,* 1845-1848, 1850-1854; *Hannibal Journal,* 1846-1850, 1851-1853; *Daily Louisville Democrat,* 1851-1854.

19. It is difficult to estimate the amounts of fixed and working capital needed or used by pork merchants. Statistics of fixed capital should be available in the returns of the manuscript censuses, but examination of these records reveals that the marshals failed to distinguish between plant and equipment and operating costs. Reports of prominent pork men with similar establishments range widely not only between cities but also within cities. In Cincinnati, at mid-century, capital invested varied from a low of $11,000 to a high of $75,000; in Louisville it fluctuated between $30,000 and $180,000; the comparative figures for St. Louis were $20,000 and $107,800, and in Madison the main establishment had a capital of $50,000. Manuscript Census, 1850, Products of Industry, Schedule 5, Hamilton County, Ohio, Jefferson County, Kentucky, St. Louis County, Missouri, and Jefferson County, Indiana.

20. *Peoria Register,* Dec. 16, 1837; *Quincy Whig,* Jan. 19, Mar. 9, 1838; Mar. 30, 1839; Jan. 1, Nov. 5, 1842; Feb. 27, 1849; Oct. 1, 1850; *Maysville Eagle,* Jan. 6, Nov. 17, 1846; Jan. 28, 1851; Nov. 11, 1852; *Hamilton Intelligencer,* Oct. 21, 1847; Nov. 30, 1848; Feb. 1, 1849; *Peoria Democratic Press,* Nov. 23, 1853; *Lafayette Journal,* Jan. 11, Oct. 22, 1856. Simeon de W. Drown, *Peoria City Record or Drown's Statistics for 1849* (n.p., n.d.), n.p.; idem, *Peoria Record and Advertiser for August 1856* (Peoria, 1856), 7, 12, 13; John M.D. Burrows, *Fifty Years in Iowa . . . Personal Reminiscences . . .* (Davenport, Iowa, 1888), 99.

Merchants participating in the early pork trade might have their slaughtering carried out by butchers, but as they became more committed to the business they integrated backward. By mid-century most packers slaughtered their own animals. Only in Cincinnati did a distinct slaughtering business emerge. John W. Coleman, "Contract for the merger of various slaughter houses in Cincinnati, 1839" (Western Reserve Historical Society); *Quincy Whig,* Nov. 5, 1842; Dec. 11, 1844; Dec. 4, 1849; *CPC,* Nov. 15, 1848; *Daily Louisville Democrat,* Oct. 28, 1853; *Daily Cincinnati Gazette,* Dec. 19, 22, 23, 1853; *Lafayette Journal,* Nov. 28, 30, Dec. 7, 13, 20, 21, 28, 29, 1854; *Peoria City Directory* (1844), 126; Charles Cist, *Sketches and Statistics of Cincinnati in 1851* (Cincinnati, 1851), 279–81.

21. *Wabash Express,* Mar. 16, 1842; *Illinois Palladium,* Aug. 3, 1842; *Peoria Register,* Feb. 3, 1843; *Quincy Whig,* Mar. 15, 1843; *Dayton Transcript,* Mar. 2, 1844; *Maysville Eagle,* Feb. 18, 1847; Nov. 11, 1852; *Hannibal Gazette,* Nov. 4, 1847; *Hannibal Journal,* Dec. 30, 1847; *Des Moines Whig and Register,* Nov. 22, 1849; Oct. 3, 7, 17, 1850; Nov. 13, 1851; *Cincinnati Gazette,* July 23, Nov. 22, 1850; *CPC,* Oct. 27, 1852; *Milwaukee Sentinel,* July 13, 1853; *Lafayette Journal,* Jan. 10, 1855; *Weekly Hawkeye and Telegraph,* Dec. 5, 1855; *Indiana State Journal,* Oct. 29, 1857; Nov. 11, 1858; William Rees, *Description of the City of Keokuk, Lee County* (Keokuk, 1854), 18; *Keokuk City Directory* (1857), 181.

22. *Cincinnati Daily Gazette,* Nov. 25, 1835; Aug. 30, 1849; *Louisville Daily Courier,* Nov. 20, 1844; Nov. 25, 1848; Dec. 2, 1848; *CPC,* Nov. 19, 1845; Oct. 7, 1846; Dec. 20, 1848; Sept. 19, 1849; Nov. 5, 1851; Oct. 27, 1852; Nov. 23, 1853; *Kentucky Yeoman,* Oct. 29, 1846; *Cists's Advertiser,* Nov. 2, 1847; Oct. 31, 1849; July 25, 1850; Feb. 7, 1851; Cist, *Cincinnati in 1851,* 228–29, 230–31; *Louisville City Directory* (1848/49), 51; Benjamin Casseday, *The History of Louisville . . . to 1852* (Louisville, 1852; rpt., 1970), 36; Richard Deering, *Louisville, Her Commercial, Manufacturing and Social Advantages* (Louisville, 1859), 86, 88.

23. Stagg & Shay's new ham-curing house in Cincinnati in 1849 warranted a capital investment of $20,000, while Evans & Swift's new operations in Cincinnati in 1852 were estimated to have cost $18,000. *CPC,* Sept. 19, 1849; Oct. 27, 1852.

24. These figures must be regarded as estimates. Though local sources regularly report the market prices of hogs, they only intermittently record transport charges, the costs of cooperage and salt, wage rates, and insurance premiums. Furthermore it is not possible to ascertain when and at what cost any pork merchant bought his materials, how much his hogs weighed, how many were live rather than dressed, and what kinds of pork products he processed. But these estimates are not completely ahistorical because they are based on average figures for the locations cited. *Scioto Gazette,* Nov. 2, 16, Dec. 7, 14,

21, 28, 1843; Jan. 4, 11, 18, Nov. 21, 1844; Dec. 23, 1845; Feb. 13, Dec. 9, 23, 1846; Jan. 6, 13, 20, Nov. 10, Dec. 8, 1847; Jan. 12, 19, Feb. 23, Nov. 15, 22, 29, Dec. 13, 20, 1848; Jan. 17, 31, 1849; Manuscript Census, 1850, Products of Industry, Ross County, Ohio; Berry, *Western Prices,* 557-96; Charles T. Leavitt, "Some Economic Aspects of the Western Meat Packing Industry, 1830-1860," *Journal of Business of the University of Chicago* 4 (1931):73.

25. *Quincy Whig,* Mar. 26, Sept. 24, 1842; Oct. 25, Nov. 29, Dec. 6, 13, 1843; Nov. 27, Dec. 11, 1844; Jan. 1, 29, Nov. 12, 26, Dec. 10, 17, 24, 31, 1845; Jan. 7, 21, 28, Dec. 2, 9, 16, 23, 30, 1846; Jan. 13, 27, Feb. 3, 17, Nov. 3, 17, 24, Dec. 1, 8, 1847; Jan. 5, 12, 19, 26, Feb. 2, 9, 16, 23, Mar. 1, 8, 22, 1846; *Beardstown Gazette,* Dec. 20, 27, 1848; Jan. 10, 1849; *Drown's Statistics for 1849,* n.p.; Henry Asbury, *Reminiscences of Quincy, Illinois . . .* (Quincy, 1882), 113-15; William V. Pooley, *The Settlement of Illinois from 1830 to 1850* (Madison, Wis., 1908), 4, 18-19.

26. The costs of city packers' operations are also estimates. Published sources offer guides on hog prices, numbers of establishments, and transport charges. Supplementary but fragmentary information is available in contemporary descriptions of packing operations and in trade reports. Cincinnati firms were smaller than expected, possibly due to the division of the city's business between slaughterers and packers. There were larger establishments in both Louisville and Madison. *Dollar Farmer* 2 (1843): 81; *CPC,* Nov. 2, 23, 30, Dec. 7, 21, 28, 1844; Jan. 4, 11, 18, Feb. 2, 1845; Nov. 15, 1848; Nov. 5, 1851; *Hamilton Intelligencer,* Nov. 14, 1844; *Louisville Daily Courier,* Nov. 20, 1844; *Liberty Hall and Cincinnati Gazette,* Jan. 30, 1845; *Louisville Weekly Journal,* Nov. 12, 19, 26, Dec. 3, 10, 17, 24, 31, 1845; Nov. 21, Dec. 5, 12, 19, 24, 1846; Jan. 9, 16, 1847; *Louisville Examiner,* Nov. 6, 20, 27, Dec. 4, 18, 25, 1847; Jan. 8, 15, 22, 1848; *Louisville Weekly Courier,* Nov. 25, 1848; *Madison Weekly Courier,* Nov. 8, 15, 22, 29, Dec. 6, 27, 1845; Jan. 3, 10, 17, 31, 1846; *Cincinnati Almanac for 1846,* 81; *Cist's Advertiser,* Feb. 29, 1848; Feb. 7, 1851; Manuscript Census, 1850, Products of Industry, Hamilton County, Ohio; ibid., Jefferson County, Kentucky; ibid., Jefferson County, Indiana; Cist, *Cincinnati in 1851,* 281-87; *Louisville City Directory* (1848/49), 51; John B. Newhall, *The British Emigrants' Hand Book and Guide to the New States of America . . .* (London, 1844), 68-71; Berry, *Western Prices,* 557-96.

27. For general descriptions of the "all-purpose" midwestern merchant see Atherton, *The Pioneer Merchant*; and Fred M. Jones, *Middlemen in the Domestic Trade of the United States* (Urbana, Ill.,

1937). More detailed insights into early rural mercantile transactions can be gleaned from the papers of Samuel Moore of Mooresville on the White River in Indiana (Indiana State Library). Moore sent cargoes of pork and bacon downriver both to southern markets and to the major northeastern meat center of Baltimore.

28. For random information gleaned from western newspapers, see *Peoria Register,* Dec. 16, 1837; Mar. 10, 1838; Nov. 19, Dec. 2, 1841; Jan. 28, Dec. 23, 1842; *Quincy Whig,* Jan. 19, 1838; Mar. 9, Nov. 30, Dec. 7, 14, 1839; Jan. 4, Oct. 24, 31, 1840; Oct. 2, Dec. 11, 1841; Jan. 1, Sept. 24, Oct. 8, 15, Nov. 5, 1842; Jan. 25, Feb. 1, Oct. 25, Nov. 8, 29, Dec. 13, 1843; Oct. 16, 23, Dec. 11, 1844; Jan. 8, 29, 1845; *Scioto Gazette,* Nov. 24, Dec. 8, 1842; Jan. 12, Nov. 9, 23, 1843; Nov. 28, 1844; *Wabash Express,* Jan. 18, 1843; *Dayton Transcript,* Nov. 1, 1845; *Madison Weekly Courier,* Nov. 8, 1845; *Maysville Eagle,* Nov. 8, 1845; Oct. 14, Nov. 11, 18, 1847; *Circleville Watchman,* Jan. 16, Dec. 4, 1846; Mar. 3, 1848; *Hamilton Intelligencer,* Oct. 21, 1847; Nov. 30, 1848; Dec. 14, 1848; Feb. 1, 1849. For information on the Indianapolis branch of the Indiana State Bank, see Gayle Thornbrough and Dorothy L. Riker, eds., *The Diary of Calvin Fletcher,* vol. 3 (Indianapolis, 1974), passim; Gayle Thornbrough, Dorothy L. Riker, and Paula Corpuz, eds., *The Diary of Calvin Fletcher,* vols. 4-6 (Indianapolis, 1975-1978), passim.

29. *Maysville Eagle,* Oct. 29, Nov. 8, 1845; Jan. 27, Feb. 28, Nov. 24, 1846; Feb. 16, Oct. 14, Nov. 11, 1847; Nov. 19, 23, 1850; Jan. 28, 1851; Nov. 6, 11, 18, 1852; Nov. 17, 23, 1853; RG Dun & Co., Kentucky, 31: 13, 41, 67, 247, 250; Manuscript Censuses, 1850 and 1860, Products of Industry, Mason County, Kentucky.

30. Manuscript Census, 1850, Products of Industry, Vigo County, Indiana; *Terre Haute City Directory* (1864), 21-33; RG Dun & Co., Indiana, 119: 2; Condit, *History of Early Terre Haute,* 143-48; Oakey, *Greater Terre Haute,* 2:202-3; *Biographical History of Eminent and Self-Made Men of the State of Indiana,* 2:11-12.

31. Manuscript Census, 1850, Products of Industry, Madison County, Illinois; *Peabody's Weekly Markets,* Jan. 23, 1846; *Maysville Eagle,* Oct. 26, 1848; *Hannibal Journal,* Nov. 30, Dec. 14, 1848; Jan. 20, 1853; *Peoria Democratic Press,* Oct. 29, 1851; *Alton City Directory* (1858), 80, 132; *Missouri State Gazeteer and Business Directory* (1860), 114; RG Dun & Co., Illinois, 139: 136, 164; ibid., Missouri, 25:256, 257; ibid., Indiana, 109:23, 80; Wilbur T. Norton, *Centennial History of Madison County, Illinois* (Chicago, 1912), 1166; *Biographical Encyclopaedia of Illinois* (Philadelphia, 1875), 202; *History of Marion County, Missouri* (St. Louis, 1884), 898-904.

32. Berry, *Western Prices*, 226–28, specifically analyzes banks and hog packing. The general discussion on "Currency and Banking, Speculation and Investment, and the Price Level," 357-542, is also helpful in assessing the financial situation.

33. For general statements about trading networks, see James E. Vance, Jr., *The Merchants' World: The Geography of Wholesaling* (Englewood Cliffs, N.J., 1970), 80–128.

34. RG Dun & Co., Ohio, 78:437, 443; ibid., Missouri, 37:95, 407; 38:235; CCC *AR* (1899), "Obituary Notice," 320–21; *Leading Manufacturers and Merchants of Cincinnati and Environs* (New York, 1886), 90; George M. Roe, *Cincinnati: The Queen City of the West . . .* (Cincinnati, 1895), 363; Elstner, *Centennial Review of Cincinnati*, 116, 149; Logan U. Reavis, *St. Louis: The Future Great City of the World*, Biographical Ed. (St. Louis, 1875), 161-65; *Missouri Republican*, Feb. 15, 1870, in "Charles Van Ravenswaay Files" (Missouri Historical Society). General references to trading relationships are scattered widely in midwestern newspapers. John J. Roe in the 1840s has been excluded from the sample.

35. Lard was widely used for cooking. In its more refined form of lard oil and stearine, it was sold for lighting purposes and for making soap and candles. Initially packers regarded these by-products as inferior to pork cuts and they often ignored them, but by mid-century they were showing marked interest in producing them not only as a means of reducing wastage but as a valuable product for which there was a large demand. Indeed, in the 1850s the annual lard figure per hog killed ranged between 28 and 35 pounds, or 40 percent of the maximum possible. *PF* 2 (1842): 71; 3 (1843): 2-3; *Quincy Whig*, Dec. 31, 1842; *CPC*, Feb. 22, 1845; Mar. 14, 1849; Feb. 12, 1851; Mar. 22, 1854; Jan 24, 1855; Feb. 2, 1859; *Western Journal and Civilian* 2 (1849): 38–39; Charles Cist, "The Hog and Its Products," in U.S., Congress, House, Serial 519, "Report of the Commissioner of Patents (1847)," *House Documents*, 30 Cong., 1 sess. (1847/48), 529–30; Manuscript Census, 1850, Products of Industry for the States of Illinois, Indiana, Iowa, Kentucky, Missouri, and Ohio.

36. *Quincy Whig*, Nov. 8, 1843; *PF* 3 (1843): 14; 7 (1847): 32–33; 14 (1854): 22-24; CCC *AR* (1849–1859), passim; St. Louis Chamber of Commerce, *Annual Reports* (1848), 8; (1849), 8; (1852), 9-10; (1854), 23-24; (1855), 22-23; (1856), 16-17; (1857), 23-25; (1858), 25-27; (1859), 29-30 (Missouri Historical Society; hereafter cited as SLCC *AR*); Cist, "Hog and Its Products," passim; Kentucky State Agricultural Society, *Second Report to the Kentucky Legislature, 1858/59*, 75–76.

37. Cures were individual but most pork merchants first steeped the hams in a salt, sugar, and saltpeter solution. After several weeks, hams were moved to the smokehouse where they were hung several feet away from the smoke pits to absorb the flavor of the hickory, beech, or maple sugar smoke. The smoking process could last days or weeks. Then ordinary hams were placed in casks or boxes to be sold by weight or were canvased in bulk. Quality hams for the expensive market were wrapped individually in brown paper, canvased, yellow-washed, and stenciled, or were dipped in a special composition to prevent deterioration.

Quincy Whig, Feb. 27, 1841; Nov. 8, 1843; Jan. 2, 1849; Jan. 22, Feb. 19, 1850; Jan. 21, 1851; *PF* 3 (1843): 14; 7 (1847): 32; *CPC,* Sept. 19, 1849; Nov. 6, 1850; Nov. 23, 1853; Nov. 1, 1854; Oct. 31, 1855; Nov. 9, 1859; *Beardstown Gazette,* May 1, 1850; Mar. 17, 1852; *Cist's Advertiser,* Feb. 7, 1851; *HMM* 28 (1853): 431; *Peru Daily Chronicle,* Apr. 1, 1854, in AC Cole Notes (University of Illinois, Champaign-Urbana); Casseday, *History of Louisville,* 36; Kentucky State Agricultural Society, *Second Report,* 75–76; *Cincinnati City Directory* (1851/52), 303; (1852), 172–173; (1853), 334; (1855), 201–2; (1856), 188, 190; (1857), 331; (1858), 315; (1859), 339; (1860), 417.

38. Mess pork consisted of the sides of corn-fattened hogs weighing at least 250 pounds. If the ribs and backbone were removed, the barrel could be stamped a superior marking of "clear" or "clear mess." Prime pork was composed of meat from lighter hogs weighing at least 150 pounds net, and had a maximum of inferior cuts like legs, necks, and heads, with sides filling the remainder of the barrel. Cargo pork was "merchantable" meat consisting of sides, four shoulders, and not more than 30 pounds of heads.

Wabash Express, Mar. 9, 1842; *Quincy Whig,* Nov. 8, 1843; Dec. 3, 1845; *HMM* 15 (1846): 185–86; 36 (1856): 744–45; *Madison Daily Courier,* Nov. 15, 1859; *Revised Ordinances of St. Louis* (1836), 78–82; (1850), 236–38; *Revised Ordinances of St. Louis* (1851), 168–69; CBT *AR* (1858), 30; Cist, "Hog and Its Products," passim.

39.

Year	Urban Population of U.S.	Military Personnel on Active Duty	Labor Force on Ocean Vessels
1830	1,127,000	11,942	70,000
1840	1,845,000	21,616	95,000
1850	3,544,000	20,824	135,000

Source: *Historical Statistics of the United States, Colonial Times to 1957* (Washington, D.C., 1960).

Season	No. of Hogs Packed in West[1]	Meat (lbs.)[2]
1832/33	283,333	42,499,950
1839/40	650,000	97,500,000
1849/50	1,652,220	247,733,000

Source: Table 6 above; and Berry, *Western Prices,* 223.

1. No figures are reported for the West in 1832/33 and 1839/40. These figures are based on the assumption that Cincinnati packed 30% of the regional total.

2. Assumes that each hog weighed 200 lbs. gross and yielded 150 lbs. of meat.

Year	Urban and Institutional Population of U.S.[1]	Annual Pork Consumption[2] (lbs.)
1830	1,159,800	141,495,600
1840	1,891,800	230,799,600
1850	3,606,400	439,980,800

1. Urban population plus 40% of military personnel and 40% of merchant marine. It is assumed that the remainder of the army were fed with fresh beef while the navy and merchant marine were partly provisioned with fish and from foreign sources.

2. The upper bound estimate for per capita meat consumption in the U.S. is 225 lbs. Slaves consumed 146 lbs. meat each. Assuming that the average urban consumption fell between these two figures at 185 lbs., and that two-thirds of the meat eaten was pork, then the average pork consumption was 122 lbs. See Robert E. Gallman, "Self-Sufficiency in the Cotton Economy of the Antebellum South," in William N. Parker, ed., *The Structure of the Cotton Economy of the Antebellum South* (Washington, D.C., 1970), 18–19.

Midwestern packers produced 70 percent of the American meat outputs. U.S., Congress, Senate, Document 39, "A Digest of the Statistics of Manufactures According to the Returns of the Seventh Census," *Senate Executive Documents,* 35 Cong., 2 sess. (1858/59); and William N. Parker, "Pork Production in the United States, 1840–1910: Estimates and Sources, Notes" (unpublished paper, 1966), 29.

Year	70% of Commercial Meat Requirements (lbs.)
1830	99,046,920
1840	161,559,720
1850	307,986,560

40. U.S., Congress, Senate, Document 259, "Exports . . . to Foreign Countries, 1789–1893," pt. 2, "Exports and Imports," *Senate Documents,* 53 Cong., 2 sess. (1893/94), 36–39, 172–79; Richard Perren, *The Meat Trade in Britain, 1840–1914* (London, 1978), 69–74.

41. There is very little consistent information on what proportion of the hog pack entered local city trade. There are also only a few references to the butchering business. *Peoria Democratic Press,* Dec. 13, 1854; CDP *AR* (1857), 15; *Indiana State Sentinel,* Nov. 16, 1858; CCC *AR* (1859), 29; Charles Cist, *Sketches and Statistics of Cincinnati in 1859* (Cincinnati, 1859), 264. City directories record an abundance of butchers, however. See, for example, *Alton City Directory* (1858), 132; *Burlington City Directory* (1859), 104; *Chicago City Directory* (1854/55), 8, 22; (1855/56), 169, 190; (1858), 338-39, 369; (1859), 158-60, 170-72; *Indianapolis City Directory* (1855), 46; (1857), 11; *Keokuk City Directory* (1846/57), 38; (1859/60), 109; *Peoria City Directory* (1859), 23.

42. "In Relation to the Improvement of the Mississippi River," St. Louis Chamber of Commerce, *Proceedings* (1842), 18; SLCC *AR* (1848), 8; St. Louis Chamber of Commerce, Committee on Trade, *Report* (1852), 9; *CPC,* Mar. 6, 1850; Feb. 18, 1852; *HMM* 25 (1851), 488; 26 (1852), 432; CCC *AR* (1853), 17; (1855), 29; (1858), 33; CDP *AR* (1858), 21; (1859), 19; MCC *AR* (1858), 19; (1860), 39.

43. Scattered references suggest an active interest in the southern market. See, for example, *Missouri Republican,* Feb. 17, 1843; *Dollar Farmer* 2 (1843): 80; *Louisville Daily Courier,* Nov. 23, 1844; *CPC,* Mar. 14, 1849; Oct. 29, 1851; Cist, "Hog and Its Products," 527-28; CCC *AR* (1848), 7; (1853), 17; (1855), 29; SLCC *AR* (1858), 37; (1860), 39, 41, 43; *Daily Louisville Democrat,* Feb. 28, 1854. It is, however, difficult to turn this partial evidence into precise statements, owing to the fluctuating nature of the pork industry.

44. Extant records do not suggest how much of the midwestern hog product dispatched downriver was destined for southern consumption. Some cargoes were shipped directly to consumers, but more were sent to New Orleans to await purchase and dispatch both in and beyond the South. Even when meat was shipped by ocean steamer its destination may have been the upper South. For totals of pork and bacon shipped downriver, see Table 11.

The self-sufficiency of the antebellum South in foodstuffs is a historical perennial. Recent work suggests that the western trade to the South was small. Gallman, "Self Sufficiency in the Cotton Economy," 5-24; Parker, "Pork Production in the United States, 1840-1910," 1-30; and William K. Hutchinson and Sam. H. Williamson, "The Self Sufficiency of the Antebellum South," *Journal of Economic History* 31 (1971): 591-612. But the size of the southern market for imported pork is still debatable in terms of both fluctuations over time and intraregional patterns of agriculture. See Sam B. Hilliard, *Hog Meat and Hoecake: Food Supply in the Old South, 1840-1860* (Carbondale, Ill., 1972), 186-212.

45. *HMM* 7 (1842): 391; 9 (1843): 570; 30 (1854): 457; *Missouri Republican,* Feb. 17, 1843; *Cincinnati Gazette,* Feb. 9, 1843; Jan 18, 1844; *PF* 3 (1843): 2-3; *CPC,* Nov. 2, Dec. 7, 1844; Mar. 11, 1849; Mar. 11, 1857; Feb. 17, 1858; *De Bow's Review* 2 (1846): 422; 6 (1848): 437; 16 (1854): 409; *Gem of the Prairies,* Nov. 16, 1850; Nov. 8, 1851; *Milwaukee Sentinel,* Jan. 24, 1860; Cist, "Hog and Its Products," 527-28; CCC *AR* (1848), 7; (1857), 23; (1859), 28; CDP *AR* (1853), 7-8; (1854), 14; SLCC *AR* (1852), 10-11; Milwaukee Board of Trade, *Annual Reports* (1858), 21; (1859), 37.

46. National Archives Record Group 92, Entry 67, "Register of Proposals, 1831 and 1832"; Entry 69, "Register of Contracts and Purchases, 1819-1847"; Entry 74, "Register of Beef and Fresh Meat Contracts, 1820-1856"; Entry 76, "Contracts," vol. 5, 1843-1851; vol. 6, 1851-1853; "In Relation to the Improvement of the Mississippi River," St. Louis Chamber of Commerce, *Proceedings* (1842), 18; *Missouri Republican,* Nov. 23, 1842; Cist, "Hog and Its Products," 527-28; *CPC,* Mar. 14, 1849; *Gem of the Prairies,* Nov. 15, 1850; Nov. 8, 1851; Lewis E. Atherton, "Western Foodstuffs in the Army Provision Trade," *AH* 14 (1940): 161-69.

47. *Report of the Commissioner of Patents* (1842), 104-7; (1843), 213-27; (1844), 414-31; (1845), 1155-64; Her Majesty's Customs, "Bills of Entry for Liverpool Bill A," Entries for 1847, 1849, 1852, and 1855; *PF* 2 (1842): 86-87; 3 (1843): 2-3, 43-44; 4 (1844): 284-85; *Quincy Whig,* Oct. 22, 1842; Dec. 9, 23, 1854; *Dollar Weekly* 1 (1842): 49-50, 76-77; 2 (1843): 63, 79; *Missouri Republican,* Jan. 10, Feb. 17, 1843; *HMM* 9 (1843): 570; 26 (1852): 431; 32 (1855): 501; *CPC,* Nov. 9, 1844; Nov. 15, 1848; Mar. 14, Oct. 10, 31, 1849; Mar. 6, 1850; Dec. 12, 1855; Dec. 31, 1856; Cist, "Hog and Its Products," 528; *Gem of the Prairies,* Nov. 10, 1849; Nov. 8, 1851; *Peoria Democratic Press,* Dec. 19, 1855; CCC *AR* (1850), 4-5; (1857), 23; (1858), 23; (1859), 11; CDP *AR* (1854), 14; MCC *AR* (1860), 37; U.S., Congress, Senate, Document 259, "Exports . . . to Foreign Countries, 1789-1893," pt. 2, "Exports and Imports," *Senate Documents,* 53 Cong., 2 sess. (1893/94), 36-39, 172-79; Perren, *Meat Trade in Britain,* 69-74.

48. *Missouri Republican,* Feb. 12, 1841; *CPC,* Nov. 2, 1844; Mar. 14, 1849; *Dollar Farmer* 1 (1842): 95; 2 (1844): 110; *HMM* 7 (1842): 391; 9 (1843): 570; 25 (1851): 605; 26 (1852): 432; 29 (1853): 629; *De Bow's Review* 2 (1846): 42; 6 (1848): 437; Cist, "Hog and Its

Products," 528; *Beardstown Gazette,* Nov. 8, 1848; *Western Journal and Civilian* 5 (1850): 124; 14 (1855): 425.

49. Two sources supply unsatisfactory attempts to assess the intricacies of the existing and potential markets for midwestern meats. Berry, *Western Prices,* 215-46, provides an overview from the perspective of Cincinnati, but this needs to be extended to other packing points. Leavitt, "Some Economic Aspects," attempts to construct some tentative marketing flows for provisions.

Chapter 3

1. *Peoria Democratic Press,* Jan. 2, 1856; *Peoria Weekly Transcript,* Nov. 24, Dec. 15, 22, 29, 1857; Jan. 5, 12, 19, 26, Feb. 2, 9, 16, 23, Mar. 2, 9, 16, Nov. 19, 26, Dec. 3, 10, 17, 24, 31, 1858; Jan. 7, 21, 28, Feb. 4, 11, 1859; CDP *AR* (1856), 14-15; (1857), 25-26; (1858), 14-16, 31-32; (1859), 21-25, 27-28; (1860), 19-22. Manuscript Census, 1860, Products of Industry, Peoria County, Illinois; Burrows, *Fifty Years in Iowa,* 98-102.

2. Alexandria recorded an average output of 16,154 hogs packed in the three winter seasons 1856/57-1858/59, making the town the twenty-third leading packing place in the West. *CPC,* Mar. 24, 1858, Feb. 2, 1859. Maxwell & Johnson were the only packers operating in the town in these years. They are not included in the sample of meatpackers for the late 1850s, but they are discussed here because they provide the best extant records of meatpackers in the mid-nineteenth century Midwest.

3. Maxwell, "Letterbook, 1857-1859," contains numerous letters mainly directed to J.J. Roe & Company of St. Louis concerning the purchase of hogs. Though some of the letter copies are blurred, it is still possible to follow the activities of the firm for most of the period. The earlier "Record Book, 1853-1856" also provides numerical information on hog purchases. Estimates of the operating costs of Maxwell & Johnson for the 1857/58 season are derived from figures in the manuscript sources and from the general cost of packing enterprises as set out in the text in chapter 2.

4. Maxwell, "Letterbook, 1857-1859," passim; RG Dun & Co., Missouri, 8:334, 345, 352b; 36:95, 407; 38:235.

5. "Frederick Layton: Field Notes for a Biographical Sketch," Wis. Mss MM (State Historical Society of Wisconsin, Madison); *Peoria Democratic Press,* Nov. 28, 1855; *Tazewell Register,* Dec. 17, 1857; *Peoria Record . . . for . . . 1856,* 13; *Edwards' Peoria Census Report and Historical and Statistical Review* (Peoria, 1876), n.p.; RG Dun & Co.,

Illinois, 173:132, 227, 259; 211:172, 192, 219, 227, 235; *History of Peoria County*, 543; *Portrait and Biographical Album of Peoria County*, 349-50; Newton Bateman and Paul Selby, eds., *Historical Encyclopaedia of Illinois and History of Tazewell County*, 2 vols. (Chicago, 1905) 2:910.

6. Manuscript Census, 1850, Products of Industry, Lee County, Iowa; ibid., 1860, Adams County, Ill.; *Quincy Whig*, Oct. 2, 1841; Nov. 5, 1842; Oct. 16, 1844; Oct. 15, 1845; Oct. 14, 1846; Oct. 24, 1848; Oct. 1, 1850; *Valley Whig and Keokuk Register*, Nov. 22, 1849; Oct. 3, 17, 1850; Feb. 6, 18, Nov. 13, 1851; Jan. 14, 1857; Feb. 8, Dec. 6, 1858; Sept. 5, 1849; Jan. 16, 1860; Jan. 21, 1861; *Quincy City Directory* (1855/56), n.p.; (1857/58), n.p.; (1859/60), 153; *Keokuk City Directory* (1857), 125, 181; Joseph T. Holmes, *Quincy in 1857* (Quincy, 1857), 53-54; Nathan Parker, *Iowa as It Is in 1855* (Chicago, 1855), 151; RG Dun & Co., Illinois, 4:146; 20:180; ibid., Iowa, 31: 129; Patrick H. Redmond, *History of Quincy and Its Men of Mark* (Quincy, 1869), 228-29; Henry Ashbury, *Reminiscences of Quincy, Illinois* . . . (Quincy, 1882), 113-15; *The History of Lee County, Iowa* (Chicago, 1879), 619-24, 708; *Portrait and Biographical Album of Lee County* (Chicago, 1887), 404-6; Harold H. McCarty and C.W. Thompson, *Meat Packing in Iowa* (Iowa City, 1933), 14-15; Faye E. Harris, "A Frontier Community: The Economic, Social and Political Development of Keokuk, Iowa, 1820-1866" (Ph.D. diss., Univ. of Iowa, 1965), 192-97, 363-66.

7. Manuscript Census, 1850, Products of Industry, Vigo County, Ind., Hamilton County, Ohio; ibid., 1860, Vigo County, Ind.; *Beardstown Gazette*, Feb. 4, 1852; *Wabash Express*, Jan. 19, 1859; *Terre Haute City Directory* (1864), 21-23; *Cincinnati City Directory* (1850/51), 56, 73, 90, 265; (1853), 69, 93, 117, 330, 332, 334, 383; (1855), 43, 57, 69, 200, 202, 213; (1856), 51, 67, 83, 190, 265; (1857), 61, 81, 83, 103, 250, 331; (1858), 71, 83, 95, 237, 315; (1859), 75, 99, 101, 114, 275, 338; (1860), 113, 114, 129, 284, 417; RG Dun & Co., Indiana, 119:2; ibid., Ohio, 78:153, 176, 437, 443; 79:230, 232; 80: 231; *Biographical History of Eminent . . . Indiana*, 2:11-12.

8. A.L. Kohlmeier, *The Old Northwest, as the Keystone of the Arch of American Federal Union: A Study in Commerce and Politics* (Bloomington, Ind., 1938), passim; Wyatt W. Belcher, *The Economic Rivalry between St. Louis and Chicago, 1850-1880* (New York, 1947), passim; Sherry O. Hessler, "Patterns of Transport and Urban Growth in the Miami Valley, Ohio, 1820-1860" (M.A. thesis, Johns Hopkins Univ., 1961), 124-34; Bessie L. Pierce, *A History of Chicago*, 3 vols.

(Chicago, 1937-1947) 2:37-62; Charles T. Leavitt, "Transportation and the Livestock Industry of the Middle West to 1860," *AH* 8 (1934), 25-33; Howard C. Hill, "The Development of Chicago as a Center of the Meat Packing Industry," *Mississippi Valley Historical Review* 10 (1923): 253-73. Frederick L. Paxson, "The Railroads of the Old Northwest before the Civil War," *Transactions of the Wisconsin Academy of Sciences, Arts and Letters* 17 (1914): 243-74. For further information on the construction of railroads in the various states, consult local history volumes, as, for example, Francis P. Weisenburger, *The Passing of the Frontier, 1825-1850,* vol. 3 of *History of the State of Ohio* (Columbus, Ohio, 1941), 110-18; Emma Lou Thornbrough, *Indiana in the Civil War Era, 1850-1880,* vol. 3 of *The History of Indiana* (Indianapolis, 1965), 318-61; Arthur C. Cole, *The Era of the Civil War, 1848-1870,* vol. 3 of *Centennial History of Illinois* (Chicago, 1922), 27-52, 357-61; Richard N. Current, *The Civil War Era, 1848-1873*, vol. 2 of *The History of Wisconsin* (Madison, 1976), 29-41, 437-45.

9. Pork packing in Madison in the 1840s:

Season	No. of Hogs Packed	Season	No. of Hogs Packed
1843/44	65,000	1847/48	98,000
1844/45	45,000	1848/49	95,500
1845/46	63,000	1849/50	87,709
1846/47	45,000		

Sources: Various contemporary newspapers.

Donald T. Zimmer, "Madison, Indiana, 1811-1860: A Study in the Process of City Building" (Ph.D. diss., Indiana Univ., 1974), 113-43; *Daily Louisville Courier,* Nov. 14, 1844; *Daily Louisville Democrat,* Dec. 13, 1851, Jan. 28, 1852.

10. Manuscript Censuses, 1850 and 1860, Products of Industry, Jefferson County, Ind.; *Daily Louisville Democrat,* Jan. 28, 1852; *Lafayette Journal,* Jan. 13, 1854; *Madison Evening Courier,* Dec. 4, 1856; *Madison Courier,* Nov. 17, 1857; Feb. 3, 1858; Dec. 6, 1859; Jan. 11, Dec. 31, 1860; *Madison City Directory* (1859), 73, 95; *Madison Business Directory* (1860), 33; RG Dun & Co., Indiana, 50: 59, 105; *Biographical History of Eminent . . . Indiana,* 1:50; *Biographical and Historical Souvenir for the County of Clark . . . Jefferson . . .* (Chicago, 1889), 192; Zimmer, "Madison, Indiana, 1811-1860," xii, 57-58, 150-67.

11. *Burlington Hawkeye and Telegraph,* Mar. 3, Oct. 31, Nov. 14, Dec. 5, 1855; Jan. 2, 9, Feb. 20, Nov. 12, 1856; Jan. 14, Dec. 2, 1857;

Feb. 2, 9, Oct. 28, 1858; Jan. 18, 1859; Feb. 11, 1860; Jan. 26, Feb. 2, Dec. 7, 1861; Jan. 4, 25, Dec. 6, 1862; Jan. 31, Dec. 12, 1863; *Burlington Business Directory* (1856), 4–6; *Burlington City Directory* (1857), 3–7; (1859), 718; CBT *AR* (1858), 27; (1859), 55; (1860), 33; (1861), 33; (1862), 34; (1864), 48; (1865), 38; Edwards' *Commercial Directory of the Mississippi Valley* (1866), 411-12; Western Historical Company, *History of Des Moines County, Iowa* (Chicago, 1879), 484–85; McCarty and Thompson, *Meat Packing in Iowa,* 14, 19–20.

Pork packing in Burlington, Iowa, in 1847-1860:

Season	No. of Hogs	Season	No. of Hogs
1847/48	17,000	1854/55	28,000
1848/49	15,000	1855/56	49,574
1849/50	29,000	1856/57	24,500
1850/51	19,000	1857/58	16,100
1851/52	11,000	1858/59	32,300
1852/53	6,000	1859/60	43,600
1853/54	11,000	1860/61	37,781

Sources: Various contemporary newspapers.

12. *The Diary of Calvin Fletcher* 3:214; 4:80; Thornbrough, *Indiana in the Civil War Era,* 322–36, 418, 557–59; James H. Madison, "Businessmen and the Business Community in Indianapolis, 1820–1860" (Ph.D. diss., Indiana Univ., 1972), 120–22; Bernard A. Hewes, "The Rise of the Pork Industry in Indiana" (M.A. thesis, Indiana Univ., 1939), 53–62; RG Dun & Co., Indiana, 67: 9, 171; 68: 205, 384.

13. *Indiana State Journal,* Nov. 23, Dec. 13, 27, 1855; Dec. 30, 1856; Jan. 21, 1860; *Indianapolis City Directory* (1857), 241; (1858/59), 192; (1859/60), 76; Madison, "Businessmen and the Business Community," 122–23; B.R. Sulgrove, *History of Indianapolis and Marion County, Indiana* (Philadelphia, 1884), 225–26.

14. Pork packing in Cincinnati in the 1840s:

Season	Variant A	Variant B	Season	Variant A	Variant B
1840/41	160,000	160,000	1845/46	205,000	287,000
1841/42	220,000	220,000	1846/47	250,000	250,000
1842/43	250,000	250,000	1847/48	475,000	498,000
1843/44	240,000	240,000	1848/49	410,000	310,000
1844/45	196,000	213,000	1849/50	393,000	401,755

Sources: Variant A: CCC *AR* (1857), 18; Variant B: Cist, *Cincinnati in 1851,* 279. Early reports for Cincinnati hog packing vary. Variant A agrees with the figures given in Berry, *Western Prices,* except for 1845/46, which is stated as 305,000. Annual figures for the "Packing of the West" are not available until 1842/43.

15. Cist, *Cincinnati in 1851,* 278–88; James Hall, *The West: Its Commerce and Navigation* (Cincinnati, 1848), 263–328; Berry, *Western Prices,* 224–26; Scheiber, *Ohio Canal Era,* 381–43; Edward K. Muller, "The Development of Urban Settlement in a Newly Settled Region: The Middle Ohio Valley, 1800-1860" (Ph.D. diss., Univ. of Wisconsin, 1972), 54–56, 336–430.

16. *Railroad Record* 2(1854): 517–18, 565; CCC *AR* (1855), 10–13; Hessler, "Patterns of Transport . . .," passim; Paxson, "The Railroads of the Old Northwest," passim; Eugene H. Roseboom, *The Civil War Era, 1850–1873,* vol. 4 of *The History of the State of Ohio* (Columbus, Ohio, 1944), 22-24, 111–13.

17. CCC *AR* (1851), 4; (1855), 11; Deering, *Louisville: Her Commercial . . .,* 86, 88; Kohlmeier, *Old Northwest,* 97–208; Hessler, "Patterns of Transport . . .," passim; Roseboom, *Civil War Era,* 111–13; Percy Bidwell and John Falconer, *History of Agriculture in the Northern United States, 1620–1860* (Washington, D.C., 1925), 440.

18. CCC *AR* (1859), 37; (1860), 7, 30; Berry, *Western Prices,* 224–26; Paxson, "Railroads of the Old Northwest," passim; Leavitt, "Transportation and the Livestock Industry," 26–33; John F. Stover, *Iron Road to the West: American Railroads in the 1850s* (New York, 1978), 114–41.

19. CCC *AR* (1850), 14; (1851), 3–5; (1862), 5–6; (1853) 17; (1855), 29; (1858), 33; (1859), 37; (1861), 6–7, 38, 50; (1862), 32, 34–35; *Cincinnati Daily Commercial,* Dec. 2, 1861; Sherry O. Hessler, "The Great Disturbing Cause and the Decline of the Queen City," Historical and Philosophical Society of Ohio, *Bulletin* 20 (1962): 169–82.

20. Slaughtering in Cincinnati was not part of an integrated packing process as it was in most other places of the West. It remained a separate function undertaken by slaughterers. This division of labor may account for the Cincinnati packers' early decision to specialize in fancy cured ham—a specialization that was to continue and to mark the city's packers as quality rather than quantity producers.

21. Manuscript Census, 1850, Products of Industry, Hamilton County, Ohio; *CPC,* Jan. 1, Nov. 6, 1850; Nov. 1, 1854; Mar. 30, 1859; *Daily Cincinnati Chronicle,* Nov. 1, 1850; *Cincinnati City Directory* (1850/51), 56, 73, 90, 265; (1853), 69, 93, 117, 330, 332, 334, 383; (1855), 43, 57, 69, 157, 200, 202, 213; (1856), 51, 67, 83, 190, 195, 265; (1857), 61, 81, 83, 103, 204, 250, 331; (1858), 71, 83, 95, 176, 237, 315; (1859), 75, 99, 101, 114, 176, 275, 338; (1860), 113, 114, 129, 205, 284, 417; RG Dun & Co., Ohio, 78:8, 12, 153,

156, 437, 443; 79:230, 232; 80:231; 82:7, 253; Albert N. Marquis, ed. *The Industries of Cincinnati* (Cincinnati, 1883), 127; Roe, *Cincinnati: The Queen City,* 963; *History of Cincinnati and Hamilton County Ohio* (Cincinnati, 1894), 489, 900; Joblin, *Cincinnati Past and Present,* 114-16, 301-3; *City of Cincinnati and Its Resources,* 114.

22. Manuscript Census, 1860, Products of Industry, Jefferson County, Ky.; *De Bow's Review* 12 (1852):68; *Louisville Democrat,* Jan. 4, 1853; Jan. 16, 1854; Dec. 25, 1858; Dec. 28, 1859; *Indiana State Journal,* Jan. 3, 1855; Jan. 26, 1856; Jan. 12, 1857; *Madison Daily Courier,* Feb. 8, 1858; *Louisville City Directory* (1858/59), 295; (1859/60), 294; RG Dun & Co., Kentucky, 24:5; 25:128, 302; ibid., Indiana, 14:63.

23. Pierce, *History of Chicago,* 2:35-149.

24. Chicago's early reputation as a meat packing center was dependent on beef rather than pork packing. Both quantitative and qualitative reports stressed the importance of the beef trade with the Northeast and with Europe. See *Chicago Democrat,* Jan. 13, 1846, Oct. 16, 1847, in Bessie Louise Pierce Notes (Chicago Historical Society Library); *Gem of the Prairies,* Nov. 16, 1850; Nov. 8, 1851; CDP *AR* (1852-1858), passim.

Beef packing in Chicago in the 1850s:

Year	No. of Cattle Packed	Year	No. of Cattle Packed
1850	27,500	1855	28,972
1851	59,000	1856	14,977
1852	24,343	1857	34,675
1853	25,435	1858	45,504
1854	23,691	1859	51,606

Sources: Various contemporary newspapers and trade reports.

25. Alfred T. Andreas, *History of Chicago from the Earliest Period to the Present Time,* 3 vols. (Chicago, 1884), 1:560-64; James W. Putnam, *The Illinois and Michigan Canal: A Study in Economic History* (Chicago, 1918), passim; Pierce, *History of Chicago,* 2:37-39; Whitaker, *Feedlot Empire,* 35-38.

26. Pierce, *History of Chicago,* 2:40-76; Cole, *Era of the Civil War,* 27-52; Paxson, "Railroads of the Old Northwest," passim; Stover, *Iron Road to the West,* 114-58; Hill, "Development of Chicago," 260-61; B.H. Myer, comp., *History of Transportation in the United States before 1860* (Washington, D.C., 1917), 509-13.

27. Chicago's receipts of hogs by railroad:

Railroad	1858	1859	1860
Galena and Chicago	50,497	56,600	56,464
Illinois Central	87,359	64,072	76,532
Chicago, Burlington and Quincy	205,117	66,906	102,138
Chicago, Alton and St. Louis	129,992	30,209	40,658
These four railroads	472,965	217,787	278,792
All railroads	540,486	271,204	392,864

Sources: CBT *AR* (1858), 27; (1859), 55; (1860), 33.

28. Belcher, *Economic Rivalry,* passim; Pierce, *History of Chicago,* 2:40-76; Cole, *Era of the Civil War,* 27-52; Stover, *Iron Road to the West,* 114-48; Walsh, "Spatial Evolution," 12, 14; Riley, *Development of Chicago and Vicinity,* 86-89, 93-98; William E. Derby, "A History of the Port of Milwaukee" (Ph.D. diss., Univ. of Wisconsin, 1963), 168-93.

29. CDP *AR* (1853), 6-7; (1857), 26; (1858), 14; (1859), 17-24; (1861), 21; CDP, "Railroads, History and Commerce," 61-62; CBT *AR* (1859), 58-59; (1860), 36-38; *Chicago City Directories* for 1851, 1852/53, 1853/54, 1854/55; 1855/56, 1857, 1858, 1859/60, 1860, 1861/62, passim; Andreas, *History of Chicago,* 1:560-63.

30. *Chicago City Directories* (1856), 65; (1857), n.p.; (1858), 172; (1859), 172; (1860), 470; *Daily Democratic Press,* Feb. 3, 1855, in B.L. Pierce Notes; CBT *AR* (1857-1860), passim; RG Dun & Co., Illinois, 28:171; 33:240; ibid., New York, 319:410, 459; 323:873; Andreas, *History of Chicago,* 1:562; 2:331-32; *United States Biographical Dictionary, Illinois Volume* (Chicago, 1883), 759-60; *Biographical Encyclopaedia of Illinois,* 351; *Biographical Sketches of the Leading Men of Chicago* (Chicago, 1868), 157-61; Pierce, *History of Chicago,* 2:40-60, 95-101.

31. CDP *AR* (1853), 7-8; (1855), 14-15; (1856), 15-16; (1857), 27; (1858), 16; (1859), 17-21; (1860), 17; (1861), 19; CDP, "Railroads, History and Commerce," 62-63; CBT *AR* (1859), 59; (1860), 38.

32. CDP *AR* (1855), 15; (1856), 15, 16; (1857), 25, 26; (1858), 15, 16, 17; (1859), 22, 24, 25-28; (1860), 19-21; (1861), 21, 23; CBT *AR* (1858), 24-25, 28-30; (1859), 54, 55, 56, 57; (1860), 33, 35.

Chapter 4

1. Discussion is limited to the Union army, since contracts for naval supplies were not tendered at midwestern cities. The numbers in the Union army varied.

Year	Active Soldiers, Union Army
1861	186,845
1862	637,264
1863	918,354
1864	970,905
1865	1,000,692

Source: *Historical Statistics of the United States, Colonial Times to 1957* (Washington, D.C., 1961), Table Y, 763-75, 737.

The army ration consisted of 12 oz. of pork or bacon or 20 oz. of salt or fresh beef; 18 oz. of soft bread or flour or 12 oz. of hard bread or 18 oz. of cornmeal; and for every 100 rations, 15 lbs. of beans or peas or 10 lbs. of rice or hominy; 10 lbs. of green coffee or 8 lbs of roasted coffee or 1.5 lbs. of tea; 15 lbs. of sugar, 4 qts. of vinegar, 3 lbs. 12 oz. of salt; 1 qt. of molasses; and 30 lbs. of potatoes when practicable. See *Regulations for the Army of the United States,* Article 42 (New York, 1961). There was little change in the basic ration throughout the war. A contract for rations dated Aug. 20, 1864, at Dixon, Illinois, stated the same requirements, further noting that fresh beef should be issued at least twice a week and oftener if required by the provost marshal. See National Archives, R.G. 192, Box 3.

2. These estimates are based on the following official purchase figures: 223,711,399 lbs. of bacon, 1,559,864 barrels of salt pork, 613,870 lbs. of salt beef, and 322,581 head of cattle. A barrel usually contained 200 lbs. of salt meat. A steer could weigh 500-800 lbs. net. The lower figure has been used in view of the weight loss in transit to army camps and the complaints about the quality of animals slaughtered for fresh beef. The army also bought 15,411,766 lbs. of ham. See Palmer H. Boeger, "Hardtack and Burned Beans," *Civil War History* 4 (1958):90.

To place the army purchases in perspective it should be noted that Cincinnati packers dispatched 334,021,950 lbs. of pork and bacon in the decade before the outbreak of war, or about 62 percent of the amount bought by the army (See Table 11).

3. During the first year of the war, before the commissary offices were fully organized, haste, carelessness, and collusion led to numerous opportunities for swindling and for speculation. Following public

outrage and a propaganda campaign, the situation was soon altered. From June of 1862 all provisions were supplied by contractors who had submitted the lowest bids for specific quantities of particular kinds of meat. Further legislation designed to ensure the honest operation of this contract system required the publication in the local newspapers of lists of all tenders that were proposed or accepted. Such a system favored the larger packer who was well organized, but it neither prevented suppliers from bidding for small amounts when advertised, nor discriminated against those who bid for several lots and in different locations. For general discussions of subsistence operations, see Fred A. Shannon, *Organization and Administration of the Union Army,* 2 vols. (Cleveland, 1928; rpt. 1965), 1:53-103; Erna Risch, *Quartermaster Support of the Army: A History of the Corps, 1775-1939* (Washington, D.C., 1962), 382-87, 447-52; James A. Huston, *The Sinews of War: Army Logistics, 1775-1953* (Washington, D.C., 1966), 159-75, 184-85; Boeger, "Hardtack and Burned Beans," 73-92.

4. Receipts and shipments of livestock to and from Chicago are recorded in the annual reports of the Board of Trade. For the years 1858-1864, the years are calendar years. In 1864 the reports start to use the year ending March 31. All figures quoted here are for years ending on March 31. A small number of cattle—20,000 in 1860 and 40,000 in 1865—were driven in to Chicago. Otherwise all livestock were shipped in by rail. CBT *AR* (1860-1870), passim; Pierce, *History of Chicago,* 2:91-94; Belcher, *Economic Rivalry,* 153-57.

5. CBT *AR* (1860), 37, 38; (1861), 36, 37; (1862), 33, 36; (1864), 47, 53; (1865), 37, 44.

6. *Chicago City Directory* (1859), 172; (1860), 470; (1860/61), 439; (1861/62), 432; (1862/63), 449-50; (1863/64), 596; (1864/65), 699; (1866), 1032-33; (1866/67), 106-7; (1867/68), 99; (1868), 1291; *CPC,* Jan. 20, Feb. 3, 1864; Apr. 5, 1865; National Archives, R.G. 192, Entry 68: 61; RG Dun & Co., Illinois, 28:171; 33:240; ibid., New York, 319:459; 322:873; 323:900 G.G.; CBT *AR* (1859-1869), passim; *Biographical Sketches of the Leading Men of Chicago,* 157-61; *Biographical Encyclopaedia of Illinois,* 351; Andreas, *History of Chicago,* 2:331-32.

7. Manuscript Census, 1870, Products of Industry, Cook County, Ill.; *Chicago City Directory* (1859/60), 516; (1860/61), 439; (1861/62), 432; (1862/63), 499; (1863/64), 564; (1864/65), 699; (1865/66), 815-16; (1866), 1032-33; (1866/67), 1067; (1867/68), 99; (1868), 1291; (1868/69), 143-44; *CPC,* Apr. 5, 1865; National Archives, R.G. 192, Entry 68: 12, 61, 75; RG Dun & Co., Illinois, 34:235; ibid., Indiana, 117:40; CBT *AR* (1859-1869), passim; Chicago Tribune,

Chicago in 1864 (Chicago, 1865), 13; *Biographical Sketches of the Leading Men of Chicago,* 127, 129, 144–45; *Biographical Encyclopaedia of Illinois,* 10; Andreas, *History of Chicago,* 2:335.

8. Manuscript Census, 1870, Products of Industry, Cook County, Ill.; *Chicago City Directory* (1862/63), 449–50; (1863/64), 546; (1864/65), 669; (1865/66), 815–16; (1866), 1032–33; (1866/67), 106–7; (1868), 99; (1868/69), 1291; (1870), 1069–71; *CPC,* Feb. 3, 1864; Apr. 5, 1865; National Archives, R.G. 192, Entry 68: 11, 61, 75; CBT *AR* (1860–1870), passim; RG Dun & Co., Illinois, 28:169; ibid., New York, 349:919; *Chicago in 1864,* 14; *Scientific American* 11 (1864): 354–55; *Chicago Tribune,* Jan. 9, 1901 (obituary notice); *Encyclopaedia of Biography of Illinois,* 1:324–326.

9. *Chicago City Directory* (1862/63), 499-500; (1863/64), 564; (1864/65), 699; (1865/66), 815–16, (1866), 1032–33; (1866/67), 106–7; (1867/68), 99; (1868), 1291; (1868/69), 143–44; (1870), 1069–71; RG Dun & Co., Illinois, 34:236; CBT *AR* (1861-1871), passim; *Chicago Tribune,* Apr. 2, 1904 (obituary notice).

10. Manuscript Census, 1870, Products of Industry, Cook County, Ill.; *Chicago City Directory* (1858), 170; (1859), 170; (1860), 470; (1860/61), 439; (1862/63), 499-500; (1863/64), 546; (1865/66), 815–16; (1866), 1032–33; (1868), 1291; (1868/69), 143–44; RG Dun & Co., Ill., 27:16, 249, 304; CBT *AR* (1848-1870), passim; *Biographical Sketches of Leading Men of Chicago,* 149–51; David W. Wood, ed., *Chicago and Its Distinguished Citizens* (Chicago, 1881), 36–39; Josiah B. Currey, *Chicago: Its History and Its Builders,* 5 vols. (Chicago, 1912), 1:84–85.

11. Manuscript Census, 1870, Products of Industry, Cook County, Ill.; *Chicago City Directory* (1858), 170; (1859), 170; (1860), 470; (1860/61), 439; (1862/63), 499; (1863/64), 546; (1865/66), 815–16; (1866), 1032–33; (1866/67), 106–7; (1867/68), 99; (1868), 291; (1868/69), 143–44; (1870), 1069–71; (1871), 1056; *Gem of the Prairies,* Nov. 16, 1850; RG Dun & Co., Illinois, 27:83; CBT *AR* (1858–1870), passim; Andreas, *History of Chicago,* 2: 338–39.

12. *Cincinnati Daily Commercial,* Nov. 25, Dec. 2, 13, 1861; Feb. 5, Nov. 12, 30, Dec. 10, 1862; Jan. 7, 1863; CCC *AR* (1861), 7, 35, 37, 38; (1862), 7, 32, 35, 36; (1863), 33, 36, 37; (1864), 41; (1866), 61; (1867), 54; (1868), 68, 69; (1869), 175, 176, 187; (1870), 98-99; (1871), 81; (1873), 123; (1874), 135; Semi Annual Report of Officers of Cincinnati Board of Trade for Year Ending Mar. 31, 1869, Report of Committee on Manufactures, 30–32.

13. Manuscript Census, 1870, Products of Industry, Hamilton County, Ohio; *Cincinnati City Directory,* (1860), 113, 114; (1861),

120, 121; (1862), 114, 115; (1863), 142; (1864), 101, 102; (1865), 105, 110; (1866), 131; (1867), 150, 151; (1868), 153, 155; (1869), 171, 173; (1870), 172, 173, 175; *CPC*, Nov. 5, 1862; Feb. 25, Nov. 13, 17, 18, 25, 1863; June 1, Nov. 24, 1864; July 19, 1865; National Archives, R.G. 192, Entry 68:28, 44, 108; RG Dun & Co., Ohio, 78: 426, 437, 443; 79:230; Elstner, *Centennial Review of Cincinnati*, 116; *Leading Manufacturers and Merchants of Cincinnati*, 90, 224; Roe, *Cincinnati: The Queen City of the West*, 363; *City of Cincinnati and Its Resources*, 114.

14. Manuscript Census, 1870, Products of Industry, Hamilton County, Ohio; *Cincinnati City Directory* (1860), 129, 284; (1861), 137, 332; (1862), 130, 312; (1863), 157, 330; (1864), 129, 351; (1865), 138, 367; (1866), 153, 403; (1867), 179, 458; (1868), 185, 498; (1869), 209, 548; (1870), 210, 593; *CPC*, Sept. 30, 1863; Feb. 3, 8, 1864; National Archives, R.G. 192, Entry 68:26, 28, 57, 107, 109; *Cincinnati Daily Commercial*, Nov. 7, 1863; RG Dun & Co., Ohio, 79: 232; 82:193; 83:129; Joblin, *Cincinnati Past and Present*, 115, 116, 302-3.

15. Manuscript Census, 1870, Products of Industry, Hamilton County, Ohio; *Cincinnati City Directory* (1860), 417; (1861), 398; (1862), 375; (1863), 395; (1864), 409; (1865), 430; (1866), 488; (1867), 543; (1868), 613; (1869), 676; (1870), 757; *CPC*, Sept. 30, Nov. 13, 17, 18, 1863; Feb. 3, 8, June 1, 1864; National Archives, R.G. 192, Entry 68:44, 107, 108; RG Dun & Co., Ohio, 78: 176; *City of Cincinnati and Its Resources*, 114; *History of Cincinnati*, 489.

16. *Cincinnati Daily Commercial*, Jan. 20, Dec. 16, 1864; *CPC*, Mar. 14, 1864; CCC *AR* (1861), 38; (1862), 32; (1863), 34; (1864), 39; (1865), 42; (1866), 61, 62; (1867), 53, 54; (1868), 68; (1869), 186, 187; RG Dun & Co., Kentucky, 25: 128; Johnson, *Memorial History of Louisville*, 2:261-64, 525-26; Louisville Chamber of Commerce, "Louisville: The Civil War: A Business History," *Louisville Magazine* 12 (1961): 5-8; Charles K. Messmer, "City in Conflict: A History of Louisville, 1860-1865" (M.A. thesis, Univ. of Kentucky, 1953), passim; E. Merton Coulter, *The Civil War and Readjustment in Kentucky* (Chapel Hill, N.C., 1926), 215-38; Henry C. Symonds, *Report of a Commissary of Subsistence, 1861-65* (Sing Sing, N.Y., 1888), 170-83; Palmer H. Boeger, "The Great Kentucky Hog Swindle of 1864," *Journal of Southern History* 28 (1962): 59-70.

17. St. Louis Merchants' Exchange, *Annual Report* (1865), 54; (1866), 63-64; (1867), 52-53; (1868), 49 (Missouri Historical Society; hereafter cited as SLME *AR*); *Cincinnati Daily Commercial*, Feb. 19, 1862; Nov. 4, 1864; *CPC*, Jan. 24, July 1, 1863; Jan. 20, Feb. 3, 10,

Mar. 20, 1864; Apr. 5, June 7, 1865; National Archives, R.G. 192, Entry 68: 20, 21, 32, 33, 47, 48, 64, 67, 73, 108; RG Dun & Co., Missouri, 37:496, 508; Belcher, *Economic Rivalry*, 139-76; Thomas J. Scharf, *History of St. Louis City and County* . . ., 2 vols. (Philadelphia, 1883), 1:614, 617-19; Walter B. Stevens, *St. Louis, the Fourth City, 1764-1909*, 3 vols. (St. Louis, 1909), 1: 637-39; *Edwards' Commercial Directory of the Mississippi Valley* (1866), 499-501; Harry L. Purdy, *An Historical Analysis of the Economic Growth of St. Louis, 1840-1945* (n.p., 1946), 32, 43-53.

18. *Milwaukee Sentinel*, Jan. 24, 1860; Dec. 29, 1862; Jan. 21, 1864; Oct. 19, 1865; Mar. 22, 1866; Oct. 23, 1867; MCC *AR* (1859), 29, 30; (1861), 19-21; (1862), 32-34; (1863), 32-35; (1864), 32-34; (1865), 31-35; *Weekly Gate City*, Jan. 6, Feb. 12, 1862; Feb. 4, 1863; *Edwards' Commercial Directory of the Mississippi Valley* (1866), 432; "John Plankington: Field Notes for a Biographical Sketch," Wis. Mss MM (State Historical Society of Wisconsin, Madison); R.G. Dun & Co., Wisconsin, 36: 311; Frederick Merk, *Economic History of Wisconsin during the Civil War Decade* (Madison, Wis., 1916), 150-51, 271-307; Derby, "History of the Port of Milwaukee," 168-279; Harris, "Frontier Community," 364-69; Frank A. Flower, ed., *History of Milwaukee from Pre Historic Times* . . ., (Chicago, 1881), 1146-49.

19. *CPC*, Mar. 27, 1861; Apr. 16, 1862; Apr. 15, 1863; Apr. 13, 1864; Mar. 22, 1865; Mar. 21, 1866; Mar. 27, 1867.

20. Manuscript Census, 1860, Products of Industry, Peoria County, Ill.; *Quincy Whig*, Feb. 28, 1863; Feb. 27, 1864; Jan. 21, 1865; Mar. 10, 1866; Nov. 28, 1868; Jan. 29, 1869; Feb. 12, 1870; *Des Moines Valley Whig*, Jan. 16, 1860; Jan. 21, 1861; Feb. 12, Dec. 17, 1862; *Weekly Gate City*, Feb. 13, 1866; Jan 13, 1869; Feb. 8, 1871; *Peoria Transcript*, Feb. 1, Dec. 28, 1866; RG Dun & Co., Illinois, 4:32, 127, 195, 275; 28:304; 173:132, 227; ibid., Iowa, 31:129, 227; *Quincy City Directory* (1859/60), 153; (1861), 157; (1863), 169; (1864/65), 157; (1866), 213; (1871), 211; *Keokuk City Directory* (1859/60), 116; (1866/67), 131; (1871/72), 34; *Peoria City Directory* (1860), 164; (1861), 20; (1865), 251; (1867/68), 30; (1868/69), 38; Redmond, *History of Quincy*, 119-20; David F. Wilcox, *Representative Men and Homes, Quincy, Illinois* (Quincy, 1899), 873-74; *Portrait and Biographical Album of Peoria*, 349-50; *History of Lee County*, 708; *Portrait and Biographical Album of Lee County*, 404-6.

21. Manuscript Census, 1860, Products of Industry, Tippecanoe and Vigo County, Ind.; ibid., 1870, Products of Industry, Tippecanoe County, Ind.; *Terre Haute City Directory* (1864), 23; RG Dun & Co., Indiana, 109:81; 119:2; *Past and Present of Tippecanoe County, Indi-*

ana (Indianapolis, 1909), 688-90; *Biographical History of Tippecanoe, White . . . Counties, Indiana,* 2 vols. (Chicago, 1899), 2:946-48; *Biographical History of Eminent . . . Indiana,* 2:11-12; Oakey, *Greater Terre Haute,* 202-3.

22. Manuscript Census, 1870, Products of Industry, Buchanan County, Mo.; *St. Joseph City Directory* (1867/68), 181; (1868/69), 192; *St. Joseph Morning Herald,* Oct. 30, 1862; Dec. 1, 1863; Dec. 9, 1865; *St. Joseph Weekly Gazette,* Jan. 6, 1870; RG Dun & Co., Missouri, 4:27; *The History of Buchanan County, Missouri* (St. Joseph, 1881), 768, 858-59.

Chapter 5

1. Pork Packers' Association of Chicago, *Annual Report of the Packing of the West. . .* (Chicago, 1876), 7-8.

2. The number of separate stockyards existing in 1865 varies between four and six, according to the source of information. The six herein referred to are the Sherman Yards, the Bulls' Head Yards, the Cottage Grove Yards, the Pittsburgh and Fort Wayne Yards, the Michigan Southern Yards, and the Chicago, Burlington & Quincy and Northwestern Yards. See Jack Wing, *The Great Union Stock Yards of Chicago . . .* (Chicago, 1865), 8-11; and Alfred T. Andreas, *History of Cook County, Illinois* (Chicago, 1884), 655.

3. Nine different railroad companies took $925,000 of the stock; packers provided $50,000 and the remainder was subscribed by the public. Among the directors were the packers Roselle M. Hough, Charles N. Culbertson, Virginius A. Turpin, and John L. Hancock; *PF* 19 (1867): 9; Wing, *Great Union Stock Yards,* passim; Illinois State Agricultural Society, *Transactions* 6 (1865/66): 314-24; *Chicago Tribune,* Jan. 1, 1866; *A Strangers' and Tourists' Guide to the City of Chicago* (Chicago, 1866), 59-66; Pierce, *History of Chicago,* 2:93-94.

4. *Great Union Stock Yards,* 29.

5. CBT *AR* (1860-1875), passim; Wing, *Great Union Stock Yards,* passim; Illinois State Agricultural Society *Transactions* 6 (1865/66): 321; J. M. Wing & Co., *Seven Days in Chicago* (Chicago, 1877), 46-49; Andreas, *History of Cook County,* 665-68; *A Strangers' and Tourists' Guide,* 60-63; T.E. Zell & Co., *A Guide to the City of Chicago* (Chicago, 1868), 69-72; Directors of the Union Stock Yard and Transit Co., *Annual Reports* (1869-1871), passim; Joseph G. Knapp, "A Review of Chicago Stock Yards History," *University Journal of Business* 2 (1924): 331-47.

6. Wing & Co., *Seven Days in Chicago*, 49–50; Andreas, *History of Cook County*, 667–69; Illinois State Agricultural Society *Transactions* 6 (1865/66): 320–21; Wing, *Great Union Stock Yards*, 23–29; *Strangers' and Toursists' Guide*, 61–65; *Guide to the City of Chicago*, 70–72.

7. SLME *AR* (1873), 64; (1874), 73; Scharf, *History of St. Louis*, 1:1311–13; Purdy, *Economic Growth of St. Louis*, 74; John W. Leonard, *Industries of St. Louis* . . . (St. Louis, 1887), 148, 187; Joseph A. Dacus and James W. Buel, *A Tour of St. Louis* . . . (St. Louis, 1878), 331–33; Andrew Morrison and John H.C. Irving, *The Industries of St. Louis* . . . (St. Louis, 1885), 95–96.

8. *Cincinnati Gazette*, Sept. 4, 1874; *CPC*, Sept. 5, 1873; Oct. 8, 1875; CCC *AR* (1874), 154; (1875), 164; (1876), 164; (1878), 172; Albert N. Marquis, ed., *The Industries of Cincinnati* . . . (Cincinnati, 1883), 135–36; Roe, *Cincinnati: The Queen City of the West*, 238.

9. Stockyards were not new features of the postwar period. In the riverine period packers and slaughterers had provided pens, but the advent of railroads entailed a relocation of enclosures with ready access to rails. These new compounds were satisfactory by the standards of the 1850s, but the large upsurge in livestock traffic in the 1860s soon meant that they were both too small physically and lacked the supporting services required by brokers and dealers who were transacting business in an impersonal market.

10. Burlington Board of Trade, *Annual Report* (1877), 31; Louisville *Courier Herald* Scrapbooks, Book 3, n.p. (Kentucky Room, Louisville Public Library); *History of Peoria County*, 542–43; John Gregory, *Industrial Resources of Wisconsin* (Milwaukee, 1870), 1:220–21; Max R. Hyman, ed., *Hyman's Handbook of Indianapolis* (Indianapolis, 1897), 266; Clemen, *American Livestock*, 82–91, 203–7.

11. *Kansas City Daily Journal of Commerce*, July 27, 1870; Joseph G. McCoy, *Historic Sketches of the Cattle Trade of the West and Southwest* (Kansas City, Mo., 1874; rpt., Glendale, Cal., 1940), 325–31; Cuthbert Powell, *Twenty Years of Kansas City's Livestock and Traders* (Kansas City, 1893), 15–23; William H. Miller, *The History of Kansas City* (Kansas City, 1881), 164–69; A. Theodore Brown, *Frontier Community: Kansas City to 1870* (Columbia, Mo., 1963), 31–81, 115–56; Charles N. Glaab, *Kansas City and the Railroads* (Madison, Wis., 1962), 168–69; Eva L. Atkinson, "Kansas City Livestock Trade and Packing Industry, 1870–1914: A Study in Regional Growth" (Ph.D. diss., Univ. of Kansas, 1971), passim.

12. Ober, Day & Co., *The Commerce of American Cities: Kansas*

City, the Metropolis of the New West (Kansas City, Mo., 1879), 17–20; Powell, *Twenty Years of Knasas City* . . ., 67–75; Atkinson, "Kansas City Livestock Trade," 278–81; Kansas City Stock Yards Co., *Seventy-Five Years of Kansas City Livestock Market History, 1871-1946* (Kansas City, 1946), 4–10.

13. Plankington & Armour operated in a rented plant in Kansas City in 1870, but they built their own establishment in 1871. *Kansas City Daily Journal of Commerce,* Oct. 26, 1870; July 22, 1871; Jan. 1, 1876; *Kansas City Weekly Journal of Commerce,* Nov. 19, 1870; Nov. 10, Dec. 15, 1871; Jan. 23, 1874; Jan. 1, 1876; Kansas City Board of Trade, *Annual Report,* 1: 12–15; 3: 12–14; 12 (1891), 56–57; Powell, *Twenty Years of Kansas City,* 86–95; McCoy, *Historic Sketches of the Cattle Trade,* 325–62; Miller, *History of Kansas City,* 169–71; Theodore S. Case, ed., *History of Kansas City, Missouri* (Syracuse, N.Y., 1888), 216–21; Goodspeed Publishing Co., *Wyandotte County and Kansas City, Historical and Biographical* (Chicago, 1890), 447–54.

14. Neither Ottumwa nor Omaha, with hog outputs of 23,044 and 15,603 respectively, was among the leading packing points of the West in the mid-1870s (1873/74–1875/76). But both places grew rapidly in the later 1870s and have been used here as illustrations, though neither John Morrell & Co. nor James E. Boyd is included in the sample. *Omaha Republican,* Jan. 2, Feb. 14, 1875; Jan. 8, Oct. 21, 1876; Jan. 3, 1877; Jan. 18, Oct. 18, 1878; Jan. 23, Mar. 12, 1880; *Ottumwa Democrat and Times,* Dec. 5, 1878; RG Dun & Co., Iowa, 51: 341; *Nebraska State Gazeteer for 1879/80,* 100: *for 1882/32,* 236–37; *Cedar Rapids City Directory* (1881), 40; *The History of Linn County, Iowa* (Chicago, 1878), 525–26, 667–78; *Portrait and Biographical Album of Linn County* (Chicago, 1887), 165–66, 939; S.B. Evans, ed., *History of Wapello County* (Chicago, 1901), 151, 197–98; Alfred T. Andreas, *History of the State of Nebraska,* 2 vols. (Chicago, 1882), 1: 757–58, 773, 796; *Industries of Omaha* (Omaha, 1887), 46–47, 99; McCarty and Thompson, *Meat Packing in Iowa,* 30–35; Lawrence O. Cheever, *The House of Morrell* (Cedar Rapids, Iowa, 1948), 73–79.

15. In 1870, 5,448,000 people lived in cities in the Northeast and 2,700,000 people lived in cities in the Midwest, which is here synonymous with the North Central region. Assuming that the average per capita consumption of pork was 122 lbs., the urban market of these two regions required 994,056,000 lbs. of pork. In the 1869/70 packing season, midwestern entrepreneurs put up 2,595,240 hogs. If these hogs averaged 200 lbs. gross and if 50 lbs. is allowed for removing the blood and entrails and for some rendering down to lard, the total pork

product would weigh 388,286,000 lbs. Though midwestern men only packed about 70 percent of the national hog crop, there was clearly a shortfall in supplying the main urban markets. Furthermore there was also a small urban market of 1,007,000 in the South, part of which was supplied by midwestern packers. The smaller Far Western urban market was mainly supplied locally. See chapter 2, note 39, for an explanation of the calculations. Lampard, "The Evolving System of Cities," 103; *Historical Statistics of the United States,* Series A, 123-80, 12-13.

16. U.S., Congress, Senate, Document 259, "Exports . . . to Foreign Countries, 1789-1893," pt. 2, "Exports and Imports," *Senate Documents,* 53 Cong., 2 sess. (1893/94), 174, 175.

17. Most local newspapers reported pork packing data when they became available. *The Cincinnati Prices Current,* as the main commercial sheet, made a deliberate point of obtaining figures from correspondents in all packing points; see, for example, *CPC,* Jan. 2, 1856; Dec. 8, 1858. Other papers were more random in their coverage; see, for example, *Scioto Gazette,* Dec. 12, 1849; *Keokuk Whig and Register,* Nov. 14, 1850; *Daily Louisville Democrat,* Jan. 4, 1854.

18. For a discussion of the spread of the telegraph, see Robert L. Thompson, *Wiring a Continent: The History of the Telegraph Industry in the United States, 1832-1866* (Princeton, N.J., 1947). There are scattered references in the newspapers to the use of news brought by telegraph, but the precise dating of regular wire services varies from point to point. For information on telegraph offices in stockyards, see *Strangers' and Tourists' Guide,* 65; and *Cincinnati Gazette,* Sept. 4, 1873.

19. *Revised Ordinances of St. Louis* (1836), 78-82; (1850), 236-38; (1866), 436-38; *Quincy Whig,* Dec. 3, 1845; *HMM* 34 (1856), 744-45; Pork Packers Association of Chicago, "Directions for Cutting, Packing and Curing Pork and Beef . . ." (Chicago, 1865); *Chicago Tribune,* Jan. 1, 1866; *PF* 43 (1872): 268; *CPC,* Aug. 16, Sept. 20, 1872; Aug. 29, Sept. 19, 1873; July 17, 31, Sept. 4, 18, 1874; Oct. 22, 1875; *Kansas City Daily Journal of Commerce,* Jan. 29, 1873; CBT *AR* (1866), 16-21; (1870), 20-23; (1871), 22-25; Indianapolis Board of Trade, *Annual Report* (1876), 89-92 (hereafter cited as IBT *AR*); Second National Convention of Pork Packers and Provision Dealers, *Proceedings* (Chicago, 1873); Charles H. Taylor, ed., *History of the Board of Trade of the City of Chicago,* 3 vols. (Chicago, 1917), 1:413.

20. *Kansas City Daily Journal of Commerce,* July 22, 1871.

21. *Omaha Daily Bee,* Dec. 12, 1872; *Omaha Republican,* Feb. 14, 1874; Jan. 2, 1875; *Milwaukee Sentinel,* Mar. 21, 1874; *Ottumwa*

Democrat and Times, Dec. 5, 1878; *Nebraska State Gazeteer and Business Directory* (1879/80), 100; *History of Linn County, Iowa,* 525-26.

22. *Boston Courier,* Jan. 19, 1835; *CPC,* Nov. 15, 1848; Cist, *Cincinnati in 1851,* 278-88; Richard G. Arms, "From Disassembly to Assembly: Cincinnati: The Birthplace of Mass Production," *Bulletin,* Historical and Philosophical Society of Ohio, 17 (1959): 197-203; Carl M. Becker, "Evolution of the Disassembly Line: The Horizontal Wheel and the Overhead Railway Loop," *Bulletin* of the Cincinnati Historical Society, 26 (1968): 277-82.

23. *PF* 13 (1864): 116-17; *Scientific American* 11 (1864): 354-55; Chicago Tribune, *Chicago in 1864* (Chicago, 1864); *HMM,* 54 (1866): 376-79; *Chicago Tribune,* Jan. 1, 1866; Dec. 11, 1866, in B.L. Pierce Notes; CBT *AR* (1863-1873), passim; *Strangers' and Tourists' Guide,* 33-34; Wing & Co., *Seven Days in Chicago,* 51-57.

24. IBT *AR* (1872), 23-24; (1873), 12; (1874), 23; (1876), 28-29; *Indianapolis City Directory* (1868), 58; William R. Holloway, *Indianapolis: A Historical and Statistical Sketch of the Railroad City* (Indianapolis, 1870), 129, 312; Jacob P. Dunn, *History of Greater Indianapolis,* 2 vols. (Chicago, 1910), 1: 348-49; RG Dun & Co., New York City, 370:698.

25. *Milwaukee Sentinel,* Oct. 19, 20, 1865; Oct. 23, 1867; Dec. 31, 1870; Jan. 26, June 14, Nov. 25, 1871; Feb. 3, July 28, 1873; Nov. 21, 1874; July 10, 1876; Aug. 20, 21, 1878; May 22, 1879; MCC *AR* (1866-1878), passim; James S. Buck, *Pioneer History of Milwaukee,* 4 vols. (Milwaukee, 1876-1888), 2: 210-13; Flower, *History of Milwaukee,* 1146-48, 1218.

26. These figures are conservative estimates, given the range of hog prices in the 1870s. They are derived from the *Annual Reports* of the Chicago Board of Trade and from scattered descriptions in newspapers. They assume that live hogs cost $4.25 per 100 lbs. and dressed hogs $5.25 per 100 lbs., and that an establishment purchased 80 percent of its animals, weighing 200 lbs., live. Adding 15 percent to the price of the animals to cover other materials like salt, cooperage, and coal, and allowing a work force of thirty men working for three months for a daily wage of $1.50 each, the running costs would be $199,200. No allowance has been made for rendering byproducts other than lard, lard oil, and tallow, and transport charges have not been included.

27. *St. Joseph Daily Morning Herald,* Dec. 11, 18, 1867; Jan. 1, 1875; *Kansas City Daily Journal of Commerce,* June 23, Dec. 1, 1868; Oct. 26, 1870; July 22, 1871; Jan. 1, 1876; *Omaha Daily Bee,* Dec. 12,

1872; *Omaha Republican,* Feb. 14, 1874; Jan. 2, 1875; Jan. 8, Oct. 21, 1876; *Ottumwa Democrat and Times,* Dec. 5, 1878; *Nebraska State Gazeteer and Business Directory* (1879/80), 100; *Cedar Rapids City Directory* (1881), 40; *History of Linn County,* 525–26; McCoy, *Historic Sketches,* 349–59; Powell, *Twenty Years,* 89–91; *United States Biographical Dictionary, Missouri Volume* (Chicago, 1878), 431–34; Cheever, *House of Morrell,* 73–79.

28. There were also numerous experiments with mechanical refrigeration in the 1870s, but none of the diverse resulting systems yet supplanted natural ice refrigeration. Schooley, *Process of Obtaining a Dry Cold Current*; *Peoria Transcript,* Nov. 10, 1870; Dec. 14, 1871; *CPC,* June 20, 1873; Feb. 18, 1874; CCC *AR* (1872–1878), passim; CDP *AR* (1858), 23; CBT *AR* (1872–1878), passim; "The Ice Industry—Portrait," in Chauncey M. Depew, ed. *One Hundred Years of American Commerce,* 2 vols. (New York, 1895), 2:466–69; Richard O. Cummings, *The American Ice Harvests: A Historical Study of Technology, 1800–1918* (Berkeley, 1949), passim; Oscar E. Anderson, Jr., *Refrigeration in America* (Princeton, N.J., 1953), passim; Clemen, *American Livestock,* 211–24.

29. Summer packing in four leading midwestern centers, 1872–1877 (as a percentage of their total packing):

Year	Indianapolis	St. Louis	Cincinnati	Chicago	Midwest
1872	32.6	15.4	13.1	6.7	8.3
1873	46.8	22.2	13.2	16.8	16.0
1874	42.3	24.6	19.6	20.9	17.4
1875	21.6	23.8	17.4	31.4	20.1
1876	49.1	24.0	18.8	44.8	31.3
1877	43.1	22.5	17.5	37.6	28.1

Source: CCC *AR* (1872–1878).

30. Summer packing in Chicago's leading pork establishments, 1872–1877 (as a percentage of the establishment's annual output):

Establishment	1872	1873	1874	1875	1876	1877
Anglo American Packing & Provision Co.	...	...	1.7	48.5	57.5	44.5
Armour & Co.	...	7.0	16.8	44.3	52.8	40.4
Chicago Packing & Provision Co.	...	2.3	...	...	...	33.8

(continued)

Establishment	1872	1873	1874	1875	1876	1877
Tobey & Booth	10.4	14.9	17.7	60.0	64.8	59.8
Davies, Atkinson & Co.	1.3	12.9	13.3	60.1	49.8	42.6
George W. Higgins & Co.	...	...	...	...	14.7	...
H. Botford & Co.	...	...	...	7.2	48.1	...
S.A. Ricker	9.8	...	...	48.2	65.3	41.5

Source: CBT *AR* (1872-1878).

31. IBT *AR* (1872), 23-24; (1873), 12; (1874), 23-24; (1876), 28-29; *Cedar Rapids City Directory*, (1876/77), 126, 156; (1881), 40; RG Dun & Co., Indiana, 68: 352, 423; 71: 238; ibid., Iowa, 33: 169, 395; ibid., New York, 348: 900J, 900 a/47, 900 a/56, 900 a/120; 370: 700S, 700A/46; Dunn, *Greater Indianapolis*, 1: 348-49; *Hyman's Handbook of Indianapolis*, 279-80; *History of Linn County*, 525-26, 677-78; *Portrait and Biographical Album of Linn County*, 165-66, 939; McCarty and Thompson, *Meat Packing in Iowa*, 33-35.

32. Neither the *Annual Reports* of the Cincinnati Chamber of Commerce nor the *Cincinnati Prices Current* record the annual business of individual meat packing establishments in Cincinnati. Estimates of the size of particular enterprises are based on the Manuscript Census, 1870, Products of Industry, Hamilton County, Ohio; ibid., 1880, State of Ohio, Special Schedules Numbers 9 and 10: "Slaughtering and Meat Packing, Salt Works"; and CCC *AR* (1869-1880). For qualitative evidence see *CPC*, Nov. 1, 1872; Dec. 5, 1873; Oct. 8, Nov. 5, 1875; RG Dun & Co., Ohio, 78: 1/1, 426, 443, 470; 79: 230; 80:179, 231; 87: 125; 88:256, 303; *Leading Manufacturers and Merchants of Cincinnati*, 90, 224; *City of Cincinnati and Its Resources*, 114.

33. *Peoria City Directory* (1870/71), 25; (1871/72), 41; (1872/73), 34; (1873/74), 34; (1875), 25; (1876), 405; (1877/78), 353; *Keokuk City Directory* (1871/72), 5, 34, 225; (1873/74), 43-44, 253; (1877/78), 185; (1879/80), 191, *Quincy City Directory* (1871), 212; (1873/74), 208; (1875/76), 247; *Peoria Transcript*, Nov. 10, 1870; Nov. 23, Dec. 14, 1871, Nov. 23, 1876; *Weekly Gate City*, Feb. 8, 1871; *Quincy Whig*, Feb. 12, 1870; Peoria Board of Trade, *Annual Report* (1871), 36; (1872), 42; (1873), 29; (1874), 31; (1875), 28; RG Dun & Co., Illinois, 4: 275, 306[16]; 173: 2611; 174: 412, 498, 597, 833; ibid., Iowa, 31: 227; 32: 401, 516; *History of Lee County*, 708; Redmond, *History of Quincy*, 119-20.

Chapter 6

1. By far the best account of big business in the meat packing industry is Mary Yeager, *Competition and Regulation: The Development of Oligopoly in the Meat Packing Industry* (Greenwich, Conn., 1981).

2. The "Big Five" or the packing corporations, Armour & Company, Swift & Company, Morris & Company, Wilson & Company, and the Cudahy Packing Company, together with their subsidiaries and affiliated companies, had an olipolistic grip over the American meat industry in the early twentieth century. They handled from 61 to 86 percent of the principal lines in the meat business and owned a high percentage of stockyards, car lines, cold-storage plants, branch houses, and other essential facilities for the distribution of perishable foods. See United States Federal Trade Commission, *Report on the Meat Packing Industry,* pts. 1-6 (Washington, D.C., 1919).

Appendix

1. The techniques of sampling are explained in most statistical textbooks. See, for example, Hubert M. Blalock Jr., *Social Statistics* (New York, 1960), 392-412; or Herman J. Loether and Donald G. McTavish, *Inferential Statistics for Sociologists* (Boston, 1974), 42-65. For sampling as applied to historical work, see R.S. Schofield, "Sampling in Historical Research," in E.A. Wrigley, ed., *Nineteenth Century Society: Essays in the Use of Quantitative Methods for the Study of Social Data* (Cambridge, England, 1972), 146-90.

2. The annual statements of the "Packing of the West" in *CPC* only list packing points. The annual reports of the chambers of commerce and boards of trade of the major midwestern cities usually cite pork packers, but no similar records are available for small centers. City directories also enumerate pork packers but their classification schemes and dates of compilation vary. The census schedules only supply a partial listing of meat packing establishments (see chapter 1, note 8).

3. Recent collective biographical studies demand that precise categories of information be collected for each member of the group, for example, age, wealth, length of time in business, religion, nationality, father's occupation, education, and family status. The R.G. Dun & Company Collection is the best source of qualitative information, but it does not provide this data systematically. In some cases it states the precise age of the entrepreneur; in other cases it gives age within a five-

year time-span or in more general terms, such as young, middle-aged, or elderly; or it may give financial status exactly for one year but in broader bands, such as small, moderate, or large, for other years. Biographical sketches in county histories may supply some information, but only for the better known entrepreneurs. The census only provides partial evidence for a proportion of pork packers.

4. The "new" quantitative history is based on "full data banks," particularly those provided by the manuscript schedules of the federal censuses and by voting statistics. See, for example, "The Philadelphia Social History Project," a special issue of *Historical Methods Newsletter* 9 (1976): 41-184; Kathleen N. Conzen, *Immigrant Milwaukee, 1836-1860: Accommodation and Community in a Frontier City* (Cambridge, Mass., 1976); Howard P. Chudacoff, *Mobile Americans: Residential and Social Mobility in Omaha, 1880-1920* (New York, 1972); Allan G. Bogue et al., "Members of the House of Representatives and the Processes of Modernization, 1789-1960," *Journal of American History* 63 (1976): 275-302; and Richard Jensen, *The Winning of the Midwest: Social and Political Conflict, 1888-1896* (Chicago, 1971).

5. For other types of collective biography, see William Miller, "American Historians and the Business Elite," *Journal of Economic History* 9 (1949): 184-208; C. Wright Mills, "The American Business Elite: A Collective Portrait," in Irving L. Horowitz, ed., *Power, Politics and People: The Collected Essays of C. Wright Mills* (New York, 1962), 110-39; Reinhard Bendix and Frank W. Howton, "Social Mobility and the American Business Elite," in Reinhard Bendix and Seymour M. Lipset, eds., *Social Mobility in Industrial Society* (Berkeley, 1959), 114-43; Frances W. Gregory and Irene D. Neu, "The American Industrial Elite in the 1870's: Their Social Origins," in William Miller, ed., *Men in Business: Essays on the Historical Role of the Entrepreneur* (Cambridge, Mass., 1952); Herbert G. Gutman, "The Reality of the Rags-to-Riches Myth: The Case of the Paterson, New Jersey, Locomotive, Iron and Machinery Manufacturers, 1830-1880," in Stephan Thernstrom and Richard Sennett, eds., *Nineteenth Century Cities: Essays in the New Urban History* (New Haven, 1969), 98-124; Richard H. Peterson, *The Bonanza Kings: The Social Origins and Business Behavior of Western Mining Entrepreneurs, 1870-1900* (Lincoln, Neb., 1977); and John N. Ingham, *The Iron Barons: A Social Analysis of an American Urban Elite, 1874-1965* (Westport, Conn., 1978).

6. This sample is not static and attempts to reflect the changing characteristics of the pork industry. Too many researchers group indi-

viduals either at the terminal point of the study and work backwards or at the beginning of the study and work forwards.

7. It is not possible to isolate a regular cycle in the output of the pork packing industry in the mid-nineteenth century, but moving averages of the annual data suggest that a two- to three-year period is the best means of moderating the seasonal fluctuations. The choice of a single year can present an aberration from the norm, while the more standard period of a decade masks frequent instabilities. The use of irregular intervals between the three-year periods provides another method of dealing with the vacillations in the industry.

8. As there are twenty individuals or firms in each time-period, 5 percent of the regional pack provides a rough guideline for selecting the number of cases from each place having an output higher than 5 percent. For example, in the mid 1840s when Cincinnati is responsible for 24.9 percent of the packing of the West, five entrepreneurs represent "Hogopolis." Places having an output smaller than 5 percent of the regional total were chosen from the rank-order list of the leading packing points. If qualitative information was not available for entrepreneurs in one of the selected points, either a similar packing point or the next packing point on the list was selected. In the mid-1840s Maysville substitutes for Westport.

9. An arbitrary decision was taken on the number of individuals in the collective biography. Statistical soundness had to be balanced against the time-consuming task of searching through numerous and diverse local records for minimal or nil returns. While eighty may not be significant statistically, the sample has been stratified to provide greater validity. Few historicans can afford either the time or the expense of tracing individuals chosen at random through their life cycle. For an exceptional study, see Peter R. Knights, *The Plain People of Boston, 1830-1860: A Study in City Growth* (New York, 1971). Even detailed work on a specific group of "ordinary persons" is rare. See, for example, Charlotte Erickson, *Invisible Immigrants: The Adaptation of English and Scottish Immigrants in Nineteenth Century America* (Coral Gables, Fla., 1972).

10. The quantitative data banks used for the analysis of anonymous Americans—census records and city directories—are not particularly helpful in constructing portraits of meat packers. They supply only supplementary information. Other sources like the R.G. Dun & Co. Collection, newspapers, and county histories provide more evidence, but only for upper- and middle-level entrepreneurs. This group of pork packers may thus fail adequately to represent short-lived or young firms.

Selected Bibliography

MANUSCRIPT SOURCES

There is a lamentable lack of business papers for early midwestern meat packers. Existing records are negligible and usually disappointing in quality.

The most valuable manuscript source available for the whole region for the mid-nineteenth century is the R.G. Dun and Company Collection of Credit Rating Reports, located at the Baker Library of Harvard Business School. These reports, made semiannually, give the wealth of the individual or the value of the firm, their estimated worth in capital invested, real estate and personal property, length of operation, prospects, and credit worthiness. Occasionally a special (and fuller) report was made on a particular firm's operations. The data provide reasonable business profiles, but they are not sufficiently robust to satisfy quantitative analysis.

The other, less valuable, source available at regular intervals, on a regional basis, is the Federal Manuscript Census schedules, Products of Industry, 1850, 1860, and 1870, for the states of Illinois, Indiana, Iowa, Kentucky, Minnesota, Missouri, Ohio, and Wisconsin. This material is disappointing because meat packing was frequently not recorded, either because it was regarded as commerce rather than manufacturing, or because the seasonal operations were not conducted in the summer, when the census marshalls collected data. The resulting partial information is of limited use.

The most informative business source is the Letterbook, 1857–1859, of the pork packer A. Maxwell of Alexandria, Missouri, in the Western Historical Collection at Columbia, Missouri. Some additional insights into his operations are available in the Record Book, 1853–1856, of Maxwell & Johnson of Alexandria. Other fleeting glimpses of entrepreneurial endeavor are scattered in the letters, papers, and records of merchants and packers, as for example, in the papers of Samuel Moore of Mooresville, Indiana, Indiana State Library, Indianapolis; in the Joseph Rawson & Sons' "Accounts and Trial Balances," Cincinnati Historical Society; in the letters from David Keigh & Co., Chicago, Warshaw Collection of the Smithsonian Institution, Washington, D.C.; and in the financial records, 1866–1887, of Plankington & Armour Co., Milwaukee, Milwaukee County Historical Society. Information of a more general commercial nature can be found in the minutes of the Cincinnati Chambers of Commerce and Merchants' Exchange; in the minutes of the Louisville Board of Trade, 1862–1870; and in the correspondence of Sidney D. Maxwell, superintendent of the Cincinnati Chamber of Commerce in the 1870s.

Knowledge about contracts and proposals for supplying the army can be gleaned from National Archives Record Group 192, "Records of the Office of the Commissary General of Subsistence." The most useful information is located in Entries 68 and 69, "Registers of Accepted Proposals, 1863–1871" and "Registers of Contracts, 1819–1907." Other marginal references are in Entries 74, 76, and 77, "Registers of Beef and Fresh Meat Contracts, 1820–1894," "Contracts, 1825–1853," and "Contracts, 1866"; and also in Record Group 92, "The Quartermaster's Consolidated File."

The notes of two Illinois historians proved useful. Arthur C. Cole left a collection of thirty-one boxes of notes used when writing volume 3 of *The Centennial History of Illinois: The Era of the Civil War, 1848–70*; these are located in the library of the University of Illinois, Champaign-Urbana. Bessie L. Pierce bestowed an accumulation of papers from producing volumes 1–3 of her *History of Chicago*; these are housed with the Printed Collections at the Chicago Historical Society.

GOVERNMENT SOURCES

Federal

United States, Bureau of the Census. *Sixth Census* (1840).

——. *Sixth Census: Compendium.*

——. *Seventh Census* (1850).

——. *Statistical View of the United States: A Compendium of the Seventh Census.*

——. *Eighth Census* (1860). vol. 1: *Population*; vol. 2: *Agriculture*; vol. 3: *Manufactures.*

——. *Ninth Census* (1870), vol. 1: *The Statistics of Population*: vol. 2: *The Statistics of Wealth and Industry.*

——. *Ninth Census: A Compendium.*

——. *Tenth Census* (1880). vol. 2: *Manufactures.*

——. *Twelfth Census* (1900). vol. 9: *Manufactures,* pt. 3: "Special Report: Slaughtering and Meat Packing."

——. *Census of Manufactures* (1905): "Slaughtering and Meat Packing, Manufactured Ice and Salt."

United States, Commissioner of Patents, *Annual Reports.* 1841–1861.

United States, Congress, House. "First Annual Report of the Bureau of Animal Industry for the Year 1884." *House Miscellaneous Documents,* no. 25, serial 2311, 48 Cong., 2 sess. (1884/85).

——. Report of Committees of the House, "Government Contracts." *Report,* no. 2, serial 1142, 1143, 37 Cong., 2 sess. (1861/62).

——. "Report of the Commissioner of Corporations on the Beef Industry." *House Documents,* vol. 54, no. 382, serial 4833, 58 Cong., 3 sess. (1905).

United States, Congress, Senate. Andrews, Israel D., "Report of the Trade and Commerce of the British and North American Colonies and upon the Trade of the Great Lakes and Rivers." *Senate Documents,* Doc. 112, serial 622, 32 Cong., 1 sess. (1853).

——. "Report from the Select Committee on the Transportation and Sales of Meat Products." *Senate Reports,* no. 829, serial 2705, 51 Cong., 1 sess. (1889/90).

——. "Wholesale Prices of Farm Products for 52 Years." *Senate Reports,* no. 1394, pt. 2, serial 3074, 52 Cong., 2 sess. (1893).

United States, Department of Agriculture. *Annual Reports.* 1862–1876.

United States, Department of Commerce and Labor, Bureau of Statistics. *Monthly Summary of the Commerce and Finance of the United States for the Fiscal Year, 1900.* pt. 3, "The Provision Trade of the United States."

United States, Department of the Treasury, Bureau of Statistics. *Annual Report on the Internal Commerce of the United States, October 1881.* Appendix no. 7; Joseph Nimmo, Jr., "The Commercial, Industrial and Transportation Interests of the City of Cincinnati."

United States, Federal Trade Commission. *Report on the Meat Packing Industry.* 6 vols., 1918–1920.

State

Illinois, Board of Agriculture. *Transactions of the State Agricultural Society.* 1859–1880.

Indiana, Board of Agriculture. *Reports.* 1851–1880.

Iowa, Agricultural Society. *Reports.* 1853–1880.

Kentucky, Bureau of Agriculture, Horticulture and Statistics. *Reports,* nos. 2 and 4. 1879, 1881.

Missouri, Board of Agriculture. *Reports.* 1865–1873.

Ohio, Board of Agriculture. *Reports.* 1846–1880.

Ohio, Commissioner of Statistics. *Reports to the General Assembly.* 1857–1880.

Wisconsin, Agricultural Society. *Transactions.* 1851–1868.

COMMERCE AND TRADE REPORTS

Chicago Board of Trade. *Annual Reports* 1–22 (1858–1878).

Chicago Daily Democratic Press. *Annual Reviews* 1–8 (1852–1860). [Title varies.]

Chicago Tribune Press. *Annual Reviews* 12 (1860); 15 (1863); 17 (1865); 21 (1869); 22 (1870). [Title varies.]

Cincinnati Chamber of Commerce. *Annual Reports* 1–32 (1847–1880). [Title varies.]

Cleveland Board of Trade. *Annual Statements* (1865–1870).

Des Moines Board of Trade. *Annual Report* 1 (1880).

Indianapolis Board of Trade. *Annual Reports* 1–6 (1871–1875).

Kansas City Board of Trade. *Annual Reports* 1–4 (1878–1881); 12 (1891).

Louisville Board of Trade. *Annual Reports* 2 (1880); 5 (1883).

Milwaukee Board of Trade. *Annual Reports* 1–3 (1854–1857).

Milwaukee Chamber of Commerce. *Annual Reports* 1–23 (1858–1880).

Omaha Board of Trade. *Annual Report* (1885).

The Packing of the West. *Annual Reports* (1876, 1877).

Peoria Board of Trade. *Annual Reports* 1 (1870); 3 (1872); 6 (1875); 9 (1878).

St. Louis Chamber of Commerce. *Annual Reports* (1848, 1852, 1854, 1858, 1860). [Title varies.]

St. Louis Merchants' Exchange. *Annual Statements* (1865–1875).

St. Paul, Chamber of Commerce. *Annual Reports* (1867–1874).

NEWSPAPERS

Newspaper reports for the packing months from October to March provided the majority of the material for many aspects of meat packing. Brackets [ ] indicate an incomplete file.

Beardstown Gazette, [1847-1848], [1849-1852].
Burlington Hawkeye, 1855-1864, 1865.
Chicago Tribune, 1861-1862.
Cincinnati Chronicle, 1840-1841.
Cincinnati Commercial, [1861-1865].
Cincinnati Gazette, 1835-1836, 1842-1847, 1850-1851.
Cincinnati Prices' Current, 1845-1846, 1848-1863, 1865-1867, 1872-1877.
Circleville Watchman, 1844-1848.
Cist's Advertiser (Cincinnati), 1845-1853.
Dayton Transcript, 1843-1846.
Des Moines Register, [1871-1874].
Gate City Weekly (Keokuk), [1849-1861].
Gem of the Prairies (Chicago), [1844-1845], [1847-1852].
Hamilton Intelligencer [1843-1849].
Hannibal Gazette, 1846-1848.
Hannibal Journal, 1846-1850, [1851-1853].
Indiana State Sentinel, 1855-1859.
Kansas City Times, 1874, 1875.
Kentucky Yeoman (Frankfort), 1846-1849.
Lafayette Daily Journal, 1853-1859.
Louisville Democrat, 1851-1854, 1857-1859, 1859-1860.
Madison Courier, [1845-1847], [1856-1864].
Maysville Eagle, 1845-1848, [1850-1854].
Milwaukee Sentinel, 1838-1865.
Missouri Argus (St. Louis), [1835-1839].
Missouri Republican (St. Louis), 1841-1843.
Muscatine Enquirer, 1856-1860.
Omaha Republican, 1869-1880.
Peoria Weekly Democratic Press, [1851-1857].
Peoria Weekly Transcript, 1857-1859, [1863], 1865-1873, 1876-1877.
Quincy Whig, [1838-1857], [1860-1871].
St. Joseph Morning Herald, 1862-1864, 1866-1868, 1872-1876.
St. Louis Intelligencer, 1850-1851.
St. Louis Price Current and Commercial Record, 1854-1855, 1861, 1867-1872.

Scioto Gazette, 1841–1849.
Valley Whig and Keokuk Register, [1849–1861].
Wabash Express, [1842–1860].

Note: A useful index to Cleveland newspapers is: Works Progress Administration. *Annals of Cleveland, 1818–1935: A Digest and Index of the Newspaper Record of Events and Opinion.* Cleveland, 1938. A similar index, compiled on cards, and available at the Milwaukee Public Library, is: Works Progress Administration. "Index to the Milwaukee Sentinel."

PERIODICALS

Chicago Magazine, 1857.
De Bow's Review, 1844–1864, 1866–1870.
Dollar Farmer, 1842–1844, 1845–1846.
Genius of the West, 1854–1856.
Hazard's United States' Commercial and Statistical Register, 1839–1841.
Hunt's Merchants' Magazine, 1839–1870.
Illinois Farmer, 1856–1864.
Niles' National Register, 1835–1849.
North-Western Review, 1857–1858.
Ohio Valley Farmer, 1857–1860.
Prairie Farmer, 1841–1875.
Railroad Record, 1853–1868.
Western Journal and Civilian, 1848–1856.
Wisconsin Farmer, 1849–1865.

CITY DIRECTORIES

The titles of city directories vary considerably, so for convenience they have been listed by city consulted, and grouped by state. For the specific years used, see the notes.

Illinois: Alton, Chicago, Galena, Peoria, Quincy, Springfield.
Indiana: Indianapolis, Madison, Terre Haute.
Iowa: Burlington, Des Moines, Dubuque, Keokuk, Muscatine.
Kentucky: Louisville.
Michigan: Detroit.
Missouri: Hannibal, St. Joseph, St. Louis.
Ohio: Chillicothe, Cincinnati, Circleville, Cleveland, Columbus, Dayton, Hamilton.
Wisconsin: Milwaukee.

CONTEMPORARY GAZETEERS, GUIDES, AND HISTORIES

Allen, Thomas. *The Commerce and Navigation of the Valley of the Mississippi.* . . . St. Louis, 1847.

Alton, Illinois. *Revised Ordinances of the City of Alton.* . . . Alton, 1851.

Barrows, Willard. *Notes on Iowa Territory*. Cincinnati, 1845.

Baylies, A. *An Exposition of the Business of Milwaukee.* Milwaukee, 1863.

Bebb, William. *Cincinnati: Her Position, Duty and Destiny.* Cincinnati, 1848.

Blanchard, Rufus. *Handbook of Iowa*. . . . 2nd ed. Chicago, 1869.

Buckingham, James S. *The Eastern and Western States of America.* London, 1842.

Burrows, John M.D. *Fifty Years in Iowa . . .: Personal Reminiscences . . . of Men and Events . . . of Davenport and Scott County, 1838-1888.* Davenport, Iowa, 1888.

Campbell, A. *A Glance at Illinois: Her Lands and Their Comparative Value* . . . . La Salle, Ill., 1856.

Campbell, John D. *Campbell's Shippers' Guide for Indiana, Illinois . . . and Classified Business Directory of Towns on the Illinois Central.* Cincinnati, 1870.

Campbell's Gazeteer of Missouri. rev. ed. St. Louis, 1875.

Chambers, William. *Things As They Are in America.* London, 1854.

Chandler, H.C., & Co. *Railroad Business Directory and Shippers' Guide for Indiana.* Indianapolis, 1868.

——. *Railway, Business Directory and Shippers' Guide for Illinois.* Indianapolis, 1868.

Chapman, S. *Handbook of Wisconsin.* Milwaukee, 1855.

Chicago in 1860: A Glance at Its Business Houses. . . . Chicago, 1860.

Chicago Tribune. *Chicago in 1864.* Chicago, 1865.

Cist, Charles. *Cincinnati in 1841.* Cincinnati, 1841.

——. *Sketches and Statistics of Cincinnati in 1851.* Cincinnati, 1851.

——. *Sketches and Statistics of Cincinnati in 1859.* Cincinnati, 1859.

——. *The Cincinnati Miscellany*. . . . Cincinnati, 1846.

Colby, Charles G. *Handbook of Illinois.* New York, 1854.

Colton, Joseph H. *The State of Indiana Delineated.* New York, 1838.

Commercial Directory of the Western States and Rivers . . . 1867/8. St. Louis, 1867.

Curtiss, Daniel S. *Western Portraiture and Emigrants' Guide.* New York, 1852.

Deering, Richard. *Louisville: Her Commercial, Manufacturing and Social Advantages, Including a Sketch of her History, Geography, Topography.* . . . Louisville, 1859.

Disturnell, John. *The Travellers' Guide through the State of Illinois.* New York, 1838.

Drake, Benjamin. *Cincinnati in 1826.* Cincinnati, 1827.

Drake, Daniel. *Natural and Statistical View or Pictures of Cincinnati and the Miami Country.* Cincinnati, 1815.

Drown, Simeon de W. *Drown's Record and Historical Review of Peoria.* Peoria, 1851.

——. *Peoria Record and Advertiser for August, 1856.* Peoria, 1856.

Edwards, Richard. *Edwards' Great West and Her Commercial Metropolis.* . . . St. Louis, 1860.

Edwards' Descriptive Gazeteer and Commercial Directory of the Mississippi Valley. St. Louis, 1860.

Edwards' Peoria Census Report and Historical and Statistical Review. Peoria, 1876.

The Emigrant's Instructor on Wisconsin and the Western States of America. Liverpool, 1844.

Ensign and Thayer's Travellers' Guide through the States of Ohio, Michigan, Indiana, Illinois. . . . New York, 1852.

Flint, Charles L. *One Hundred Years of Progress of the United States.* Hartford, Conn., 1872.

Gazeteer and Directory of the Hannibal and St. Joseph Railroad and of the Missouri River. . . . Detroit, 1873.

Gazeteer of the State of Missouri. St. Louis, 1837.

Gerhard, Fred. *Illinois As It Is.* Chicago, 1857.

Gregory, John. *Industrial Resources of Wisconsin.* Milwaukee, 1855; rev. ed., 1870.

A Guide to the City of Chicago: Its Public Buildings. . . . Chicago, 1868.

Hall, James. *Statistics of the West.* Cincinnati, 1836.

——. *The West: Its Commerce and Navigation.* Cincinnati, 1848.

Hawes, George W. *Commercial Gazeteer and Business Directory of the Ohio River.* Indianapolis, 1861.

——. *The Illinois State Gazeteer for 1857/8.* Chicago, 1858.

——. *Indiana State Gazeteer and Business Directory.* Indianapolis, 1858, 1860, 1862, 1864.

——. *Kentucky State Gazeteer and Business Directory, 1859/60.* Louisville, 1859.

——. *Michigan State Gazeteer and Business Directory for 1860.* Detroit, 1860.

——. *Missouri State Gazeteer, Shippers' Guide and Business Directory for 1865.* Indianapolis, 1865.

——. *Ohio State Gazeteer and Business Directory.* Cincinnati, 1859; Indianapolis, 1860.

Holmes, Joseph T. *Quincy in 1857.* Quincy, 1857.

Horsford, Eben N. *The Army Ration.* 2nd rev. ed. New York, 1864.

Illinois Annual Register and Western Business Directory. Chicago, 1847.

Illinois State Business Directory, 1860. Chicago, 1860.

Illinois State Gazeteer and Business Directory for the Years 1864/5. Chicago, 1864.

The Indiana Gazeteer or Topographical Dictionary. Centreville, 1826.

Indiana Gazeteer or Topographical Directory. Indianapolis, 1833; 3rd ed., 1849.

Indianapolis Board of Trade. *Indianapolis: Its Manufacturing Interests, Wants, Facilities.* Indianapolis, 1857.

Indiana State Gazeteer and Shippers' Guide for 1866/7. Lafayette, 1866.

Iowa State Gazeteer. . . . Chicago, 1865.

Jenkins, Warren. *The Ohio Gazeteer and Travellers' Guide.* rev. ed. Columbus, 1841.

Jones, A.D. *Illinois and the West.* Philadelphia, 1838.

Jones, J.W., & Co. *An Address to the Merchants of the Northwest. . . .* Chicago, 1856.

Kansas State Gazeteer and Business Directory. vols. 1-4. Detroit, 1878, 1880, 1882, 1884.

Kentucky State Gazeteer and Business Directory. Louisville, 1876, 1879.

Kilbourn, John. *The Ohio Gazeteer or Topographical Dictionary.* Columbus, 1816, 1819, 1821, 1826, 1829, 1831, 1833.

Kimball, J.F., & Co. *Eastern, Western and Southern Business Directory. . . .* Cincinnati, 1846.

Louisville, Kentucky. *Revised Ordinances of the City of Louisville. . . .* Louisville, 1854.

Lyford, William G. *The Western Address Directory. . . .* Baltimore, 1837.

Michigan State Gazeteer and Business Directory, 1863/4. Detroit, 1863.

Milwaukee in 1860: A Glance at Its Business Houses. . . . Milwaukee, 1860.

Minnesota Gazeteer and Business Directory for 1865. n.p., 1865.

Missouri State Gazeteer and Business Directory. St. Louis, 1860.

Mitchell, S. August. *Illinois in 1837: A Sketch Descriptive of the Situation. . . .* Philadelphia, 1837.

Montague's Illinois and Missouri State Directory for 1854. St. Louis, 1854.

National Convention of Pork Packers and Provision Dealers. *Proceedings of the National Convention.* Chicago, 1873.

Nebraska State Gazeteer and Business Directory. Omaha, 1879, 1882.

Newhall, John B. *The British Emigrants' Hand Book and Guide to the New States of America. . . .* London, 1844.

——. *A Glimpse of Iowa in 1846. . . .* Burlington, 1846.

——. *Sketches of Iowa. . . .* New York, 1841.

Northern Cross Railroad. *Travellers' Guide to the North and East.* Quincy, 1856.

The Ohio Railroad Guide. Cincinnati, 1852.

Ohio State Business Directory for 1853/4. Cincinnati, 1853.

Ohio State Register and Business Mirror for 1857. Cincinnati, 1857.

Ottawa, Illinois. *By-Laws and Ordinances of the Town of Ottawa.* Ottawa, 1849.

Parker, Nathan H. *Iowa As It Is in 1855.* Chicago, 1855.

——. *The Iowa Handbook for 1857.* Boston, 1857.

——. *Missouri As It Is in 1867.* Philadelphia, 1867.

——. *The Missouri Hand Book.* St. Louis, 1865.

Peck, John M. *A Gazeteer of Illinois.* Jacksonville, 1834; 2nd rev. ed., 1837.

——. *The Traveller's Directory for Illinois.* New York, 1839.

Pekin, Illinois. *The City Charter and Ordinances.* Pekin, 1864.

Peoria Transcript. *A Descriptive Account of the City of Peoria.* Peoria, 1859.

Platt, Montague T. *Illinois State Business Directory, 1871/2.* Chicago, 1871.

Price Current. *Review of the Trade and Commerce of Kansas City for 1879.* Kansas City, 1879.

Quincy, Illinois. *Charters, Ordinances. . . .* Quincy, 1864.

Quincy Citizens' Association. *The Advantages As a Manufacturing and Commercial Point. . . .* Quincy, 1871.

Rees, William. *The Mississippi Bridge Cities, Davenport, Rock Island and Moline.* Rock Island, 1854.

Ritchie, James S. *Wisconsin and Its Resources with Lake Superior, Its Commerce and Navigation.* Chicago, 1857.

Ross, James. *Wisconsin and Her Resources for Remunerating Capital and Supporting Labor.* Madison, 1871.

St. Louis Chamber of Commerce. *Report of Committee . . . upon Trade, Commerce and Manufactures. . . .January, 1852.* St. Louis, 1852.

St. Louis City. *Revised Ordinances.* St. Louis, 1836, 1843, 1846, 1850, 1853, 1856, 1861, 1866.
Sargent, George B. *Notes on Iowa. . . .* New York, 1848.
Schooley, John A. *A Process of Obtaining a Dry Cold Current of Air from Ice. . . .* Cincinnati, 1855.
Skillman, W.C. *The Western Metropolis or St. Louis in 1846.* St. Louis, 1846.
State Gazeteer and Business Directory for Michigan for 1875 and 1877. Detroit, 1875, 1877.
A Strangers' and Tourists' Guide to the City of Chicago in the Early Days. Chicago, 1866.
Wells, John G. *Pocket Hand-Book of Iowa.* New York, 1857.
Wing, Jack. *The Great Union Stock Yards of Chicago.* Chicago, 1865.
Wing, J.M., & Co. *Seven Days in Chicago.* Chicago, 1877.
Wisconsin State Directory. Madison, 1853; Milwaukee, 1857, 1858.
Youatt, William. *The Pig: A Treatise on the Breeds, Management, Feeding and Medical Treatment of Swine. . . .* London, 1847.

BOOKS

Ambler, C.H. *History of Transportation in the Ohio Valley.* Glendale, Cal., 1932.
[American Meat Institute.] *The Packing Industry.* Chicago, 1924.
Anderson, Oscar E. *Refrigeration in America.* Princeton, N.J., 1953.
Andreas, Alfred T. *History of Chicago from the Earliest Period to the Present Time.* 3 vols. Chicago, 1884.
——. *History of Cook County, Illinois.* Chicago, 1884.
——. *History of the State of Kansas.* Chicago, 1883.
——. *History of the State of Nebraska.* Chicago, 1882.
Antrobus, Augustine M. *History of Des Moines County Iowa and Its People.* 2 vols. Chicago, 1915.
Asbury, Henry. *Reminiscences of Quincy, Illinois. . . .* Quincy, 1882.
Ashton, John. *A History of Hogs and Pork Production in Missouri.* Jefferson City, Mo., 1923.
Atherton, Lewis E. *The Pioneer Merchant in Mid-America.* Columbia, Mo., 1939.
Austerlitz, Emanuel H. *Cincinnati from 1800 to 1875: A Condensed History. . . .* Cincinnati, 1875.
Barringer, John W. *Legislative History of the Subsistence Department of the United States.* Washington, D.C., 1877.
Barton, Elmer E. *A Business Tour of Chicago Depicting Fifty Years' Progress.* Chicago, 1887.

——. *Industrial History of Milwaukee: The Commercial Manufacturing. . . .* Milwaukee, 1886.

Bateman, Newton, and Selby, Paul, eds. *Historical Encyclopaedia of Illinois and History of Cass County.* 2 vols. Chicago, 1915.

——. *Historical Encyclopaedia of Illinois and History of Peoria County.* 2 vols. Chicago, 1902.

——. *Historical Encyclopaedia of Illinois and History of Tazewell County.* Chicago, 1905.

Belcher, Wyatt B. *The Economic Rivalry between St. Louis and Chicago, 1850-1880.* New York, 1947.

Benner, Samuel. *Benner's Prophecies of Future Ups and Downs in Prices.* Cincinnati, 1884.

Bennett, Henry H., ed. *The County of Ross.* State Centennial History. Madison, Wis., 1902.

Benton, Elbert J. *The Wabash Trade Route in the Development of the Old Northwest.* Baltimore, 1903.

Berry, Thomas S. *Western Prices before 1861: A Study of the Cincinnati Market.* Cambridge, Mass., 1943.

Bidwell, Percy, and Falconer, John. *History of Agriculture in the Northern United States, 1620-1860.* Washington, D.C., 1925.

Biographical and Historical Souvenir of the Counties of Clark, Crawford, Harrison, Floyd, Jefferson, Jennings, Scott and Washington, Indiana. Chicago, 1889.

Biographical Cyclopaedia and Portrait Gallery with an Historical Sketch of the State of Ohio. 6 vols. Cincinnati, 1883-1895.

The Biographical Dictionary and Portrait Gallery of Representative Men of Chicago, Wisconsin. . . . Chicago, 1895.

Biographical Encyclopaedia of Illinois. Philadelphia, 1875.

Biographical Encyclopaedia of Kentucky of the Dead and Living Men of the Nineteenth Century. Cincinnati, 1878.

The Biographical Encyclopaedia of Ohio of the Nineteenth Century. Cincinnati, 1876.

Biographical History of Eminent and Self-Made Men of the State of Indiana. 2 vols. Cincinnati, 1880.

Biographical Record and Portrait Album of Tippecanoe County, Indiana. Chicago, 1888.

Biographical Review of Lee County, Iowa. Chicago, 1904.

Biographical Sketches of the Leading Men of Chicago. Chicago, 1868.

Bogue, Allen G. *From Prairie to Corn Belt: Farming on the Illinois and Iowa Prairies in the Nineteenth Century.* Chicago, 1963.

Bross, William. *History of Chicago: Historical and Commercial Statistics. . . . What I Remember of Early Chicago. . . .* Chicago, 1876.

Brown, A. Theodore. *Frontier Community: Kansas City to 1870.* Columbia, Mo., 1963.

Buck, James S. *Pioneer History of Milwaukee.* 4 vols. Milwaukee, 1876-1886.

Buley, R. Carlyle. *The Old Northwest: Pioneer Period, 1815-1840.* 2 vols. Bloomington, Ind., 1950.

Bushnell, Joseph P., ed. *Des Moines Illustrated.* Des Moines, 1889.

Case, Theodore S., ed. *History of Kansas City, Missouri.* Syracuse, 1888.

Casseday, Benjamin. *The History of Louisville from Its Earliest Settlement till the Year 1852.* Louisville, 1852; rpt. 1970.

Cavanagh, Helen M. *Funk of Funk's Grove: Farmer, Legislator and Cattle King of the Old Northwest, 1797-1865.* Bloomington, Ill., 1952.

A Centennial Biographical History of the City of Columbus and Franklin County. Chicago, 1901.

Chamberlin, Everett. *Chicago and Its Suburbs.* Chicago, 1874.

Cheever, Lawrence O. *The House of Morrell.* Cedar Rapids, Iowa, 1948.

[Chicago Historical Publishing Co.] *History of Chicago.* Chicago, 1889.

[Cincinnati Times Star Co.] *The City of Cincinnati and Its Resources.* Cincinnati, 1891.

Clark, John G. *The Grain Trade in the Old Northwest.* Urbana, Ill., 1966.

Clark, Victor S. *History of Manufactures in the United States.* 3 vols. Washington, D.C., 1929; rpt. 1949.

Cleaver, Charles. *Early Chicago Reminiscences.* Fergus Historical Series, no. 19. Chicago, 1882.

——. *History of Chicago from 1833 to 1892.* Chicago, 1892.

Clemen, Rudolph A. *The American Livestock and Meat Industry.* New York, 1923.

——. *Byproducts in the Packing Industry.* Chicago, 1927.

——. *George H. Hammond (1838-1886): Pioneer in Refrigerator Technology.* New York, 1946.

Cobb, Henry. *Industrial Interests of Missouri.* St. Louis, 1870.

Colbert, Elias. *Chicago: Historical and Statistical Sketch of the Garden City. . . .* Chicago, 1868.

Cole, Arthur C. *The Era of the Civil War, 1848-1870.* vol. 3 of *Centennial History of Illinois.* Chicago, 1922.

Collins, Lewis. *Collins' Historical Sketches of Kentucky: History of Kentucky.* Louisville, 1877; rev. ed., 2 vols., Covington, 1882.

Collins, William H. *Past and Present of the City of Quincy and Adams County, Illinois. . . .* Chicago, 1905.

Commemorative Biographical Record of Prominent and Representative Men of Indianapolis and Vicinity. Chicago, 1908.

Condit, Blackford. *The History of Early Terre Haute*. New York, 1900.

Cone, Stephen D. *Biographical and Historical Sketches: A Narrative of Hamilton and Its Residents, from 1792–1896*. Hamilton, Ohio, 1896.

Corey, Lewis. *Meat and Men: A Study of Monopoly Unionism and Food Policy*. New York, 1950.

Coulter, E. Merton. *The Civil War and Readjustment in Kentucky*. Chapel Hill, 1926; rpt. 1966.

[Courier Press Club.] *Cincinnati, the Queen City; Newspaper Reference Book*. Cincinnati, 1914.

Crittendon, George A. *The Industries of Louisville*. . . . Louisville, 1881.

Cummings, Richard O. *The American Ice Harvests: A Historical Study of Technology, 1800–1918*. Berkeley, 1949.

Current, Richard N. *The Civil War Era, 1848–1873*. vol. 2 of *The History of Wisconsin*. Madison, 1976.

Currey, Josiah S. *Chicago: Its History and Its Builders. A Century of Marvelous Growth*. 5 vols. Chicago, 1912.

——. *Manufacturing and Wholesale Industries of Chicago*. 3 vols. Chicago, 1918.

The Daily News History of Buchanan County and St. Joseph, Missouri. St. Joseph, 1898.

Danhof, Clarence H. *Change in Agriculture: The Northern United States, 1820–1870*. Cambridge, Mass., 1969.

Depew, Chauncey M., ed. *One Hundred Years of American Commerce, 1795–1895*. New York, 18 9

Descriptive Illustrated Review of Ottumwa Iowa, Trade. . . . n.p., 1890.

Dixon, J.M. *Centennial History of Polk County*. Des Moines, 1876.

Drury, John. *Rare and Well Done: Some Historical Notes on Meats and Meatmen*. Chicago, 1966.

Dunn, Jacob P. *Greater Indianapolis: The History, the Industries, the Institutions*. 2 vols. Chicago, 1910.

Elstner, Charles E. *The Industries of Louisville Kentucky and New Albany Indiana*. . . . Louisville, 1886.

[Elstner, J.M., & Co.] *The Centennial Review of Cincinnati*. . . . Cincinnati, 1888.

Encyclopaedia of Biography of Illinois. 3 vols. Chicago, 1892–1902.

Englhardt, George W. *Cincinnati, the Queen City*. . . . Cincinnati, 1901.

Esarey, Logan. *History of Indiana from Its Exploration to 1922.* 2 vols. Fort Wayne, Ind., 1924.

Finley, Isaac J., and Putnam, Rufus. *Pioneer Record and Reminiscences of the Early Settlers and Settlement of Ross County, Ohio.* Cincinnati, 1871.

Fishlow, Albert. *American Railroads and the Transformation of the Ante-Bellum Economy.* Cambridge, Mass., 1965.

Fite, Emerson D. *Social and Industrial Conditions in the North during the Civil War.* New York, 1910.

Fite, Gilbert C. *The Farmers' Frontier, 1865-1900.* New York, 1966.

Fletcher, Calvin. *The Diary of Calvin Fletcher,* ed. Gayle Thornbrough. vol. 1. Indianapolis, 1972.

Flower, Frank A., ed. *History of Milwaukee, Wisconsin from Pre Historic Times. . . .* Chicago, 1881.

Ford, Henry A., and Ford, Kate. *History of Cincinnati, Ohio.* Cleveland, 1881.

——. *History of Hamilton County, Ohio.* Cleveland, 1881.

Fowler, Bertram B. *Men, Meat and Miracles.* New York, 1952.

Gates, Paul W. *Agriculture and the Civil War.* New York, 1965.

——. *The Farmers' Age: Agriculture, 1815-1860.* New York, 1960.

Gephart, William. *Transportation and Industrial Development in the Middle West.* New York, 1909.

Giedion, Siegfried. *Mechanization Takes Command.* New York, 1948.

Glaab, Charles N. *Kansas City and the Railroads: Community Policy in the Growth of a Regional Metropolis.* Madison, Wis., 1962.

Goodspeed, Weston A., and Healy, Daniel D., eds. *History of Cook County Illinois.* 2 vols. Chicago, 1909.

[Goodspeed Bros.] *Pictorial and Biographical Memoirs of Indianapolis and Marion County.* Chicago, 1893.

Goss, Charles F. *Cincinnati, the Queen City, 1788-1912.* 4 vols. Cincinnati, 1912.

Grand, W. Joseph. *Illustrated History of the Union Stockyards.* Chicago, *ca.* 1896.

Greve, Charles T. *Centennial History of Cincinnati and Representative Citizens.* 2 vols. Chicago, 1904.

Guyer, Isaac D. *History of Chicago, Its Commercial and Manufacturing Interests.* Chicago, 1862.

Haites, Erik F.; Mak, James; and Walton, Gary M. *Western River Transportation: The Era of Early Internal Development, 1810-1860.* Baltimore, 1975.

Half Century's Progress of the City of Chicago: The City's Leading Manufacturers and Merchants. . . . Chicago, 1887.

Hassam, Loren. *A Historical Sketch of Terre Haute, Indiana. . . .* Terre Haute, 1873.

Henlein, Paul C. *Cattle Kingdom in the Ohio Valley, 1783-1860.* Lexington, Ky., 1959.

Hieronymus, Thomas A. *Economics of Futures' Trading.* New York, 1971.

Hilliard, Sam B. *Hog Meat and Hoecake: Food Supply in the Old South, 1840–1860.* Carbondale, Ill., 1972.

A History and Biographical Cyclopaedia of Butler County, Ohio. Cincinnati, 1882.

History of Adams County, Illinois. . . . Chicago, 1879.

History of Brown County, Ohio. Chicago, 1883.

The History of Buchanan County, Missouri. St. Joseph, 1881.

History of Cincinnati and Hamilton County, Ohio. . . . Cincinnati, 1894.

History of Circleville and Pickaway Counties. Cleveland, 1880.

History of Columbus, Franklin County Ohio, Pictorial and Biographical. Chicago, 1909.

History of Des Moines County, Iowa. Chicago, 1879.

History of Franklin and Pickaway Counties, Ohio. Cleveland, 1880.

The History of Jackson County, Missouri. Kansas City, Mo., 1881.

The History of Lee County, Iowa. Chicago, 1879.

History of Lewis, Clark, Knox and Scotland Counties, Missouri. St. Louis, 1887.

The History of Linn County, Iowa. Chicago, 1878.

History of Madison County, Illinois . . . with Biographical Sketches. Edwardsville, Ill., 1882.

History of Marion County, Missouri. St. Louis, 1884.

The History of Muscatine County, Iowa. Chicago, 1879.

History of Peoria County, Illinois. Chicago, 1880.

The History of Polk County, Iowa. Des Moines, 1880.

History of Ross and Highland Counties, Ohio. Cleveland, 1880.

History of Sangamon County, Illinois. Chicago, 1881.

History of Tazewell County, Illinois. Chicago, 1879.

History of Wapello County, Iowa. Chicago, 1901.

Holloway, William R. *Indianapolis: A Historical and Statistical Sketch of the Railroad City.* Indianapolis, 1870.

Hopkins, John A., Jr. *Economic History of the Production of Beef Cattle in Iowa.* Iowa City, 1928.

Hubbard, Henry C. *The Older Middle West, 1840–1880.* New York, 1936.

Hunter, Louis C. *Steamboats on the Western Rivers.* Cambridge, Mass., 1949.

——. *Studies in the Economic History of the Ohio Valley: Seasonal Aspects of Industry and Commerce before the Age of Big Business.* Northampton, Mass., 1935.

Huston, James A. *The Sinews of War: Army Logistics, 1775-1953.* Washington, D.C., 1966.

Hyde, William, and Conrad, Howard L. *Encyclopaedia of the History of St. Louis.* 4 vols. St. Louis, 1899.

Hyman, Max R. *Handbook of Indianapolis.* Indianapolis, 1897.

Industrial Chicago. 6 vols. Chicago, 1891-1896.

The Industries of Cleveland. Cleveland, 1888.

Industries of Omaha. Omaha, 1887.

[Inter Ocean.] *Centennial History of the City of Chicago: Its Men and Institutions.* Chicago, 1905.

——. *A History of the City of Chicago: Its Men and Institutions.* Chicago, 1900.

Joblin, M., & Co. *Cincinnati Past and Present: Its Industrial History.* . . . Cincinnati, 1872.

——. *Louisville Past and Present: Its Industrial History.* Louisville, 1875.

Joblin, Maurice. *Cleveland Past and Present: Representative Men.* Cleveland, 1869.

Johnson, Crisfield, comp. *History of Cuyahoga County, Ohio.* Cleveland, 1879.

Johnston, Josiah S., ed. *Memorial History of Louisville from Its First Settlement to the Year 1896.* Chicago, 1896.

Kansas City Stock Yards Co. *Seventy-Five Years of Kansas City Livestock Market History, 1871-1946.* Kansas City, Mo., 1946.

Kirkland, Joseph. *The Story of Chicago.* Chicago, 1892.

Kohlmeier, A.L. *The Old Northwest: As the Keystone of the Arch of American Federal Union; A Study in Commerce and Politics.* Bloomington, Ind., 1938.

Lampard, Eric E. *The Rise of the Dairy Industry in Wisconsin: A Study in Agricultural Change, 1820-1920.* Madison, Wis., 1963.

The Leading Industries of Kansas City, Missouri. Chicago, 1882.

Leading Manufacturers and Merchants of Cincinnati and Environs. Cincinnati, 1886.

Leech, Harper, and Carroll, John C. *Armour and His Times.* New York, 1938.

Leonard, John. *Industries of St. Louis. . . . Her Relations as a Center of Trade, Manufacturing.* . . . St. Louis, 1887.

Leonard, L.A., ed. *Greater Cincinnati and Its People: A History.* 4 vols. New York, 1927.

Lippincott, Isaac. *A History of Manufactures in the Ohio Valley to The Year 1860.* New York, 1914.

Lurie, Jonathan. *The Chicago Board of Trade, 1859-1905: The Dynamics of Self-Regulation.* Urbana, Ill., 1979.

McCarty, Harold H., and Thompson, C.W. *Meat Packing in Iowa.* Iowa City, 1933.

McCoy, Joseph G. *Historic Sketches of the Cattle Trade of the West and Southwest.* Kansas City, Mo., 1874; rpt., 1940.

McDowell, Robert E. *City of Conflict: Louisville in the Civil War, 1861-65.* Louisville, 1962.

Manufacturing and Mercantile Resources of Indianapolis. Indianapolis, 1883.

Marquis, Albert N. *The Industries of Cincinnati: The Advantages, Resources. . . .* Cincinnati, 1883.

[Merchants and Manufacturers' Bureau.] *The Advantages of Kansas City, Missouri, As a Mercantile and Manufacturing Center.* Kansas City, Mo., 1887.

Merk, Frederick. *Economic History of Wisconsin during the Civil War Decade.* Madison, Wis., 1916.

Miller, William H. *The History of Kansas City.* Kansas City, 1881.

[Morrison, Andrew.] *The Industries of Cincinnati.* Cincinnati, 1886.

Morrison, Andrew, and Irwin, John H.C. *The Industries of St. Louis: Her Advantages. . . .* St. Louis, 1885.

Moses, John, and Kirkland, Joseph. *History of Chicago, Illinois.* 2 vols. Chicago, 1895.

[National Provisioner.] *The Significant Sixty: An Historical Report of the Progress and Development of the Meat Packing Industry, 1891-1951.* Chicago, 1952.

Neyhart, Louise A. *Giant of the Yards.* Boston, 1952.

Norton, Wilbur T. *Centennial History of Madison County, Illinois . . . 1812 to 1912.* Chicago, 1912.

Oakey, Charles C. *Greater Terre Haute and Vigo County.* 2 vols. Chicago, 1908.

[Ober, Day & Co.] *The Commerce of American Cities: Kansas City, The Metropolis of the New West.* Kansas City, 1879.

Orth, Samuel P. *A History of Cleveland, Ohio.* 3 vols. Chicago, 1910.

The Packers' Encyclopaedia. Chicago, 1922.

Parker, William N., ed. *The Structure of the Cotton Economy of the Antebellum South.* Washington, D.C., 1970.

Past and Present of Tippecanoe County, Indiana. Indianapolis, 1909.

Pease, Theodore C. *The Frontier State, 1818-1848.* vol. 2 of *Centennial History of Illinois.* Springfield, 1918.

Perren, Richard. *The Meat Trade in Britain, 1840-1914.* London, 1978.

Perrin, William H. *History of Cass County, Illinois.* Chicago, 1882.

——, ed. *Kentucky: The History of the State.* 8th ed. Louisville, 1888.

Pierce, Bessie L. *A History of Chicago.* 3 vols. Chicago, 1937, 1940, 1957.

Pooley, William V. *The Settlement of Illinois from 1830 to 1850.* University of Wisconsin Bulletin, no. 220. Madison, 1908.

Porter, Glenn, and Livesay, Harold C. *Merchants and Manufacturers: Studies in the Changing Structure of Nineteenth Century Marketing.* Baltimore, 1971.

Portrait and Biographical Album of Des Moines County, Iowa. Chicago, 1888.

Portrait and Biographical Album of Lee County, Iowa. Chicago, 1887.

Portrait and Biographical Album of Linn County, Iowa. Chicago, 1887.

Portrait and Biographical Album of Peoria County, Illinois. Chicago, 1890.

Portrait and Biographical Album of Polk County, Iowa. Chicago, 1890.

Portrait and Biographical Album of Wapello County, Iowa. Chicago, 1887.

Portrait and Biographical Record of Madison County, Illinois. Chicago, 1894.

Portrait and Biographical Record of Marion, Ralls and Pike Counties, Missouri. Chicago, 1895.

Portrait and Biographical Record of Tazewell and Mason Counties. Chicago, 1904.

Powell, Cuthbert. *Twenty Years of Kansas City's Livestock Trade and Traders.* Kansas City, Mo., 1893.

Power, J.C. *History of Springfield, Illinois, Its Attractions. . . .* Springfield, 1871.

Putnam, James W. *The Illinois and Michigan Canal: A Study in Economic History.* Chicago, 1918.

Purdy, Harry L. *An Historical Analysis of the Economic Growth of St. Louis.* n.p., 1946.

Reavis, Logan U. *St. Louis: The Future Great City of the World.* St. Louis, 1870.

Redmond, Patrick H. *History of Quincy and Its Men of Mark.* Quincy, 1869.

Richman, Irving B., ed. *History of Muscatine County, Iowa.* 2 vols. Chicago, 1911.

Riley, Elmer A. *The Development of Chicago and Vicinity as A Manufacturing Center Prior to 1880.* Chicago, 1911.

Risch, Erna. *Quartermaster Support of the Army: A History of the Corps, 1775–1939.* Washington, D.C., 1962.

Roe, George M. *Cincinnati, the Queen City of the West. . . .* Cincinnati, 1895.

Roseboom, Eugene H. *The Civil War Era, 1850–1875.* vol. 4 of *The History of the State of Ohio.* Columbus, Ohio, 1944.

Rutt, Christian L., ed. *History of Buchanan County and the City of St. Joseph.* Chicago, 1904.

Savage, James W., and Bell, John. *History of the City of Omaha, Nebraska.* Chicago, 1894.

Scharf, John T. *History of St. Louis City and County.* Philadelphia, 1883.

Scheiber, Harry N. *Ohio Canal Era: A Case Study of Government and the Economy, 1820–1861.* Athens, Ohio, 1969.

Searight, Thomas B. *The Old Pike: A History of the National Road.* Uniontown, Pa., 1894.

Shannon, Fred A. *The Farmers' Last Frontier: Agriculture, 1860–1897.* New York, 1945.

——. *The Organization and Administration of the Union Army, 1861–1865.* 2 vols. Cleveland, 1928; rpt., 1965.

Smith, Alice E. *From Exploration to Statehood.* vol. 1 of *The History of Wisconsin.* Madison, Wis., 1973.

Sorenson, Alfred. *History of Omaha: From the Pioneer Days to the Present Time.* Omaha, 1889.

Stevens, George E. *The Queen City in 1869.* Cincinnati, 1869.

Stevens, Walter B. *St. Louis: The Fourth City, 1764–1911.* St. Louis, 1909.

Still, Bayrd. *Milwaukee: The History of a City.* Madison, 1948, 1965.

Stover, John F. *Iron Road to the West: American Railroads in the 1850s.* New York, 1978.

Sulgrove, B.R. *History of Indianapolis and Marion County, Indiana.* Philadelphia, 1884.

Swift, Louis F., and Van Vlissingen, A. *The Yankee of the Yard: The Biography of Gustavus Franklin Swift.* Chicago, 1927.

Symonds, Henry C. *Report of a Commissary of Subsistence, 1861–65.* Sing Sing, N.Y., 1888.

Taylor, Charles H., ed. *History of the Board of Trade of the City of Chicago.* 3 vols. Chicago, 1917.

Taylor, George R. *The Transportation Revolution, 1815-1860.* New York, 1951.

——, and Neu, Irene D. *The American Railroad Network, 1861-1890.* Cambridge, Mass., 1956.

Thompson, James W. *A History of Livestock Raising in the United States, 1607-1860.* Washington, D.C., 1942.

Thompson, Robert L. *Wiring a Continent: The History of the Telegraph Industry in the United States, 1832-1866.* Princeton, N.J., 1947.

Thornbrough, Emma Lou. *Indiana in the Civil War Era, 1850-1880.* Indianapolis, 1965.

Towne, Charles W., and Wentworth, Edward N. *Cattle and Men.* Norman, Okla., 1955.

——. *Pigs from Cave to Cornbelt.* Norman, Okla., 1950.

United States Biographical Dictionary and Portrait Gallery of Eminent and Self-Made Men: Illinois Volume. Chicago, 1876.

United States Biographical Dictionary and Portrait Gallery of Eminent and Self-Made Men: Iowa Volume. Chicago, 1878.

United States Biographical Dictionary and Portrait Gallery of Eminent and Self-Made Men: Missouri Volume. Chicago, 1878.

United States Biographical Dictionary and Portrait Gallery of Eminent and Self-Made Men: Wisconsin Volume. Chicago, 1887.

Utter, William T. *The Frontier State, 1803-1825.* vol. 2 of *The History of the State of Ohio.* Columbus, Ohio, 1941.

Vance, James E., Jr. *The Merchants' World: The Geography of Wholesaling.* Englewood Cliffs, N.J., 1970.

Vaughan, Henry W. *Breeds of Livestock in America.* Columbus, Ohio, 1937.

Wade, Richard C. *The Urban Frontier: The Rise of Western Cities, 1790-1830.* Cambridge, Mass., 1959.

Waterman, Harrison L., ed. *History of Wapello County, Iowa.* 2 vols. Chicago, 1914.

Weisenburger, Francis P. *The Passing of the Frontier, 1825-1850.* vol. 3 of *The History of Ohio.* Columbus, Ohio, 1941.

Weld, Louis D.H. *Economics of the Packing Industry.* Chicago, 1925.

Whitaker, James W. *Feedlot Empire: Beef Cattle Feeding in Illinois and Iowa, 1840-1880.* Ames, Iowa, 1975.

Wilcox, David F. *Quincy and Adams County History and Representative Men.* Chicago, 1919.

——. *Representative Men and Homes, Quincy, Illinois.* Quincy, 1899.

Wilder, Fred W. *The Modern Packing House.* Chicago, 1905.

Williams, L.A. *History of the Ohio Falls Cities and Their Counties.* Cleveland, 1882.

Wood, David W., ed. *Chicago and Its Distinguished Citizens; or, The Progress of Forty Years.* Chicago, 1881.

Works Progress Administration. *They Built a City: 150 Years of Industrial Cincinnati.* Cincinnati, 1938.

Wright, John S. *Chicago, Past, Present, Future. . . .* Chicago, 1870.

Wyandotte County and Kansas City, Kansas: Historical and Biographical. Chicago, 1890.

Yeager, Mary. *Competition and Regulation: The Development of Oligopoly in the Meat Packing Industry.* Greenwood, Conn., 1981.

ARTICLES

Aduddell, Robert M., and Cain, Louis P. "Location and Collusion in the Meat Packing Industry." In Louis P. Cain and Paul J. Uselding, eds., *Business Enterprise and Economic Change,* pp. 85–117. Kent, Ohio, 1973.

Alvord, H.E. "The American Cattle Trade." *Journal of the Royal Agricultural Society of England,* 2nd ser., 13 (1877): 356–74.

Arms, Richard O. "From Disassembly to Assembly: Cincinnati, the Birthplace of Mass-Production." *Bulletin of the Historical and Philosophical Society of Ohio* 17 (1959): 195–203.

Arnould, Richard J. "Changing Patterns of Concentration in American Meat Packing, 1880–1963." *Business History Review* 45 (1971): 18–34.

Atherton, Lewis. "Western Foodstuffs in the Army Provisions Trade." *Agricultural History* 14 (1940): 161–69.

Bateman, Fred; Foust, James D.; and Weiss, Thomas J. "Large Scale Manufacturing in the South and West, 1850–1860." *Business History Reivew* 45 (1971): 1–17.

Becker, Carl M. "Entrepreneurial Invention and Innovation in the Miami Valley during the Civil War." *Cincinnati Historical Society Bulletin* 22 (1964): 5–28.

——. "Evolution of the Disassembly Line: The Horizontal Wheel and the Overhead Railway Loop." *Cincinnati Historical Society Bulletin* 26 (1968): 276–82.

Boeck, George A. "A Decade of Transportation Fever in Burlington, Iowa, 1845–1855." *Iowa Journal of History* 56 (1958): 129–52.

Boeger, Palmer H. "The Great Kentucky Hog Swindle of 1864." *Journal of Southern History* 28 (1962): 59–70.

———. "Hardtack and Burned Beans." *Civil War History* 4 (1958): 73-92.

Burnett, Edmund C. "Hog Raising and Hog Driving in the Region of the French Broad River." *Agricultural History* 20 (1946): 83-103.

Clark, Thomas D. "Livestock Trade between Kentucky and the South, 1840-1860." *Register of the Kentucky State Historical Society* 27 (1929): 569-81.

Coulter, E. Merton. "Commercial Intercourse with the Confederacy in the Mississippi Valley, 1861-65." *Mississippi Valley Historical Review* 5 (1919): 377-95.

———. "The Effects of Secession upon the Commerce of the Mississippi Valley." *Mississippi Valley Historical Review* 3 (1916): 275-300.

Craigie, P.G. "Twenty Years' Changes in Our Foreign Meat Supplies." *Journal of Royal Agricultural Society,* 2nd ser., 23 (1887): 465-500.

Edminster, Lynn R. "Meat Packing: History and American Developments." *Encyclopaedia of the Social Sciences* 10 (New York, 1933): 242-49.

Ezekiel, Mordecai. "The Cobweb Theorem." *Quarterly Journal of Economics* 52 (1938): 255-80.

Garfield, James R. "The Beef Industry." In Robert M. La Follette, *The Making of America,* 5 (Chicago, 1906): 174-93.

Hale, Philip H. "The Beef Packing Industry." *National Farmer and Stockgrower* (*ca.* 1900): 3-29.

Henlein, Paul C. "Cattle Driving from the Ohio Country, 1800 to 1850." *Agricultural History* 28 (1954): 83-95.

Hessler, Sherry O. "The Great Disturbing Cause and the Decline of the Queen City." *Bulletin of the Historical and Philosophical Society of Ohio* 20 (1962): 169-82.

Hill, Howard C. "The Development of Chicago as a Center of the Meat Packing Industry." *Mississippi Valley Historical Review* 10 (1923): 253-73.

Hooker, R.H. "The Meat Supply of the United Kingdom." *Journal of the Royal Statistical Society* 72 (1909): 304-76.

Hutchinson, William K., and Williamson, Samuel H. "The Self-Sufficiency of the Antebellum South: Estimates of the Food Supply." *Journal of Economic History* 31 (1971): 591-612.

Jones, Robert L. "The Beef Cattle Industry in Ohio Prior to the Civil War." *Ohio Historical Quarterly* 64 (1955): 168-94, 287-319.

———. "Ohio Agriculture in History." *Ohio Historical Quarterly* 65 (1956): 229-58.

King, I.F. "The Coming and Going of Ohio Droving." *Ohio Archaeological and Historical Publications* 17 (1908): 247–53.

Knapp, Joseph G. "A Review of Chicago Stock Yards History." *University Journal of Business* 2 (1924): 331–46.

Lawson, J.A. "The Provision Trade of Ireland." *Transactions of the National Society for the Promotion of Social Science* (1861), 700–709.

Leavitt, Charles T. "Some Economic Aspects of the Western Meat Packing Industry, 1830–1860." *Journal of Business of the University of Chicago* 4 (1931): 68–90.

——. "Transportation and the Livestock Industry of the Middle West to 1860." *Agricultural History* 8 (1934): 20–33.

Louisville Chamber of Commerce. "Louisville: The Civil War; A Business History." *Louisville Magazine* 12 (1961): 5–8.

Mabry, William A. "Antebellum Cincinnati and Its Southern Trade." In David K. Jackson, ed., *American Studies in Honor of William Kenneth Boyd* (Durham, N.C., 1940), 60–85.

Messmer, Charles. "Louisville on the Eve of the Civil War." *Filson Club History Quarterly* 50 (1976): 249–89.

Parr, Elizabeth L. "Kentucky's Overland Trade with the Antebellum South." *Filson Club History Quarterly* 2 (1929): 71–81.

Paxson, Frederic L. "The Railroads of the Old Northwest before the Civil War." *Transactions of the Wisconsin Academy of Science, Arts and Letters* 17 (1914): 247–74.

Renner, G.K. "The Kansas City Meat Packing Industry before 1900." *Missouri Historical Review* 55 (1960): 18–29.

Ross, D. Reid, and Wiester, C.W. "The Relationship between Urban Growth and Transportation Development in the Cincinnati-Northern Kentucky Area." *Bulletin of the Historical and Philosophical Society of Ohio* 21 (1963): 112–32.

Sheldon, J.P. "Report on the American and Canadian Meat Trade." *Journal of the Royal Agricultural Society of England*, 2nd ser., 12 (1877): 295–355.

Tunnell, George G. "The Diversion of the Flour and Grain Traffic from the Great Lakes to the Railroads." *Journal of Political Economy* 5 (1897): 340–75, 872–94, 969–91.

"The Union Stockyards, December 25, 1865." *Chicago History* 7 (1965/66): 289–96.

Walsh, Margaret. "The Dynamics of Industrial Growth in the Old Northwest, 1830–1870: An Interdisciplinary Approach." In Paul J. Uselding, ed., *Business and Economic History Papers Presented at the 21st Annual Meeting of the Business History Conference* (Urbana, Ill., 1975), 12–29.

——. "From Pork Merchant to Meat Packer: The Midwestern Meat Industry in the Mid-Nineteenth Century." *Agricultural History* 56 (1982): 127-37.

——. "Pork Packing As a Leading Edge of Midwestern Industry, 1835-1875." *Agricultural History* 51 (1977): 702-17.

——. "The Spatial Evolution of the Mid-Western Pork Industry,, 1835-1875." *Journal of Historical Geography* 4 (1978): 1-22.

Wilkby, Harry L. "Infant Industries in Illinois As Illustrated in Quincy, 1836-1856." *Illinois State Historical Society Journal* 32 (1939): 474-97.

Zimmerman, W.D. "Live Cattle Trade between the United States and Great Britain, 1868-1885." *Agricultural History* 36 (1962): 46-52.

THESES

Abbott, Carl J. "The Divergent Development of Cincinnati, Indianapolis, Chicago and Galena, 1840-60: Economic Thought and Economic Growth." Ph.D. diss., Univ. of Chicago, 1971.

Aduddell, Robert M. "The Packer Consent Decree." Ph.D. diss., Northwestern Univ., 1971.

Ankli, Robert E. "Gross Farm Revenue in Pre-Civil War Illinois." Ph.D. diss., Univ. of Illinois-Urbana, 1969.

Atkinson, Eva L. "Kansas City's Livestock Trade and Packing Industry, 1870-1914: A Study in Regional Growth." Ph.D. diss., Univ. of Kansas, 1971.

Derby, William E. "A History of the Port of Milwaukee." Ph.D. diss., Univ. of Wisconsin, 1963.

Glazer, Walter S. "Cincinnati in 1840: A Community Profile." Ph.D. diss., Univ. of Michigan, 1968.

Harris, Faye E. "A Frontier Community: The Economic, Social and Political Development of Keokuk, Iowa, 1820-1866." Ph.D. diss., Univ. of Iowa, 1965.

Hessler, Sherry O. "Patterns of Transport and Urban Growth in the Miami Valley, Ohio, 1820-1880." M.A. thesis, Johns Hopkins Univ., 1961.

Hewes. Bernard A. "The Rise of the Pork Industry in Indiana." M.A. thesis, Indiana Univ., 1939.

Homenuck, Henry P.M. "The Historical Geography of the Cincinnati Pork Industry, 1810-1883." M.A. thesis, Univ. of Cincinnati, 1965.

Leavitt, Charles T. "The Meat and Dairy Livestock Industry, 1819-1860." Ph.D. diss., Univ. of Chicago, 1931.

Madison, James H. "Businessmen and the Business Community in Indianapolis, 1820–1860." Ph.D. diss., Indiana Univ., 1972.

Melom, Halvor G. "The Economic Development of St. Louis, 1803–46." Ph.D. diss., Univ. of Missouri, 1947.

Messmer, Charles K. "City in Conflict: A History of Louisville, 1860–1865." M.A. thesis. Univ. of Kentucky, 1953.

Muller, Edward K. "The Development of Urban Settlement in a Newly Settled Region: The Middle Ohio Valley, 1800–1860." Ph.D. diss., Univ.of Wisconsin, 1972.

Popplewell, Frank S. "St. Joseph, Missouri As a Center of the Cattle Trade." M.A. thesis, Univ. of Missouri, 1937.

Unfer, Louis. "Swift and Company: The Development of the Packing Industry, 1875–1912." Ph.D. diss., Univ. of Illinois-Urbana, 1951.

Zimmer, Donald T. "Madison, Indiana, 1811–1860: A Study in the Process of City Building." Ph.D. diss., Indiana Univ., 1974.

Index

Adams, Sawyer & Co., 69, 104, 105
agricultural processing industries, 3, 5, 6, 7, 72, 95, 96
Alexandria, Mo., 41, 43, 126 n.2
Alton, Ill., 30, 51, 94
Ames, Henry, & Co., 66, 102, 103, 104
Anglo American Packing Co. *See* Fowler Brothers
Appalachian Mountains, 7, 19
Armour, Philip D. *See* Armour & Co.; Plankington & Armour
Armour & Co., 85, 104
army, British, 63
army, U.S., 35; commissary depots, 57, 60, 64; purchases, 57, 63, 133 n.2, 133–34 n.3; rations, 133 n.1; Union, 57, 61, 64, 65, 66, 91, 133 n.1
Atkinson, Thomas & Co., 50, 103
Atlantic ports, 45, 49, 52, 53, 54, 64, 67. *See also by name*

bacon, 33, 34, 35, 36; country cured, 23
Baltimore, Md., 35, 49, 57
banks, 29, 30–31, 37, 74, 77, 121 n. 32. *See also by name*
barrel: definition of, 34 n.1
barreled pork. *See* pork: barreled, cargo, clear, mess, prime
Bartlett, Moses R., 30, 102
Beardstown, Ill., 25, 27, 39, 44, 51, 94
beef, mess, 36
beef packing: in Chicago, 53, 131 n.24
big business, 87, 92
"Big Five," 92, 145 n.2
Billings, Horace, 44, 103
Bingham & Wilson, 30, 102
biographical illustrations. *See* sampling; *packers by name*
Blair, Lyman. *See* Culbertson, Blair & Co.
Blythe, Benjamin I., 47
Boston, Mass., 31, 35, 57, 63
Botsford, H., & Co., 104
Bourbon Stock Yards, 75
Bowling Green, Ky., 94
box: definition of, 34 n.1
Boyd, James E., 79
branch plants, 53, 60, 78, 83
Britain, 36, 50
Brotherson, P.R.K. *See* Tyng, Alexander G.
bulk meat, 32, 33, 35
Burlington, Iowa, 41, 49, 52, 94; as a packing center, 46; pork packing

Burlington, Iowa (*continued*): outputs, 129 n.11; and railroads, 46; stockyards, 75
butchers, 33, 124 n.41
Butler, S.O., 103
by-products, 18, 72, 81, 82, 83, 91, 92

canals, 48. *See also by name*
capital: mercantile sources of, 28-32, 43, 90; requirements for packing, 26-29, 41-43, 84, 117 n.19, 118 n.23, n.24, 119 n.26, 142 n. 26. *See also* costs: fixed, working
capitalists, 13, 28; East Coast, 26, 29, 31, 74, 77-78; foreign, 26, 31. *See also merchants and packing firms by name*
cargo pork. *See* pork: cargo
cattle, 77; in Midwest, 112 n.11; shipments of, to Chicago, 59, 73-74
Cedar Rapids, Iowa, 68, 77, 78, 84, 85, 97
census figures. *See* meat packing
Chapin, H.M., 103
Chicago, Ill., 41, 43, 45, 46, 47, 50, 53, 55, 60, 67, 69, 70, 73-74, 77, 82, 85, 91, 92, 94, 96, 97; beef packing outputs, 131 n.24; "Hog Butcher to the World," 51, 52; impact of Civil War on packing in, 55, 57, 58, 59-63; as a livestock center, 53, 59, 73-74, 132 n.27; as a packing center, 51, 52, 59-63, 73, 82, 131 n.24; pork packing outputs, 21; and railroads, 51-52; summer packing in, 143-44 n.30
Chicago, Alton and St. Louis Railroad, 51, 52, 132 n.27
Chicago and Rock Island Railroad, 51
Chicago, Burlington and Quincy Railroad, 46, 51, 52, 132 n.27
Chicago Packing & Provision Co., 85, 86, 104
Child, John (*also* Child, J.R., & Co.), 44, 65, 102. *See also* Rawson, Joseph
Chillicothe, Ohio, 17, 27, 30, 94; pork packing outputs, 22
Cincinnati, Ohio, 17, 25, 27, 28, 30, 31, 34, 35, 37, 45, 46, 47, 48, 49, 50, 70, 75, 82, 85, 86, 94, 96, 97; impact of Civil War on packing in, 55, 57, 59, 63-65; as a packing center, 11, 48; pork packing outputs, 20, 48, 129 n.14; and railroads, 47-50, 64; relative decline as a packing center, 48-50, 64
Cincinnati Chamber of Commerce, *Annual Reports*: as a source, 111 n.9
Cincinnati Prices Current: as a source, 111 n.9
Circleville, Ohio, 17, 34, 37, 94
Civil War, 13, 72, 79, 91, 95; impact on pork packing, 55, 57-70, 91
clear pork. *See* pork: clear
Cleveland, Ohio: pork packing outputs, 68
Coleman, J.W., 102
Collins, E., 102
Columbus, Ohio, 34, 94
competition. *See* urban rivalry
Comstock, B., & Co., 102
Confederacy: sentiment for, 64, 66
consumer tastes. *See* markets
consumption of pork: estimates of, 33, 79, 123 n.39, 140-41 n.15
contracts: with farmers, 43. *See also* army, U.S.
Coons, Charles B. (*also* Coons & Dobyns), 15, 17, 29, 102
coopers, 44, 48, 81, 83
corn-hog cycle, 11, 13, 23, 30, 147 n.7
costs: fixed, 25, 26, 27, 84, 117 n.19, 118 n.23; labor, 27, 28, 41, 142 n.26; transport, 27, 28, 41; working, 25, 27-28, 41, 43, 71, 84, 117 n.19, 118 n.24, 119 n.26, 142 n.26
Craigin & Co., 52-53, 60, 103
credit. *See* capital
Crimean War, 63

crises, 13, 14, 32. *See also* Civil War; Panic of 1857; Panic of 1873
Culbertson, Charles M. *See* Culbertson, Blair & Co.
Culbertson, Blair & Co., 60–61, 82, 103, 104
curing. *See* ham
cuts of pork, 122 n.38; regulations for, 80–81

Davis, Charles, & Co., 50, 64–65, 86, 102, 103, 104
Davis Brothers (*also* Davis & Bro.), 31, 44, 102. *See also* Davis, Charles, & Co.
Dayton, Ohio, 34, 69
"dead" meat, 7, 23. *See also* pork: dressed, net, wagon
Decatur, Ill., 69
demand. *See* markets
Des Moines, Iowa: pork packing outputs, 68
Detroit and Milwaukee Railroad, 67
disassembly line: 26, 81, 82, 84, 91
Dobyns, Jno. P. *See* Coons, Charles B.
Dold, Jacob, & Sons, 78
dressed pork. *See* pork: dressed. *See also* "dead" meat; pork: net, wagon
droving, 12, 23-24, 45, 49, 115-16 n.13
Dupee, Cyrus. *See* Hough, Roselle and Oramel

Early, Jacob D., 30, 44, 69, 102, 103, 104
entrepreneurs. *See individual packers, manufacturers, and merchants by name*
Evans, Benjamin, 65
Evans, Jason. *See* Evans and Newton; Evans & Swift
Evans & Newton, 65. *See also* Evans & Swift
Evans & Swift, 44, 50, 65, 102, 118 n.23. *See also* Swift, Briggs
exports. *See* markets

farmers: and hog raising, 11, 18-19, 23; participation in pork packing, 7, 23
Ferguson, Messrs., & Company, 83
finance. *See* capital
fire risks: to pork houses, 26, 27, 83
Flemingsburg, Ky., 30
fluctuations in pork packing, 8-9, 13, 14, 18, 23-26. *See also* corn-hog cycle
Fowler Brothers, 78, 85, 104
France, 36

Galena and Chicago Railroad, 51, 52, 132 n.27
Gano & Shields, 30, 102
Gill, T.N., 43, 102
Great Lakes, 12, 49; manufacturing complex, 1, 89
gross pork. *See* pork: gross

ham, 32, 33, 35, 36, 44, 65, 80, 86, 122 n.27
Hamilton, Ohio, 17, 30, 34, 94
Hamilton & Brothers (*also* Hamilton Bros.), 50, 66, 104. *See also* Hamilton, Ricketts & Co.
Hamilton, Ricketts & Co., 103
Hancock, John L., 52, 53, 60. *See also* Craigin & Co.
Higgins, George W., & Co., 86, 104
Higginson, G.W., 43
"Hogopolis," 18, 44
hogs: breeds, 19; for commercial slaughter, 112 n.12; numbers in the Midwest, 11; raising of, 18–19, 39, 77, 91; supply for pork packing, *passim*. *See also* corn-hog cycle
hogshead, 33; definition of, 34 n.1
Hough, Roselle and Oramel (*also* Hough, R.M. and O.S.), 62–63, 103
Hubbard, Gurdon S. (*also* Hubbard, G.S., & Co.), 62, 103
Huffman, Maxcy & Co., 102

ice packing, 13, 79, 85–86, 91, 92. *See*

ice packing (*continued*):
also pork packing: summer
Illinois, 11, 17, 40, 41, 45, 46, 48, 51, 52, 67, 98, 99, 100, 101
Illinois and Michigan Canal, 51
Illinois Central Railroad, 51, 52, 132 n.27
Illinois River, 25, 44
Indiana, 40, 45, 48, 49, 98, 99, 100, 101
Indianapolis, 44, 46, 47, 49, 60, 83, 85, 94, 96, 97; as a packing center, 47; pork packing outputs, 21; and railroads, 47
Indianapolis Belt Railroad and Stock Yard Co., 75
Indiana State Bank, 29
industry. *See* manufacturing
information: circulation or flow of, 12, 13–14, 32, 33, 36, 72, 74, 79, 80. *See also* telegraph
initial inertia, 49–50
Iowa, 40, 41, 45, 46, 52, 78, 86, 98, 99, 100, 101
Ireland, 36

Jones, Daniel A. *See* Culbertson, Blair & Co.

Kane County, Ill., 61
Kansas, 101
Kansas City, Kan. and Mo., 66, 77, 84, 97; as a livestock center, 77–78; as a packing center, 77–78; pork packing outputs, 21
Kansas City Stock Yards Co., 77–78
Kent, Albert. *See* Kent, A.E., & Co.
Kent, Sydney. *See* Kent, A.E., & Co.
Kent, A.E., & Co., 60, 61–62, 82, 103
Kentucky, 17, 18, 29, 40, 48, 64, 66, 98, 99, 100, 101
Keokuk, Iowa, 25, 41, 43, 44, 52, 62, 67, 69, 86, 94, 97; pork packing outputs, 22, 68
Kingan & Co. (*also* Kingan Brothers), 78, 83, 85, 104

labor, 23, 48, 82, 83; costs, 27, 28, 41, 142 n.26
Lafayette, Ind., 17, 30, 47, 69, 94, 96
Lake Michigan, 48, 50, 52, 74
Lamb, J.L., 103
lard, 28, 32, 33, 34, 35, 36, 81, 82, 121 n.35
Lawrenceburg, Ind., 94
Layton, Frederick (*also* Layton & Plankington), 43, 103
lead miners: as a market for pork, 34
Lewis, H., 102
Lippincott, W.J., 65
Little Miami Railroad, 48
Liverpool, England, 31, 43
Logansport, Ind., 69
Louisville, Ky., 18, 25, 27, 28, 30, 35, 37, 49, 50, 64, 66, 70, 82, 94, 96, 97; impact of Civil War on packing in, 57, 58–59, 66; pork packing outputs, 20, 66

McFerran, Armstrong & Co., 105
Madison, Ind., 18, 27, 28, 44, 47, 49, 94; as a packing center, 45–46; pork packing outputs, 22, 128 n.9; and railroads, 45–46
Madison and Indianapolis Railroad, 45, 47
Mammoth Cave Pork House, 45
Mansur & Ferguson, 103
Mansur family, 47, 103
manufacturing: in the Middle Atlantic states, 1, 2, 3, 4; in the Middle West, 1–7; in New England, 1, 2, 3, 4; in the South, 2, 3, 4; in the United States, 1–6. *See also* agricultural processing industries; processing industries
markets, 12, 32–36, 122–23 n.39; foreign, 12, 36, 50, 53, 57, 64, 80, 83, 89; institutional, 35–36, 57, 60, 61, 64, 65, 66, 91; midwestern, 33–35, 65, 86; northeastern, 35, 53, 57, 60, 61, 64, 65, 67, 89; southern, 35, 49, 64, 65,

66, 89, 124-25 n.44; urban, 12, 33, 79-80, 122-23 n.39, 140-41 n.15
Marsh, Sylvester, 63
Marshall & Ilsley, 43
mast, 19
Maxwell & Johnson, 41, 43, 126 n.2, n.3
Maysville, Ky., 15, 17, 29, 94
meat packing: in census schedules, 5, 7, 109-11 n.8; definition of, 109 n.7. *See also* beef packing; pork packing
Menomonee Valley, 75, 83
merchant marine, 35, 36
merchants: as packers, 7, 13, 15, 17-18, 25-32, 36-37, 39, 41, 43-54, 60-67, 69-70, 72, 90-92; transition to manufacturers, 13, 14, 60-62, 71-87, 89-92. *See also individual packers by name*
mess pork. *See* pork: mess
Miami River, 17, 34
Michigan, 101
Michigan Central Railroad, 51
Michigan Southern Railroad, 51
Middle West (Midwest): definition of, 107 n.1; economic development of, 1, 11; manufacturing in, 1-7; population of, 10
Milwaukee, Wis., 43, 45, 52, 70, 83, 91, 94, 96, 97; impact of Civil War on packing in, 55, 59, 67; pork packing outputs, 21; stockyards, 75
Milwaukee and Prairie du Chien Railroad, 67
Milwaukee and St. Paul Railroad, 67, 83
Minnesota, 101
Mississippi River, 18, 25, 46, 48, 51, 52, 55, 59, 74, 77. *See also* Ohio-Mississippi River
Mississippi Valley. *See* Upper Mississippi Valley
Missouri, 17, 40, 41, 45, 46, 66, 67, 70, 98, 99, 100, 101
Missouri Pacific Railroad, 81
Missouri River, 51, 69, 77
Missouri Valley, 78
Moore, Samuel, 120 n.27
Mooresville, Ind., 120 n.27
Morrell, John, & Company, 79
Morrison, James, & Company, 50, 102
Muscatine, Iowa, 61, 94

navy, 35
Nebraska, 78, 101
net pork. *See* pork: net. *See also* "dead" meat; pork: dressed, wagon
New England: fishing fleets, 36; manufacturing in, 1, 2, 3, 4
New Orleans, La., 27, 31, 35, 43, 49, 57, 64
Newport, Ind., 61
Newton, S.C., 65. *See also* Evans & Newton
New York City, 31, 35, 43, 49, 51, 52, 57, 61, 63, 83
nuisance ordinances, city, 26, 74

Ohio, 18, 40, 44, 45, 48, 49, 98, 99, 100, 101
Ohio-Mississippi River, 7, 12, 31, 36, 54, 91
Ohio River, 15, 17, 48, 49, 64
Ohio Valley, 24, 27, 33, 44, 45, 48, 49, 50, 59
Old Northwest, 48
Omaha, Neb., 77, 79, 84; pork packing outputs, 140 n.14
Ottumwa, Iowa, 77, 79, 84; pork packing outputs, 140 n. 14

packing. *See* beef packing; meat packing; pork packing
packing plants, 12, 77, 78, 79, 81-86, 91
Panic of 1857, 13, 41
Panic of 1873, 13, 77
Patterson & Timberman, 44, 62, 69, 103, 104, 105
Pekin, Ill., 27, 43, 94

Pennsylvania Canal, 49
Pennsylvania Central Railroad, 51
Peoria, Ill., 25, 27, 39, 41, 43, 51, 52, 61, 67, 69, 86, 94, 96, 97; pork packing outputs, 22, 68
Peoria Union Stock Yards, 75
Philadelphia, Penn., 35, 49, 57
pigs. *See* hogs
Pinger, David, & Co., 70, 104, 105
Pittsburgh, Penn., 49, 51
Pittsburgh, Fort Wayne and Chicago Railroad, 51
Plankington, John. *See* Layton, Frederick; Plankington & Armour
Plankington & Armour (*also* Plankington, Armour & Co.): in Kansas City, 78, 81, 105; in Milwaukee, 83-84, 104
population: midwestern, 10; urban, 12, 79, 122 n.39
pork: barrelled, 32, 33, 35, 80, 122 n. 38; cargo, 36; clear, 33, 36; consumption estimates, 33, 79, 123 n. 39, 140-41 n.15; cuts, 32-33, 122 n.38; dressed, 23, 27, 41; gross, 23, 115 n.11; mess, 33, 35, 36; net, 23, 115 n.11; prime, 33, 36; wagon, 19, 33, 90. *See also* bacon; ham
pork houses: description of, 26-27
pork packers, characteristics of, 7, 11, 13-14, 89-92; in the Civil War era, 60-67, 69-70; in pioneer days, 17-18, 26, 28-32, 36-37; in the postwar years, 72, 78-79, 81, 82-87; in the 1850s, 41, 43-44, 47, 50, 52-54. *See also* merchants; *individual packers by name*
Pork Packers' Association: Chicago, 60, 73; national, 71, 80-81
pork packing: changes in industry, 7, 11-14, 36-37, 53-54, 55, 70, 72, 79, 86-87, 89-92; in Civil War era, 55-70; concentration in cities, 12-13, 14, 55-70, 73-87, 95; geographical distribution of, 16, 42, 56, 76; interregional competition, 12-13; length of season, 24-25, 41, 89-90; number of establishments, 98-101; significance of, 7, 11-14; statistics of, 8-9, 20-21, 22, 39, 59, 68, 94, 96, 97-105; summer, 85-86, 143-44 n.29, n.30; uncertainty of, *passim*; westward movement of, 7, 11, 39-41, 55, 57, 59, 70, 75, 77
"Porkopoli," 24, 46, 67, 78
Powell, McEwen & Co., 45-46, 103
prices: in Cincinnati, 47, 49. *See also* pork: gross, net
prime pork. *See* pork: prime
processing industries: definition of, 109 n.5; in Middle West, 3, 5-7. *See also* agricultural processing industries
professional organizations, 72, 80-81. *See also* Pork Packers' Association

Queen City. *See* Cincinnati, Ohio
Quincy, Ill., 25, 27, 39, 44, 51, 52, 67, 69, 86, 94, 97; pork packing outputs, 22

railroads: impact on pork packing, 12-13, 39, 44-54, 55, 57, 64, 67, 69, 70, 72-73, 90-91, 92. *See also* stockyards; *railroads by name and by packing point*
Rawson, Joseph (*also* Rawson, Joseph, & Co.; Rawson, Joseph, & Sons), 44, 50, 65, 86, 102, 103, 104
razorbacks, 19
regulations. *See* nuisance ordinances; Pork Packers' Association
Reid, John (*also* Reid & Sherwin), 62, 82, 103
Reynolds, John L., 30, 102
Reynolds, William, & Co. (*also* Reynolds & Co.), 86, 105
Ripley, Ohio, 17, 94
riverine era, 15-37
Rock River Valley, 52
Roe, John J. (*also* Roe, J.J., & Co.), 31, 43, 126 n.3
Rose & Prentiss, 104, 105

Ruggles, S.H., & Co., 102
Rupert, C. and G.H. (*also* Rupert, Gideon), 43

St. Joseph, Mo., 67, 69, 77, 78, 84, 96, 97; as a pork packing center, 69-70; pork packing outputs, 68
St. Louis, Mo., 27, 30, 31, 33, 41, 45, 52, 66, 69, 70, 75, 85, 91, 94, 96, 97; impact of Civil War on packing in, 55, 57, 59, 66-67; pork packing outputs, 10; and railroads, 67
St. Louis National Stock Yards, 74
St. Louis Union Stockyards, 74-75
Sample, Henry T. (*also* Sample, H.T., & Co.), 69, 104
sampling: for biographical illustrations, 93-105, 147 n.8-10; in historical work, 93
Sandusky, Ohio, 48
Savage, Case & Co., 61
Schenck & Denise, 103
Scioto River, 17, 34
season, pork packing: length of, 24-25, 41, 89-90
seasonal influences. *See* weather
Second Bank of the United States: Cincinnati branch, 31
Sherwin, Joseph. *See* Reid, John
Sinclair, Thomas, & Company, 78-79, 85-86, 105
slaughtering, 26, 62, 81, 83, 84, 115 n. 11, 117 n.20, 130 n.20
South: definition of, 2 n.1. *See also* markets: southern
Springfield, Ill., 52, 94
Springfield, Ohio, 48
Stagg & Shay, 118 n.23
stockyards, 60, 72, 79, 80, 83, 91, 138 n.2, 139 n.9; impact of pork packing on, 73-75, 77-79. *See also yards by name*
structural reorganization in pork packing arrangements, 55, 72, 91, 95. *See also* packing plants; stockyards
Swift, Abraham. *See* Swift, Briggs
Swift, Briggs (*also* B. Swift & Co.), 65, 103
Swift & Co., 78

Tazewell County, Ill., 43
technology, 14, 70, 72, 79, 95. *See also* ice packing
telegraph, 14, 36, 74, 75, 80, 141 n.18
temperature control in packing, 116 n.14
Tennessee, 98, 99, 101
Terre Haute, Ind., 17, 30, 37, 44, 47, 61, 67, 69, 94, 96; pork packing outputs, 22, 68
tierce, 36; definition of, 34 n.1
transportation. *See* canals; droving; railroads; *rivers by name*
Tyng, Alexander G. (*also* Tyng & Brotherson), 43, 69, 103, 104

Union Railroad Stock Yard Co., 75, 86
Union Stock Yard National Bank, 74
Union Stock Yards, 63, 73-74, 75, 80, 82, 138 n.3
Upper Mississippi Valley, 18, 24, 27, 34, 41, 43, 52, 55, 57, 59, 67, 69, 70, 90-91
urban concentration in pork packing, 12-13, 14, 55-70, 73-79
urban rivalry, 12-13, 18, 34, 43, 44-49, 50-52, 54, 57, 63, 67, 69, 70, 86

value added by manufacture, 7; definition, 2 n.2
Virginia, 98

Wabash River, 17, 30, 69
Wade, Samuel (*also* Wade, S., & Co.), 30, 102
Wadsworth, Dyer & Co., 63
wagon pork. *See* pork: wagon
Washington, D.C., 57
weather: influence on droving, 24; influence on pork packing, 7, 12, 14, 24-25, 117 n.18

Wells, Edward, 44, 103
West. *See* Middle West
West Indies, 36
Westport, Ky., 94
West Virginia, 101
White, A.S., & Co., 102
White, Cunningham & Co., 45
White River, 47
Whittaker, F., & Sons, 104
Windy City. *See* Chicago
winter season. *See* pork packing: length of season
Wisconsin, 40, 45, 99, 100, 101
Woodburn & Shrewsbury, 102
Worster, John. *See* Hough, Roselle and Oramel